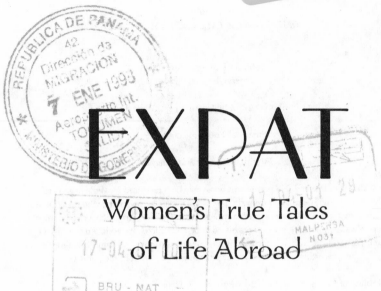

EXPAT

Women's True Tales
of Life Abroad

Edited by Christina Henry de Tessan

Seal Press

EXPAT
WOMEN'S TRUE TALES OF LIFE ABROAD

Seal Press
1400 65th Street, Suite 250
Emeryville, CA 94608

First Seal Press edition 2002

Interior design by Sue Canavan

Library of Congress Cataloging-in-Publication Data

De Tessan, Christina Henry.
  Expat : women's true tales of life abroad / by Christina Henry de Tessan.
    p. cm.
  ISBN-10: 1-58005-070-0
  ISBN-13: 978-1-58005-070-8
  1. Women travelers--Anecdotes. 2. Voyages and travels--Anecdotes. 3. Americans—Foreign countries--Anecdotes. 4. Travelers' writings, American. I. Title.

G465.E96 2002
910.4'092'2--dc21

                                                      2002510343

9 8 7 6

Printed in the United States of America by Berryville Graphics

Contents

Introduction....xi

Before and After Mexico
Gina Hyams.....1

A Taste of Home
Tonya Ward Singer.....10

The Liverpool School of Dream and Pun
Rhiannon Paine.....18

The Long Conversation
Deryn P. Verity.....44

Thirteen Ways of Looking at a Blackboard
Leza Lowitz.....58

Jean-Claude Van Damn That Was a Good Movie!
Emily Wise Miller.....81

A Mediterranean Thanksgiving, Take Two
Mandy Dowd.....89

When the Skinheads Start to Grow Hair,
It's Time to Leave Town
Angeli Primlani.....107

Watching Them Grow Up
Laura Fokkena.....120

Wasabi Was the Bitter Herb
Karen Rosenberg.....133

Making a Stir-Fry in Eastern Europe
Stephanie Loleng.....146

Muddy Waters in Borneo
Meg Wirth.....153

Never-Never
Juleigh Howard-Hobson.....170

First, the Blanket
Kate Baldus.....185

Beautiful New World
Emmeline Chang.....195

Saudades
Eliza Bonner.....211

In Search of Zorba
Marci Laughlin.....222

Living the Dream in Paris
Christina Henry de Tessan.....241

Conversation in Denmark
Lesley-Ann Brown.....252

Best Friends and Balaclavas
Erica Jacobs.....263

Growing Season
Sadie Ackerman.....276

Kashmar
Julie van Arcken.....284

About the Contributors.....299

About the Editor.....305

Acknowledgments

An anthology is a true collaborative effort. First and foremost, I want to thank the contributors for their spirited stories, as well as their endless patience and goodwill, even as I asked for "just one more round of revisions." This book would very simply not exist without them. This collection also benefited greatly from the shrewd guidance of my editor and friend Leslie Miller. Many thanks to my family, for nurturing the travel bug in me, to Ninive and Elizabeth, for believing I could do it, and of course, to Rick, for just about everything, but especially, for taking a leap of faith and running away to Paris with me and for keeping the home fires burning (quite literally) as I put this collection together.

Better be imprudent movables than prudent fixtures.
—Keats

To Rick, my very favorite imprudent movable

Introduction

My mother was born on a ranch in the Arizona desert. She loves France. My father was born in Paris and fell in love with the Wild West. While my dad loves nothing more than galloping around on horseback in search of stray cattle, Mom loves getting to know the cheese man in her neighborhood when she visits Paris. So although life at home in San Francisco was always a very fine thing, I was raised on the idea that foreign places were the stuff of real magic. Travel somehow allowed room for a fantasy that real life did not leave much time for, and my parents' adventures always seemed wonderfully romantic. They sheltered themselves from tropical storms in Guatemala with *sombrilla de pobre* leaves (poor man's umbrellas), sampled guinea pig in Peru, raced across potholed roads through Portugal's groves of cork trees, picked up hitch-hikers swathed in flowing robes and adorned with curved daggers in Morocco. Their photos told tales of fantastically different-looking places: Dad playing checkers with the local villagers in Senegal, Mom climbing to the top of Tiqual, Prague's Charles Bridge on a snowy evening. The unknown (and the more obscure the better) had a mystique all its own, and I couldn't help but get swept up in the fervor of it. I, too, became addicted to stepping out of the rut of day-to-day life and testing myself far from the familiar and comfortable routines of home. But even as I strayed further off the beaten track, I always returned home to the States after a few adventurous weeks. It was never enough. Eventually, I began to wonder what it would be like to take travel to its furthest extreme—and move someplace to *live*. After all, if one loves to travel, then isn't living abroad a natural extension of that passion?

So I went to Paris—and lived in poorly insulated, renovated maid's quarters on the ninth floor of an ancient building overlooking the chimneys and rooftops for over a year. I befriended the local merchants, learned to cope with French colleagues and became a regular in obscure North African restaurants. I sighed impatiently when the *tourists* descended upon the city in the spring. I explored beyond the glittering surface and became a local, commuting to a nine-to-five job in the icy northern European rain and reveling in the now-familiar signs of spring as the chestnuts along the Seine released their pale green leaves. All of this was heady stuff, and I loved it. But I also learned there was an unexpected dimension to living abroad that I hadn't considered before going, one my parents hadn't taught me and that I had to discover on my own. I hadn't given more than a fleeting thought to the good old-fashioned loneliness that cropped up. I no longer had the familiar clutch of friends to call and debrief with at the end of a long day. Accustomed to being efficient, competent, articulate, and able to navigate the various logistics of American life, in Paris I was often flummoxed: by doctors, medical insurance, renter's taxes, voice mail, the laundromat and that wretched foreign keyboard which turned all my letters to gibberish.

Was it worth it? Absolutely. Was it what I'd expected? Not always. Living overseas, I learned, was not the same as traveling there. And so, I became curious: how did others fare when they left to make their home in a different country? What was it like to try to gain a foothold in a foreign place, and why did they want to? And finally, how did the dream match up to the reality for them?

I was astounded by the essays I received—not only by the range of experiences and destinations, but by how different they were from traditional travel essays. When we travel, we are craving a break from routine, so we seek out the different and exotic at every turn because we know that in a week or two, we will be back in our safe little worlds. But when we *move* away, the home we've left behind can tug at us in surprising ways. We go abroad with our sights set ambitiously on change, but find we crave something recognizable and tangible, things we may never have known we needed: flavors and foods, love and companionship, routine and purpose, being understood for who we really are—whether it's our incandescent wit or our skills as a chef. Instead of fantasizing about the new and exotic, we might find ourselves daydreaming about the familiar: *No, I don't want a thimbleful of bitter French café, I want a huge paper cup full of American coffee that will last all morning.* Having wanted to take travel to its furthest extreme, we end up coming full circle as we learn to cope with the most mundane tasks in a foreign place. Ultimately, real immersion—and the real challenge—occurs during this shift. Balancing the need for the familiar with our desire for the exotic is at the heart of the expat experience.

Time and again, the women in these essays display a dazzling, inspiring resourcefulness as they struggle to find the right balance for themselves. Forced out of the familiar zone of twenty-four-hour Safeways, longtime friends, and cultural and linguistic fluency, these essays are glorious proof of our powers to adapt. They overcome fears and shyness, make themselves understood, re-create a sense of home, find what they need. These stories make me want to pack my bags once again, but they also remind me that it is not as easy as it sounds. I recall how much I craved friends and colleagues who could understand me, how humbling it was not to be able to express myself as I would have liked, and how quickly I had forgotten the hard parts. That said, I also remember how gratifying it was to assemble the myriad pieces of a life from scratch. I was as wide awake as I have ever been, for better and for worse, and for that reason alone, I would do it all over again.

Christina Henry de Tessan
Seattle, Washington 2002

Before and After Mexico

Gina Hyams

While life yet lasts, laughter and molasses
—traditional Mexican saying

January 1997. My husband, Dave, and I were deliriously happy—giddy with the reality that we were officially unemployed, homeless and about to blow our life savings by boarding Taesa flight 572 (Oakland-Zacatecas-Morelia) with one-way tickets, one two-year-old, three suitcases, a bag of books, a laptop, a pink teddy bear, a diaper bag and three saxophones. The only plan for our new life in Mexico was that Dave would play jazz, I'd finally have a go at writing and our daughter Annalena would chase lizards.

We sold nearly everything we owned to finance this escape. Our Tahitian-green Honda Civic named Uma, Macintosh computers, Navajo rugs, 50s reclining beauty-parlor chair, Bang & Olufsen stereo system, reading lamps made of twigs, goose-down comforter, garlic peeler and Weber grill: all sold to the highest bidder. People described our liquidation as "the flea market of the gods." Estranged friends descended like vultures to paw through our belongings.

Everything was gone. Dave's beloved collection of obscure R & B Christmas albums: gone. The books of French literary criticism I never actually read in college: gone. Annalena's primary-colored plastic educational toys: gone. The five bottles of extra fancy grade A pure Vermont maple syrup, four of which I bought because I never could remember if we had any, and brunch with friends was an ideal I perennially aspired to mid-supermarket-aisle: gone. Gone. Gone. Gone. Gone.

The abstract notion of lightening the load was more cathartic than the excruciating book-by-book process. I had to keep reminding myself that each item sold translated into that much more time I wouldn't have to spend in a gray cubicle. A neighbor squabbled when I refused his pitiful offer for *Italy: The Beautiful Cookbook*. He didn't understand that this was no ordinary garage sale, that we weren't getting rid of these things because we didn't like them. They were our only assets and we were exchanging them for a new life.

It's not that our old life was without its pleasures, but we were bone tired. Dave was the managing director of a Shakespeare festival and I was the assistant to a vice president of marketing at a software company (back in the glory days of corporate-sponsored staff-bonding ski trips and free Snapple lemonade for all high-tech workers). I was too lowly a peon to get stock options, but my boss was a nice guy who thanked me daily for my competence. Having spent my twenties toiling in employee-morale disaster zones at supposedly progressive political and arts organizations, the software company's esprit de corps and catered lunches had been a revelation.

Quitting was Dave's idea. He was thirty-nine and barreling his way to an ulcer from the stress of managing the theater's never-ending backstage dramas, while juggling the demands of father-hood, husbandhood and gigs with his experimental jazz ensemble. He was seeing both a therapist and a career counselor, trying to figure out a way to make money that might also make him happy, or at least happier. Architect? Therapist? Jazz history professor? Vice president of something? Bookstore owner? Record-shop clerk? Hander-outer of putters at a mini-golf course?

None of these ideas stuck. More than a new profession, he needed a break—time to catch his breath, find his bearings, rekindle his spirit. He needed a lot more than a two-week vaca-tion. While stuck in Bay Bridge traffic one Thursday night, the solution came to him. With desperate clarity, he bounded in the door and swooped Annalena up into his arms.

"Honey, I've figured it out. We don't have to buy a house. We can quit our jobs, sell everything and become expatriates instead."

We had habitually entertained fantasies of life abroad while on vacation, but this time Dave was serious. My first impulse was to dig in my heels: "But I finally like my job."

"I thought you wanted to be a writer. Think about it. We're not tied down to a mortgage. I haven't embarked on a new career. We only have one child and she's not in school yet. This is our window of opportunity."

He made it sound so reasonable. I was thirty-one and had been coasting on my "creative potential" since college. This move felt like put-up-or-shut-up time, like my artistic bluff had been called. My work at the software company was pleasant, but it was meaningless. I needed to sit still long enough to find out if I had anything to say as a writer. I also yearned to see our little girl during daylight hours.

We contemplated relocating to Holland, Spain, Italy, or France, but settled on Mexico, where we'd vacationed three times, because we loved the mariachi bands and the brilliant colors, because families were revered there and because rents were cheap. And we were, indeed, a family with limited resources—$23,732.45 after the sale, to be exact. We thought it would be enough money to carry us for a year, maybe two.

When the last of our furniture was carted away, Dave and I sat on the hardwood floor and surveyed the empty space. There was no remaining evidence of our personalities. We no longer had proof that we were intelligent people of distinguished, if modest, accomplishment and quirky good taste.

The closer we came to our departure date, the less coherent I was when people asked, "Why Morelia?" Nobody'd heard of this inland city. I tried to sound rational, explaining that we thought coastal resorts were well and good for vacations, but that at heart we weren't beach people and we didn't want to live surrounded by tourists. The guidebooks intriguingly described the state of Michoacán as the "Switzerland of Mexico," the "Hills of China of

Mexico" and the "Land that Time Forgot." We specifically chose the capital city of Morelia because we were suckers for colonial architecture and cobblestones, and, with its universities, music conservatory, and nearby crafts villages, it just seemed like the place for us.

Of course, we'd never been there, we didn't know anybody there, and we didn't speak Spanish.

We ended up spending the first of what would turn into four years in Mexico in Pátzcuaro, a Purépecha Indian town on a mountain lake about an hour's drive south of Morelia. The capital itself had felt too sprawling and cosmopolitan, too similar to California. There was a gourmet grocery where we could buy imported coffee and Häagen-Dazs, and that felt like cheating. We wanted to live in the Land that Time Forgot, and in Pátzcuaro there wasn't even coffee-to-go.

We lived on a nameless cobblestone road in a little adobe house that had no telephone, no washing machine, no microwave and no television. The kitchen counter was a glorious, crazy quilt of Talavera tiles decorated with bananas and jalapeño peppers, and the bathroom walls were painted *azul añil,* a deep ultramarine blue believed to ward off evil spirits. Two stone angels, carved in the nearby village of Tzintzuntzan, held up the mantel above the fireplace in the living room. We bought wood from an eighty-three-year-old *campesino* named Don Ambrosio who delivered it by *burro.* Stoking the fire, I felt like a pioneer bride.

Dave planted a stand of calla lilies and hung a hammock in the backyard. We learned how to finesse the water and gas tanks and (after our first miserable round of amoebas) to soak vegetables vigilantly in a disinfectant solution. Just walking to the post office was an adventure because we invariably stumbled on one fiesta or another—boys blasting fireworks at dawn in honor of the Virgin of Guadalupe, a mariachi band serenading a bride and groom on the church steps, children bashing a piñata strung up in the middle of the street, a drunken brass band careening through town in celebration of a win by their favorite soccer team.

Wandering through Pátzcuaro's outdoor market was a visual feast. Block after block was filled with the reddest tomatoes I'd ever seen, alongside pyramids of huge, ripe avocados, juicy cactus paddles, mangoes carved into flower shapes, baskets overflowing with dried chilies and pumpkin seeds, platters of chicken heads, candied sweet potatoes swarming with bees and more cow parts than I'd ever imagined. Enormous bouquets of tuberoses could be had for a song. I'd dare myself to go back by the butcher stalls to look at the ghostly tripe, pig snouts on hooks and glistening entrails. My legs would nearly buckle, the sensual overload was so confounding. When Dave wasn't around, I enjoyed a flirty dance with Juan, my favorite fruit seller. "*A su servicio, mi reina* (At your service, my queen)," he'd grin as he dug for the sweetest strawberries.

For people who had so recently shed our material trappings and piously sworn to "never accumulate that much stuff again," we had a hell of a lot of fun accumulating new stuff. There was such palpable pleasure in being surrounded by things that were *hecho a mano* (made by hand). We drank fresh-squeezed tangerine juice out of hand-blown glass goblets, wore hand-knitted wool sweaters and slept under a hand-loomed magenta bedspread. We brushed our teeth with purified water decanted from an earthenware pitcher. Annalena played with miniature toy frogs made of straw and she chased not only lizards, but dragonflies, ladybugs, grasshoppers, butterflies, pigeons and all manner of mangy street dogs as well.

We made friends with Lupita, who sold roast chickens in the market. She always gave Annalena a little *cajeta* (goat's milk caramel) cookie and advised Dave and me to make more babies. Mexicans rarely asked what we did for a living. They were more curious about the size of our family and, though ours was small, the fact that we were a family seemed to normalize us. Annalena, with her blueberry eyes and impeccable Spanish accent, became our goodwill ambassador. No matter how dusty-poor or remote the village, people made a fuss over her. *¡Qué linda!* (How pretty!), they'd exclaim. She was *preciosa* (precious), *una princesa* (a princess), *una muñeca viviente* (a living doll). By the time she was three, Annalena would answer, "*No soy una muñeca. Soy un mono.* (I'm not a doll. I'm a monkey.)" She also took to telling anyone who asked that she had forty-nine brothers and sisters.

The view from my writing desk was one-third twisting cobblestone roads and red-tiled rooftops and two-thirds sky. When I sat down to work on my novel, it seemed ludicrous to try and invent a plot when the surrealism of everyday life in Mexico felt so compelling. I found myself trying to describe the sky outside my window—surging and cleaving clouds, thunder and lightning, cotton-candy sunsets and a profusion of shooting stars. The constant drama of that sky seemed a testament to celestial will, grace and fury, an explanation of why there are so many believers in this part of the world. Instead of poetry, I wrote letters home.

Sent via e-mail, these monthly dispatches to friends and family took on a life of their own. My loved ones forwarded the letters to their loved ones, who in turn often asked to be added to my mailing list. What began as a list of thirty grew to nearly three hundred recipients. A fledgling writer couldn't ask for a greater gift. Knowing that there was an audience eager to read my words helped me develop confidence and discipline.

Through the letters, I began to discover my voice and core literary themes (death, lies, and room service). Eventually I found work as a guidebook correspondent and published two books about Mexico—one about Day of the Dead and the other about the architecture and interior decor of Mexican inns. Dave also thrived creatively. He practiced playing his horns several hours a day and found work with an art-rock band from Mexico City, as well as jazz gigs at various resorts.

We loved living in Mexico, but ultimately tired of being outsiders. The downside of a culture rooted in family clans is that friends aren't as integral. Annalena's classmates rarely invited her home to play because there they played with their cousins. We had genuinely warm, but stubbornly superficial relationships with our neighbors. While it was possible for us to feel gloriously swept away by the splendor of saint's day celebrations, these holidays would never belong to us. And because most of the expatriates we met were either cantina-hopping college students or cocktail party-hopping retirees, we didn't fit in with the foreigners either.

After four years away, it was time to engage again with our own tribe; to let Annalena get to know her own cousins; to taste Black Diamond cheddar, sushi, and real maple syrup; and to hear the thunk of the Sunday *New York Times* on our doorstep. We returned to a Victorian house in Oakland and made dates to meet old friends for lattes at our favorite cafés. Annalena learned about the wonders of drinking fountains and central heating. Dave got another arts-administration job and my old boss at the software company hired me part-time to write brochure copy. Our community welcomed us back with open arms.

But we've been home five months now, and I'm not sure we belong in California anymore either. We're struggling to reconcile the Mexican sky that now fills our hearts with the daily grind of a more or less upwardly mobile life. I find myself willfully spacing out, trying to slow down the pace, trying to hold onto the sense that time is simply time, not money. Perhaps we've become permanent expatriates—neither fish nor fowl, forever lost no matter our location. But this fluidity also means that we're now like mermaids and centaurs—magic creatures who always know there's another way.

A Taste of Home

Tonya Ward Singer

The year I taught English in China, I tried every kind of food except dog soup. I ate chicken feet, fish heads, and the gummy tendons cut from pigs' legs. I even developed a love of cold jelly-fish and cucumber salad.

"China has the best food," my students often told me. So did people I met on the bus. In fact, every stranger who got past saying hello and asking if I used chopsticks raved about the culinary superiority of China.

I didn't argue. The truth is I ate well. Aside from sea slugs and a few other meals I'd rather forget, I enjoyed banquets of sautéed snow peas, garlic shoots, sweet-and-sour pork, and steamed fish. I ate better in China than I ever had at home, and yet, six months into my life in Qingdao, I began craving roasted chicken.

Really, the craving surprised me. I hadn't eaten roasted chicken once in the previous year, when I worked in the U.S., or even during the four preceding years of college. The chicken I craved was my mother's. She baked it on special occasions, perhaps once or twice a year, when we had enough time to prepare dinner long before we were hungry. I rested my head against the kitchen counter as she worked, watching her pull out the bag of gizzards and dust the chicken with salt. She let me crush the rosemary in my hand then sprinkle it over the bumpy poultry skin. Then we waited together, playing Scrabble at the dining-room table, as our house filled with oven warmth.

When we pulled the chicken from the oven, it oozed juices through crispy skin. It was succulent, nothing like the steamed chickens with white rubbery skin hanging in Chinese restaurant windows, nothing like the chunks of meat and bone fried in a wok. No, it was my mom's chicken. A taste of home.

Unfortunately, buying chicken in China was nothing like shopping for poultry in the United States. The neighborhood market in Qingdao had no clean-plucked bodies in cellophane on yellow foam trays. These chickens had feet, feathers, heads, and, yes, life.

I had seen them crammed together in rusty wire cages stacked three high on the ground in my first weeks in Qingdao, before I made it a habit to avoid that side of the market. They were in the same aisle as the wriggling eels, fish, and crawling crabs. I preferred to shop on the other side of the warehouse along the rows of low tables piled high with green peppers, eggplants, rice, and other stationary food.

The piles of vegetables and grains were the only anchors of stillness in the bustling market. The blue and gray clothing of busy shoppers and vendors flowed down the aisles. Voices in negotiation provided a constant background hum, accompanied by the sharp rustle of plastic bags filling with produce. The smells wafted in clouds, some delicious, like the aroma of coal-roasted sweet potatoes, and others as foul as drying shrimp and chicken manure.

It was several days before I finally mustered the courage to walk to the chicken vendor and ask, "How much?"

"*10 kuài*," the man behind the cages said. I eyed his gray rumpled clothes for signs of blood, but there were none. Who would kill this chicken?

"*Tài gui le.*" I protested the price out of habit, having no real clue what a chicken should cost. Chinese came easily to me in the market, where bargaining was both a necessity and my only genuine chance to practice speaking the language. In other parts of town, I rarely got through one sentence in Chinese before a young stranger in the crowd approached to practice English. With my students and friends from the university, I was an English teacher above all else. They smiled and clapped when I spoke a word of Chinese, then turned the conversation back to the language they wished to master.

In the market, however, it was all business. Vendors wanted my money. I wanted their goods. The more Chinese I spoke, the better I could live on my university salary of $160 per month.

"*Néng bù néng pián yi diǎr.*" I asked the chicken seller if he would lower his price.

Two women left the squid table to stand beside me and stare at my strange foreign face speaking Chinese.

The man lowered his price to nine yuan per half-kilo, then pointed to a small cage crowded with four hens. The gray speckled hen pushed to the front to stare through the wire at my feet. She was cute in a pathetic way, with feathers stuck in all directions like a head of short hair first thing in the morning. I was on the verge of asking for her when she looked up and met my eyes with her own. Two empty blue disks. Forget it.

By now six more shoppers had gathered around to watch me, the outsider, trying to buy a chicken. A ten-year-old boy called "hello!" then hid behind his mother's legs. Two gray-haired women pointed at me and giggled like schoolgirls. I'd been shopping in the same market for half a year and still could not stand in one place longer than three minutes without gathering a crowd.

In the initial weeks I didn't mind the attention. It was fun to try speaking Chinese and have so many people listen and respond. After months, it got old. Really old. Some days I simply stared back in anger as if my eyes could say what I dared not shout, "I'm just another human. Stop staring. Leave me alone!"

Today I didn't have the energy to get upset, I just wanted to buy my chicken and go home. I pointed to the least scrawny of the red hens. The man leaned down to reach for her then stopped, turned and looked at me. He dragged a finger across his throat then raised his eyebrows in question. I nodded, relieved.

He grabbed my selected victim by the neck. She flapped her wings and puffed out her feathers, squawking while I struggled not to look away. My whole life I had pretended meat came from a refrigerated section in Safeway. It was time to face the truth.

With a sharp turn of his wrists, the man twisted her neck. She flapped for a minute, then went limp. Dinner.

He hooked her now-flexible neck to the end of a simple scale made of a stick and a weight on a string. Reading the scale is one of three basic elements of shopping in China: bargain, read the scale, and count your change. These I learned after being ripped-off several times in the first month. It depressed me really, the way I set out on guard as if every market vendor were out to cheat me. But I wasn't paranoid. My blond hair and round eyes were clear signs of wealth. It didn't matter that I spoke Chinese, earned a Chinese salary, and shopped in the same market every week. It didn't matter that I woke up at dawn each morning to practice tai chi. It didn't matter that I cooked in a wok, rode the bus, and lived much like my neighbors. No, in the market I was always a foreigner. Someone to stare at and overcharge.

Luckily, the poultry vendor had a contraption for removing feathers. He dropped the hen in a steaming vat that looked like an industrial washing machine, hit spin, waited a minute, then pulled out a bumpy pink body. It was half the size of the original hen. I tried not to look surprised, thinking maybe feather loss contributed to the drastic size reduction, but I had the sneaking suspicion I'd been duped.

Actually, it's a good thing the hen was small. Otherwise it would have never fit in my four-slice toaster oven. There is no such thing as a home oven in China, at least not in any apartment kitchen I ever saw. My four-foot-by-four-foot kitchen consisted of a two-burner stovetop, a gas canister, a grimy red trash bucket, and a sink balanced on cinder blocks. The toaster oven, a luxury afforded only to foreign teachers, sat on my desk in the dining room beside the phone.

When I first moved to China I was surprised to find only one choice in kitchen cutlery, a rectangular cleaver large enough to be a murder weapon in a horror film. It was overkill for mincing garlic and slicing green beans, but today it proved to be precisely the tool I needed to chop off the hen's feet and head.

The giblets, unfortunately, weren't neatly packaged in an easy-to-remove mesh bag. Knowing the hen had to be gutted, I reached into the body cavity and yanked out liver, stomach, and other tepid slimy organs I could grab with my bare fingers. Wet chicken innards rivaled the peeled grapes and cold spaghetti my friends made me touch while blindfolded at Halloween parties. I sacrificed a pair of desk scissors to cut at the remaining organs, then gave up. What didn't come out would bake as stuffing.

The skin looked much like the bumpy raw flesh of any supermarket chicken. I sprinkled it with salt and pepper, then stepped back and cocked my head like an artist pondering her next move. Rosemary, I needed rosemary. Luckily, I had some in the care package of American herbs my mother had sent me at Christmas. I poured a small pile of rosemary in my right palm and crushed it with the base of my left hand. The aroma filled my mind with images of mom's golden brown roasted chicken, the meal I was ready to bake.

I knew the numbers on the oven's thermostat dial represented degrees Celsius, not Fahrenheit. Proud of my own resourceful-ness, I copied the algebraic conversion equation from the back of my Lonely Planet guidebook and penciled calculations on a torn piece of paper bag. The numbers looked exact, so precise in fact that I set the dial and stuck the chicken in the oven without even considering that something might be wrong.

After an hour the naked hen was still pink. I then discovered the major flaw in my original plan: I had overestimated the accuracy of my Chinese toaster oven. Appliances purchased in China are nothing like the ones manufactured for export to the U.S. They may look the same on the outside, but those numbers around the temperature dial are purely for decoration, as useful as the word "Reebook" on the side of a pair of imitation tennis shoes, or the name "Everyready" on a new battery that doesn't work.

I cranked the dial up as far as it could go, set my watch timer for thirty more minutes and returned to the couch to read my book. When the timer started beeping, I ran to the toaster to reap the rewards of my hard work. This was the moment I had waited for, when mom would reach into the oven with her padded mitts and remove the baked chicken, a golden brown feast oozing rosemary juices from crispy skin.

I grabbed two dishtowels for potholders and opened the toaster-oven door. The hen was still pink. There was no delicious aroma. My apartment still smelled of dust and the steamed dumplings I had eaten for lunch. More time, I reassured myself, she needed more time.

A half-hour later, I determined it must be time for dinner. Golden brown or not, the hen *had* to be cooked after two hours of baking. I removed her from the oven and set her aluminum baking tray on a folded dishtowel in the center of the dining-room table. I stood over the pallid poultry, stuck a fork in the top and attempted to carve a slice of meat.

It was nothing like the turkeys I had carved during college Thanksgivings. It was nothing like any chicken mom ever baked. White with a pink hue, the meat felt like stringy rubber and resisted cutting. I pried out a string of breast meat with my fork and touched it to my tongue. My tongue knew better, and retracted to safety, leaving the bland semicooked strands of meat on the fork.

I felt sad for the hen at that point; a pathetic thing killed for a meal I couldn't cook. Was it too late to cube her into a stir-fry? Recooked in a pan, her meat would be as chewy and dry as the freeze-dried chicken cubes found in packaged Lipton Cup-a-Soup. Yech!

I wrapped her in the front page of last Sunday's *Washington Post* and carried her down six flights of stairs to the trash pile outside. I set her on a mound of cabbage leaves not yet swarming with flies. Perhaps the wispy-haired homeless woman who searched the trash pile daily would make her a meal. Even if she didn't, at least the rubbery hen had fulfilled her purpose: I had lost my craving for roasted chicken.

Trying to accept my defeat gracefully, I crossed the street to my favorite restaurant to order something I could count on: cold jellyfish and cucumber salad.

The Liverpool School of Dream and Pun

Rhiannon Paine

Darkness with light inside it. Illumination in an unexpected place. The bright child in the bleak house was an image to which Charles Dickens returned, time and time again. Little Nell, Florence Dombey, David Copperfield. Something appealing there, something that called to him. Perhaps it was the paradox? As a man, he liked things tidy, clean, and simple. As an artist, he knew they weren't.

I do remember bright days in Liverpool. In good weather, I used to drive down to Otterspool Promenade and walk along the Mersey, or take a ferry back and forth from Pier Head, standing out on deck to catch the sun. Another memory: a summer lawn, a pot of tea, and a plate of strawberry tarts. One January morning it snowed and then the sun came out. Devonshire Road sparkled like a white river, and the garbage cans in the courtyard wore peaked caps of snow. I had to heat the key to my Mini with a match because the lock had frozen. I was pleased to have figured out that match trick. As a native Californian, I hadn't had much experience with snow.

So it's not Liverpool's fault that most of my memories take place in gloomy interiors, or in a gloomy exterior composed of night, overcast or rain. Maybe it's a case of first impressions. I arrived in August 1978, but Lime Street Station seemed to be trapped in Dickensian winter. The station smelled like damp clothes, cigarettes, and grime-caked concrete. Dead-faced people slouched along like the ghosts of Christmas past. Discarded newspapers flapped down the platforms. The big round clock over the ticket booths ran twenty minutes slow.

"Rhiannon Paine? I'm Miriam Allott. You look just like your description."

The head of the English department at the University of Liverpool was striking in appearance, with a dramatic nose and flyaway black hair. I shook hands with her, trying to remember how I'd described myself over the telephone. "Thirty years old, slender, brown hair in an unfortunate perm that looks like a Brillo pad"? But she'd have spotted me as an American anyway. People always did, even when I was encased in an English raincoat and waterproof boots.

"My car's outside," said Professor Allott. "It's too bad about all this rain." We set off to the dorm where she'd arranged for my temporary accommodations. "You'll want to know more about the MA course," she offered. "You'll have three seminars on alternating weeks: the Victorian Novel, Thomas Hardy, and Victorian

Ideas and Beliefs. Do you know anyone in Liverpool? Never mind. I'll introduce you round. And there are two girls on the course with you, recent graduates. You're the only mature student."

We sloshed along between rows of redbrick buildings. People walked bent-shouldered under streaming umbrellas, or huddled together in bus shelters. As we rounded a corner I saw a Victorian statesman in bronze, erect on his pedestal, one arm flung out, gesturing toward new lands for Her Majesty to colonize. The pedestal was tall, but some Liverpudlian wit had taken the trouble to scale it (at night, with a stepladder? or had he gotten a leg up from a friend?) so he could hang, over the wrist of that noble out-thrust arm, the handles of a plastic shopping bag from Tesco supermarket.

Would I find anything more ironically cogent to say about Victorian ideas and beliefs in my MA seminars? It didn't seem likely.

A chain of introductions ensued. Professor Allott introduced me to John, a lecturer in communication studies. John introduced me to Clare, who was getting her M.Phil. in English. Clare promised to introduce me to other friends. Was I such a find that people couldn't wait to share me? Or was everyone desperate to hand off the odd-duck Californian to someone else? I'd lived in England on and off for three years, but I still couldn't be sure what English people were thinking.

Clare had done the Victorian MA and offered to lend me her books, so I paid her a call. First I stood and examined her building from the shelter of a new umbrella. (It was raining again.) Dark trees and diseased-looking shrubbery edged the courtyard. Scars disfigured the gray plaster around the front door. I wasn't sure how one cared for brick buildings, but whatever the process was, it had not been applied in many years to 10 Park Road.

The front door opened with a haunted-house creak. I walked down the hallway to Clare's flat.

I had been warned that she didn't clean. "She thinks housework is ideologically unsound," I'd been told. "Bourgeois. Right-wing. Boring. So it's a bit untidy, her flat. Moldy cups and plates. And dead mice on the floor."

"Dead mice?"

"The cat brings them in. And Clare doesn't hang her clothes up. She picks them off the bedroom floor, sprays them with Shalimar, and puts them on. Oh, and take some tissues. No toilet rolls. She uses newspapers. The *Daily Mail* and the *Telegraph*. It's a political statement."

No one had mentioned the dead palm plants or the bruised-olive carpet littered with cigarette butts. The walls and ceiling were dark navy blue. The light that leaked through the dirt-crusted windows shone on Clare's beautiful red hair, which edged her heart-shaped face in a fiery tangle.

"Hi man, sit down, move some books. No, that chair's broken. Shall we have a nice cup of tea? I know you'd rather have coffee but I'm sorry, Rhiannon, I haven't got any. I can make the tea very strong, you'd like that, wouldn't you?"

I looked at the mugs Clare had gathered from the two-crate coffee table. "None for me, thanks."

"It's all right, I've got clean mugs in the kitchen, honestly."

An unattractive cat appeared, sized me up—friend or foe?—guessed wrong, and started rubbing my ankles.

Clare came back carrying a warped tin tray. "Oh, you've met the Omelette, isn't he wonderful? So much character, and he's very intelligent. Roll over and play dead, Omelette." The cat rolled over, cranked its paws in the air and slitted its eyes. Clare poured the tea and curled up on the sagging sofa. "Not your scene. Right, man?"

"It's nice to see you again," I said carefully.

"No, you're an order-out-of-chaos person, I can tell. A place for everything and everything in its place."

"I can't concentrate if my apartment's messy. It's how I was raised."

"It's how all women are raised. And it's an effective way of preventing us from concentrating, isn't it? Because 'things fall apart; the centre cannot hold.' Men can concentrate in messy rooms if the alternative is to clean them. But women! The mess 'is too much with us; late and soon,' cleaning and cooking, 'we lay waste our powers: Little we see in Nature that is ours.'"

I saw a lot in Nature that was Clare's. Dust and mold, for starters. On the other hand, she'd just quoted Yeats and Wordsworth in the same paragraph. I could do that too, but there hadn't been much point until now.

"We didn't have a chance to talk properly the other night," Clare said. "Tell me, why did you choose to come to Liverpool?"

I explained that I'd been living in England off and on since 1973, going home to San Francisco occasionally to earn money. Now I wanted to get an MA. "But I'm on a tight budget, and the North is cheaper than the South, right? So I wrote to York, Newcastle, and Liverpool. From York and Newcastle, I got form letters and things. Brochures. But Professor Allott wrote to me personally."

"So you're here because Miriam Allott wrote to you? Not because you want to specialize in the period?"

I drained my mug and felt a wodge of tea leaves filter through my teeth. "I don't care about the period. I just want to go back to school."

"Fascinating." Clare looked at me as if she was a microscope and I was a bug. One of the Omelette's fleas, maybe. You knew he had them; he was that kind of cat.

"Professor Allott called me a 'mature student,'" I said.

"I know. I'm one too. I don't feel old enough to be mature. Do you?"

"No way."

The Omelette yawned. He was missing most of his teeth, I noticed. He stretched luxuriously, showing me his balls.

Clare introduced me to a couple of PhD candidates in English. Jenny was vibrant, with cropped dark hair, dark eyes, and skin like pink-gold roses. Judy was tall, blue-eyed, soft-spoken and had long, expressive hands. Within minutes, I knew I wanted them as friends. They were clearly less impressed with me, but I pursued them, like the Hound of Heaven in the Francis Thompson poem, with unperturbed pace, deliberate speed, and majestic instancy, rooting them out of their tiny study rooms in the Sydney Jones Library, or tracking them down in Cousins's, a working-class "caff" they frequented, where the coffee tasted like tea and the tea tasted like water from the Mersey.

I preferred their other haunt, the windowless, dimly lit bar at the Everyman Theatre. Its deep-purple carpet and wallpaper reminded me of the hippie pads of my youth. The black chairs and tables were crowded at all hours with cast members from the current production, students, artists, and other Liverpool riffraff. Hair on both sexes was cropped and spiky. Heels were stacked and chunky. You could tell the girls from the boys because the boys' trousers were tighter.

One day in early October, I pushed through to the bar, got a slice of pizza and a glass of wine, and joined Clare, Jenny, and Judy. With them was a diminutive dark-haired man.

"You are an artist," said the stranger, gazing at me soulfully. Maybe it was the way I was cramming pizza into my mouth and dribbling crumbs on the table, where they formed a pattern not unlike a Modigliani painting.

He pressed a round blue badge into my mozzarella-scented hand. "Come Saturday night," he said. "It's a home for artists."

The badge had a gold beetle on it. "The Liverpool School of Language, Music, Dream, and Pun," it read. "Mathew Street." When I looked up, the stranger was gone.

"'Dream and pun?'" I said. "What does that mean, 'dream and pun'?"

"Americans are so literal-minded," Jenny said.

"Boring," Clare said.

"But it's silly," I said.

"You should go," Clare said. "It's a home for artists."

"I've got a home, if you can call one room in Devonshire Road a home. What I need is a place to take a shower."

"In the conversation of Americans," Judy said dreamily, "plumbing recurs." She was wearing footless tights under her flowered dress. They looked odd to me, black tights to the ankle and then the bare tops of startlingly white feet, but it was the newest thing.

"You had Ideas and Beliefs this morning, didn't you?" Clare asked. "How did it go?"

"Oh, God. Dr. Shrimpton kept asking me about *David Copperfield*. I read *Mary Barton*. It took me three days, and he didn't ask a single question about bloody *Mary Barton*. He kept going on about Agnes and what she represents, and whether Dora tells us anything about the Victorian family. How am I supposed to know?"

"You haven't read *David Copperfield?*"

They looked at me as if I were some fabulous, legendary creature. A dragon. A unicorn. A Tory with a social conscience.

"Come on, guys. I was a history major."

"Then why aren't you doing an MA in history?" Jenny asked.

"Because I wanted to read great books and be told what to think of them. I didn't know *I* was supposed to have thoughts about them. I didn't even know I was supposed to have *read* them. There're two hundred books on the reading list, and they're all about eight hundred pages long. I'll never get through them all."

"It seems unlikely," Jenny agreed. "Unless you read nonstop. Of course, if you spent a bit less time in the Everyman. . . ."

Clare shook her head. "Oh Rhiannon, how dire! You're not supposed to be reading them for the first time! You're supposed to be refreshing your memory."

Judy stubbed out a cigarette. They smoked, all three of them. None of my friends in California smoked. Everyone knew that smoking wasn't healthy. In England, apparently, health was boring. "You don't just read one subject at university the way we do, do you?" Judy asked. "You do that course—what's it called? 'Liberal arts'?"

I explained that as an undergraduate, in addition to four years of history, French, and English, I had taken classes in biology, geology, anthropology, sociology, psychology, archery, badminton, modern dance, and a required class called Personal Hygiene. "I can tell you all about the follicle-stimulating hormone," I offered.

"I don't feel any compelling need to know," said Jenny.

I stood up. "I'm going home." Was that a gleam of relief in Jenny's eye? "To Devonshire Road," I amended.

"Quite right," Jenny said crisply. "Get started on that reading."

I drove home in the used car I'd bought, a Mini the color of a decomposing pumpkin. On the way, I assessed my progress on the friends front. Clare had spent some time in America and seemed to understand me. John was Canadian and a kindred spirit, and his wife, Ann, accepted me for John's sake. With everyone else, and even with Clare and Ann sometimes, I was still auditioning for the role of friend. I wasn't a natural for the part. I came at people directly, explained the obvious, displayed emotion.

"The cardinal sin in America is to be insincere," Clare had told me. She was quoting someone, she couldn't remember whom. "Whereas the cardinal sin in England is to be boring."

I'd promised to think about it.

I turned down Princes Street and saw the statue again, the Victorian statesman on his pedestal. He had lost his shopping bag.

It had taken weeks to find a place I could bear to live in. Most of the Liverpool "flats" I was shown consisted of one scruffy room with a bathroom down the hall ("but only five other tenants sharing, Miss Paine"). Clare explained that English laws made it almost impossible to evict people, so owners were afraid to rent out empty rooms or houses. Still, it wasn't right to put people on the streets just because they couldn't pay their rent. In principle, I agreed. In practice, I deplored the result, which was that I couldn't find a better place to live than 15 Devonshire Road.

Toxteth, Liverpool 8, would have been considered a slum in San Francisco. It was probably a slum in Liverpool too, the difference being that in Liverpool, university students lived in slums. The buildings on Devonshire Road ran the gamut from "needs a bit of work" to heaps of rubble. Number 15 was in the "needs work" category. Three story, redbrick, it had probably been as posh as a top hat in Dickens's day. My flat on the ground floor, front, was a long rectangle with a twenty-foot ceiling. A tacked-in partition down one side wrecked the proportions but housed a tiny bathroom and kitchen.

The partition was yellow. The walls were pink. The dust-furred curtains over the one big window clashed with the carpet, from which terrifying shapes in black, avocado, and gold struggled to emerge. The "three-piece suite"—a sofa and two armchairs—was upholstered in maroon with yellow splotches that looked like exploding flowers.

Life in a foreign country is a dance of submission and resistance. Self-knowledge comes in small repeated shocks as you find yourself giving in easily, with a struggle, or not at all. What can you do without? What do you cling to? I would live in a slum because students did, and go without a phone because the landlord refused to install the wiring. But I would not live with clashing colors. I bought paint and brushes, combed used-furniture shops and stood on tiptoe atop a steamer trunk that I'd set, upended, on a sideboard, to hang my new cream-colored curtains. I could have fallen to my death, but by God I'd have died in a flat where the curtains matched the woodwork.

English people put up with things that Americans wouldn't stand for. For example, relationships with utility companies are held to be lifelong arrangements, like matrimony, not to be entered into lightly by graduate students or other fly-by-night individuals living in rented accommodations. Instead of holding accounts with utility companies like responsible grown-ups, tenants push coins into meters. My flat had two meters by the bathroom: 10-pence coins for gas, 50-pence coins for electricity. I'd be reading *Mary Barton* when suddenly all the lights would go out and I'd have to crawl around in the dark trying to find my wallet. Landlords collected the meter-money and paid the utility companies, and made a useful profit into the bargain.

I shoved $100 a month into those meters, an amount that equaled my rent. It cost a dollar a day to take a bath and then it was twelve hours before the water got hot again. I'd never earned much money in San Francisco, but I'd always been warm. My utility bills had run $15 a month with all the hot water I could squander. Nor had I ever factored the price of gasoline—three times more expensive in England—into a decision about whether to drive somewhere. In California, except for a brief period in the early seventies, heat, hot water, and gasoline flowed like never-ending streams. In England they were precious, doled out a little at a time, available in large quantities only if you were rich. People with open fireplaces burned coal, not wood. The coal had to be hacked out of the ground by miners whose blackened faces and ruined lungs proved that the real cost of energy isn't measured in money.

California began to seem as unreal as Disneyland, a playground for children, a fantasy world where people couldn't grow up because the true nature of things was hidden behind special effects and spectacular scenery.

No phone, so people had to drop in if they wanted to talk to me. No doorbell either, so visitors knocked on my bathroom window. Jenny's knock was brisk, Judy's tentative, John's Canadian (unassuming, but it got the job done). Clare refused to knock. She said it was boring. She stood outside and called, "Yoo-hoo, Rhiannon!"

They dropped in to give me the news, to talk about their work, to see if I'd finished *Jude the Obscure* yet, or to ask if I wanted to go to Peter Gee's for Chinese food. Clare dropped in to invite me to poetry readings, Judy to ballet, Jenny to opera, John to movies and the theater. They dropped in singly, in pairs, in groups. After they left, I'd run to the dictionary and look up the unfamiliar words they'd used. Jenny was an especially rich source. I'm still indebted to her for adding "periphrastic" and "accidie" to my vocabulary.

I had reciprocal drop-in rights. I could go see Clare any time, although she reserved the right to send me away if she was having one of her infrequent "angsts," bouts of depression that necessitated lying in bed (a mattress on the floor) in a fog of cigarette smoke and Shalimar. "Dropping in" was a feature of that year, never to be repeated in my life until, perhaps, I move into the Retirement Home for Lint-headed Hippies. "I was just driving by," we'd say. "Yes, I'd love a cup of tea." We talked for hours about Life, Literature, Men: Why There Aren't Enough Good Ones and whether Labour had a chance of winning the next election. (They didn't. The Tories won in a landslide, and ushered in the Age of Thatcher.)

I dropped in on Clare one afternoon to talk about the sixties.

"Oh," Clare said, "I *loved* the sixties. We all lived in flats in Devonshire Road, that's why it's so nostalgic for me when I visit you, Rhiannon. I was trying to live down Roedean, and Devonshire Road was a good place to do it."

Roedean is a posh private school, the girls' equivalent of Eton. If I'd gone there, I wouldn't have tried to live it down, I'd have put *Educated at Roedean* on my business cards. Or maybe not. Maybe bragging about having gone to Roedean is one of the things you learn at Roedean not to do. It's so complicated to be English! Middle-class English, anyway. The straightforward acquisitiveness of Americans—earn as much as you can and show it off as flagrantly as possible—seems simpleminded by comparison. That's one reason the English are so endlessly interesting to me.

"But what did you do all day?" I asked.

"Well, we used to play football in Princes Park. Not your American kind, I mean, with everyone padded up and bashing about like belligerent cocoons. Soccer football. Our side was called Flared Nostril because we were spiritual and liked to sit under trees and smell the flowers. And the lot we played was called Clenched Fist, lefty political types, very militant, and must-get-on-with-the-revolution-as-soon-as-this-game-is-over. They're mostly Trades Union leaders now. Our side didn't play very well because we were always getting stoned and wandering off to look at interesting cloud formations, so Clenched Fist always won, but they didn't mind. They were the sort that always needs to win, and we were the sort that says, what's the point? And sometimes we'd get up at dawn and go pottering about Princes Park, picking up pretty rocks and leaves and things. And we'd wander around beaming at people, but only if they had good vibes."

"What did you do for money?" I asked.

"Oh, Rhiannon." (Money was boring.) "Well, some of us were at university, and some were at the Poly, and some of us had jobs in, you know, bookstores and health-food shops and things. Most of the Clenched Fists were at university because they were planning to change the system from within, so they had to get into the system first. And we thought we'd let them have a go, and if it worked, we'd have a new system, and if it didn't, we'd still have our pretty rocks and things. Why, man? What were you doing in California?"

"Protesting the war at U.C. Berkeley, in paisley bell-bottoms and a cloud of tear gas. The boys threw rocks at the cops and called them pigs. I couldn't see how that was going to end the war, but the boys said that, being a girl, I wasn't capable of understanding the complex dynamics of the revolution, and had I finished the typing yet? I was also feeling guilty about slavery and segregation and what we'd done to the Native Americans. So I decided to escape to England. Down the rabbit hole into a garden, just like Alice. Away from all that pain. Not that Liverpool's a garden."

"Or an escape. The wealth of this city was built on the slave trade. They're mortared with the blood of Africans, these buildings. Didn't you know?"

I hadn't. "Maybe that's why they're falling down," I joked. "Bad consciences."

"It's not a fairy tale," Clare said. "It's not 'Liverpool is falling down, my fair lady.' The Germans dropped bombs here, night after night, trying to stop the merchant ships from doing the North Atlantic run. In the May Blitz—1941, I think it was—there was a raid almost every night for six weeks. The sky was red. You could see the fires burning from North Wales. Twenty-five hundred people were killed on Merseyside. Over two hundred thousand houses were damaged."

I knew about the London Blitz. I'd lived in Plymouth, where most of the city center had been destroyed. I'd stood in the ruins of Coventry Cathedral and cried before the altar that German students built after the war, out of the rubble, making a cross of blackened timber and carving the words FATHER FORGIVE into the stone. But in Liverpool, I'd seen heaps of brick and I hadn't thought "bombs." I'd thought "lousy maintenance."

I said, "And the buildings can't be rebuilt because—"

"There's no money."

"I'm a twit," I said.

"Well, I wouldn't go that far. But I think it's just as well you switched from history to English."

I worked out a system for the MA course. When I ran out of time to finish a novel, I'd read the criticism, from which I could infer the plot: not the details, but enough to know that *Jude the Obscure* does not end happily. I could also pick up a line, a tack, something to say in seminar: "I agree with Blah-Boring's Marxist interpretation of the nature themes in Hardy." I didn't fool anyone, but I won points for trying, and for not making my instructors face the fact that they were sharing a room with someone who hadn't read the books. Meanwhile, I taught myself how to do literary criticism.

I got by on my wits and the strength of my writing, but I wasn't satisfied. Every book I read pointed an admonishing finger to the books I hadn't read. For every quotation I recognized, there were dozens that went past me. I wished desperately that I'd started sooner, and that, once this blessed year was over, I didn't have to go back to California and the tedious work of earning a living.

I wanted to put a glass dome over Liverpool, a life-size version of those toys that children shake to watch the snow fall. Only it would be rain that fell, not snow, and I'd be snug in 15 Devonshire Road, reading a book or writing a paper, my back against the maroon sofa, a cup of tea beside me. The gas fire would hiss, rain would drip through the tree outside my window, and then I'd hear a car door slam, feet splash across the courtyard, and someone would knock on my bathroom window. "Yoo-hoo, Rhiannon!"

Lacking that power to enchant, I knew that even if I stayed, even if I found a way to support myself in a city where a quarter of the workforce was unemployed, what I loved best would leave me. I was fond of Liverpool, but what I wanted to hang on to was the time to read and write and think. That, and the people.

Trudging away from the Modern Languages building one afternoon after a dispiriting Hardy seminar—I could tell Mr. Davies knew I hadn't finished *Jude the Obscure,* and was disappointed in me—I saw Professor Allott hailing me from under a bright yellow umbrella.

"Your essay on Carroll and Macdonald was excellent," she said. "Almost publishable, in fact."

I perked up. "Really?"

"But not quite." She cocked her head to one side, her hooded dark eyes sympathetic. "Do you know why not?"

"I haven't read enough."

"That's right."

Clare and Judy were sharing a table at the Everyman.

"You look sexy," Judy said. Caring about the working class didn't preclude an interest in fashion, although Clare limited herself to boutiques with names like Chez Guevara and clothes that were "ideologically sound." For months my friends had been saying, "If I had your body, I'd wear skin-tight trousers." A sucker for flattery, I had bought some narrow corduroy pants—I had to lie down to pull them on—and shoes with chunky heels.

"I don't feel sexy," I said. "My feet hurt and my pants keep going up my crotch. Why are you laughing?"

"Because you're funny," Clare said.

"I thought I was boring."

"You manage to be both. It's very endearing."

I didn't want to be endearing. I wanted to stun people with the weight of my intellect and dazzle them with my densely allusive discourse.

John walked in, got a glass of wine, and joined us.

"Professor Allott says my latest paper is 'almost publishable,'" I bragged. One wasn't supposed to brag—it wasn't done—but what the hell, I was American.

"Jolly good," John said warmly. He took off his rain-streaked glasses and polished them with his napkin.

"It's because you can type," Clare said wistfully.

"I think the actual words might have something to do with it," I responded, stung.

"Oh, Rhiannon, of course. But still—being able to type—it must be wonderful."

"Why don't they teach you to type in school?"

"It's something secretaries do, you see," Judy said earnestly. "Not students. Not people who are going to university."

"It's a function of the British class system," John explained.

"So working-class people learn something useful, and students have to write their papers by hand. That's silly."

"Like the Liverpool School of Dream and Pun," Clare said. "Did you ever go, by the way?"

I smiled. (People could tell I was American, John had told me, because I smiled so much.) "I don't need to," I said. "The Everyman, the books, you lot—you lot especially. You're my Liverpool School of Dream and Pun."

"Fancy that!" Judy said. "I've never been a school before."

They started to talk about structuralism. I caught the odd phrase—"the mother's phallus," "the ideal signified"—while I pondered the fact that Professor Allott had summed up my academic career in two words. Rhiannon Paine: almost publishable.

I spent the month-long Christmas break in California. The buildings were dazzling in their newness, in the perpetual sunlight that poured down like money, like hot water out of never-empty tanks. Cars gleamed, teeth sparkled, hair shone. On the torsos of my female friends, gold chains and silk blouses had broken out like an expensive rash. When people got together, they talked about things, not ideas. That cute new Mexican restaurant in the Marina. Where to buy the best silk blouses. I found the conversations boring, but I loved the Mexican restaurant.

I flew back to England, dizzy from cultural whiplash. Reflected in the eyes of my English friends, I had grown used to seeing myself as stodgy, materialistic, and a bit slow on the uptake. To the Californians, I was the next best thing to an intellectual: adventurous, free-spirited, left-wing, and eccentric as all get-out in my freaky skin-tight cords.

"So much depends on context," I told my taxi driver. My habit of engaging in long talks with taxi drivers was one of the things my English friends found endearing.

"Where you off to from Euston Station, love?"

"Liverpool."

"You won't get to Liverpool today. British Rail are on strike."

"Right. Yank the Yankee's other leg."

"No, straight up. The trains aren't running."

"Do you mean to tell me that the entire railway system of a major industrialized nation can just *shut down?*"

It seemed that it could. "Take you to a hotel, love, shall I?"

"But it's only two o'clock! Where's the nearest bus station?"

"Where you just came from. Victoria Air Terminal, across the street."

At the terminal, two porters in blue uniforms agreed to watch my luggage while I looked for alternative transportation. "But you won't get to Liverpool today," said Porter One, cheerfully.

"British Rail are on strike," explained Porter Two.

All the buses were full. All the car rental agencies were fresh out of cars. Everyone agreed, with irritating sprightliness, that I wouldn't get to Liverpool today because British Rail were on strike.

"No joy, eh?" asked Porter One.

"I can't believe it! I've just flown six thousand miles, and now people are telling me I can't do the last two hundred! I know people who'd drive that far to have dinner in an interesting new restaurant!"

"Would they, now," said Porter One.

Porter Two shook his head. "Two hundred miles is a fair old distance. I'd get a room for the night, pet. You can go to Liverpool tomorrow. Strike's meant to end at midnight."

"Although you never know," said Porter One.

At eight o'clock that night, I rang 10 Park Road. "Hi, Clare. Just wanted to let you know I'm back."

"Hi, man! Back where?"

"Liverpool."

"But you can't be! British Rail are on strike!"

"I flew."

"To Liverpool?"

"Yes."

A silence followed in which Clare seemed to be working something out. Finally she spoke. "There's an *airport* in Liverpool?"

❀ ❀ ❀

This proved, said my friends, how American I was. Go-ahead. Enterprising. Determined.

"Rubbish. I just don't like being told I can't do things. It makes me want to do them immediately."

"That's what we mean."

Here's what I wanted to say: *It was seventy-five degrees in San Francisco the day before Christmas, and I went shopping in jeans and a T-shirt, swinging along Clement Street, sunlight on my shoulders, all the shops open late and full of lovely things. But I couldn't wait to get back to this time-stained city and the smell of rain and coal fires and cigarette smoke and, when the wind is right, the Mersey River. I would rather eat cold pizza with you in the Everyman than fresh crab outdoors in San Francisco because there is something here, something I need, something that calls to me. I can't explain it. You've read everything, you're so much cleverer than I am. Please. Tell me what it is.*

But I didn't say it. Too emotional. Too sincere. Boring.

"Yoo-hoo! Rhiannon!"

Clare in a dark-gold boiler suit, fingerless mittens on a string around her neck. Rings on all her fingers. On her feet, scuffed brown cowboy boots. Her flat-mate, Les, in jeans and a ratty tweed jacket. Both excited, light pouring out of their pale faces.

"The revolution is coming!" They sat on the maroon sofa, lit cigarettes.

The lorry drivers were on strike now; also the dustbin men, the social workers, and the cemetery workers. Liverpool was storing its dead and unburiable bodies in an unused warehouse.

"The municipal water-treatment workers may come out!" Clare said.

"What happens if they do?"

"Well, that's the thing," Les said happily. "If they come out, the domestic water supply in Liverpool will be unusable!"

They beamed. Did they really expect me to share their joy, or were they hoping for a typically American reaction so they could tell their friends about it?

They could read me like *David Copperfield,* but I couldn't read them.

It had been a challenge, making friends with these people, and I had been exhilarated by the on-the-edge feeling, but now I was tired of conversations played like elaborate games. "I'm okay, you're not okay. I'm clever, you're boring." My American friends might talk about gold chains, but I didn't have to second-guess their motives. If I'd missed them, I could say so. "We missed you too," they would answer. And mean it.

But Les had spent hours helping me paint my flat. Clare had shared her books, her telephone, her friendship, her understanding of Victorian England. Angsts aside, I was welcome any time. Her house was my house. A scary thought, but still.

So I might as well give them what they wanted. I couldn't say it directly, so how else could I tell them that I loved them?

"You mean," I said, with genuine alarm, "I won't be able to take baths?"

Order out of chaos. It can't be done, but it's still my goal. I live in northern California, in a house that I try to keep clean and tidy. I edit technical documents, eat organic vegetables, practice yoga. My MA degree from the University of Liverpool is in a filing cabinet in a folder marked "Schools." There are other folders that prove I no longer attend, full-time, the School of Dream and Pun. "Retirement Savings." "Wills and Trusts." "Insurance: Home & Property." "Utility Bills." (Yes, I get to pay my own again.)

In 1995, Clare, Jenny, and Judy came to visit for two weeks. I showed them the sights. That's a redwood tree. There's the Pacific Ocean. Yes, our showers *are* better, aren't they? We talked for hours about Life, Literature, Men: Why There Aren't Enough Good Ones and whether Labour had a chance of winning the next election. (In a landslide. Clare says it hasn't made much difference.) Clare and Judy are therapists. Jenny's an academic and the author of two published novels. They can do sincerity now, and I can do clever. Not as well as they can, but well enough.

I'll see them again this year on my annual trip to England. I'll knock on Clare's door in north London, and she'll open it. "Hello, baby! You're here, fantastic! Come in, I've just washed the dog in the shower, I took him to the Heath and he rolled in badger shit, but he's all clean now, isn't he beautiful? John called, he and Ann are expecting you for dinner, and Les is coming round for lunch. Sit down—it's okay, just shove that stuff on the floor—and I'll make us a nice cup of tea."

They aren't simple, the things we keep going back for.

The Long Conversation

Deryn P. Verity

The tongue twisters that dotted the news in the 1990s—vowel-less place names like Krk and Vrba, jagged appellations like Stojkovic and Kruševac that staggered into English from their original rhythmic tongue—spoke to me privately, reminding me of past pleasures, shadowed but not entirely obliterated by current tragedy. In 1987, in the waning years of peace, I went to Yugoslavia, where I was to spend a year teaching English and linguistics to students at the Faculty of Philosophy in Niš. I ended up spending three years in that fractured country, two on the formal exchange program that sent me, and one for the sheer pleasure of the place, during which I scrounged for work and lounged by the sea.

A fever for war and retribution was certainly in the air when I lived there, but, blinded by my naive new-world optimism, truly believing that relative prosperity and relative freedom would outweigh hateful nationalism, I was shocked at the savagery that ensued. It was hard to connect the brutality of the 1990s with my memories of the people who had invited me to their houses and fed me their homemade cakes and wine. I was angry at myself, that

I had understood so poorly the sometimes corrosive mix of mysticism, manners, and mayhem that informed daily life in this country where east and west, so often described as "meeting," in fact embraced. But I was also grateful, as is common, I suppose, when a place is torn apart by war or by any searing wound, that I could remember what had been there before. As if I was listening to one radio broadcast that had constant interference from another on a nearby frequency, I followed the current news with one ear and relished, if faintly, the sights and sounds of "my" Yugoslavia with the other.

Before—the war, my trip—I was as ignorant as most other American travelers about the geography of my destination. Hungry for information, I read everything I could find about Serbia's second city, the birthplace of Constantine, Roman Naissus, an administrative center that grew up near some ancient radium springs. There is a market square, I read, the remains of a castle, some old streets and a few old stones. My subconscious cooked this information into a dreamscape that began to visit me then, and that still appears, unaltered by the reality of the place, fifteen years later. First love, it turns out, is both indelible and blind.

Set in the heartland of socialist Yugoslavia, just off the expressway linking Belgrade to Greece, Niš was not an overtly lovable place. It was dusty and breathless in the summer, damp and filthy in the winter. Air-dried clothes soon turned gray, and the tap water was, at best, stale. The people were small-city tough, one generation off the farms of their fathers, a train ride away from the villages of their grandmothers. Socialist grimness in general, and provincial socialist ugliness in particular, made Niš a kind of national joke, the Pittsburgh of the Balkans. My fellow Fulbrighters, placed in more appealing towns—bustling, intellectual Belgrade; picturesque Zagreb; alpine Ljubljana—felt bad for me. They knew the reputation this gritty provincial city had: drab, dull, narrow-minded, isolated on its dry inland plateau, convenient to neither the stunning Dalmatian coast nor the summer-cottage greenery of the forested Bosnian hills.

Yet from the minute I arrived on the dingy Niš Ekspres bus from Belgrade, I felt deeply, unexpectedly, at home. The city's rough courtesies were somehow comforting, and I cut my traveler's teeth on the new alphabet, the indecipherable bus system and the unfamiliar rhythms of the place, of a life that was neatly divided between working for the state and working for oneself. The only foreign resident in town, except for a small population of Greek university students, I was in no danger of isolation, because these casual socialists were inveterate socializers. Though a stranger, and clearly a foreigner, a lone female in a society where women rarely traveled alone, a less-than-fluent speaker of the local language—then Serbo-Croatian, now, politically correct, just Serbian—I was the person everybody talked to: bus drivers and beggars, shopkeepers and policemen, soldiers and children, janitors and hairdressers: "Where are you from? How old are you? Where are you going? Are you married? Why not? Where are your parents? How do you like our food? How long have you been here, how long will you stay?" Curiosity was the conversational currency; one day, browsing at a fruit kiosk, I heard an elderly customer ask the shopkeeper, after eyeing my jeans and parka, "Is she ours?"

I was adopted by an elderly couple who lived two floors down. Afternoons were set aside for pie or cherries or bean stew and tales of rural life. Like much of the population, the Pešićs had moved into the city from a small village. Mrs. Pešić described how, on the same day she had given birth to her fifth child, she'd been back in the fields picking vegetables. A natural teacher, she demonstrated how she used to churn her own butter and grind her own grain, using large gestures to illustrate the unfamiliar words. Wiping tears from her eyes, she told me how her daughter had been living apart from her husband for seven years (her only foreign word, "*ësieben!*", fingers held up to emphasize the number); how proud she was of her grandson, who spoke English and German, was on the chess team, was a good boy, though his father lived, like so many fathers did, in Germany, working at a factory to support his wife and son back home. Mr. Pešić told me of the time, forty-five years previous, when he'd helped rescue an American airman whose plane had come down near his house. His tears flowed at the memory of the young man's courage. America had been a friend to his land in that war. Serbs and Americans, he predicted, would always be friends.

The language rolled over and around me. I thought at first

that it was loneliness that drove these elderly people to fill the air with stories, to tell a story again rather than let the conversation die, but I soon learned that this was a national trait. Serbs hate silence. The presence of another person provides an irresistible opportunity to talk. As a language teacher, I recognized and appreciated the ways in which the most casual acquaintances abetted my efforts to speak.

A gypsy vendor at an open-air market:
"How much is this?"
"Thirty dinars."
"I take it. Thank you."
"Oh, you speak our language so well."

A vendor at a vegetable market: I saw lettuce (*ësalata'*) for the first time and I was so happy to see the soft green leaves after a winter of cabbages and onions that I decided to buy three.
"Three salads please."
"Three kilos of salad?"
"Uh, no . . . three salads."
"Only three? Three?"
"Uh, yeah."
Shaking head. "You eat like a bird," flapping arms to illustrate.

The slow Balkan trains were particularly good for language practice. An overnight trip in a six-seat compartment meant that, though I had to breathe in the smoke of the two-hundred-or-so cigarettes my five (astonished) male traveling companions consumed, I could enjoy a conversation punctuated with shared chocolates and fruit, interrupted only by the few hours we set aside for sleep, legs stretched demurely but firmly into the seat corner next to the lap of the person we faced. On another, daytime, ride, a young man in my compartment spoke to me, nonstop, for the entire twelve-hour trip. When I begged off for ten minutes and retreated behind a magazine, just for a break, he chastised me, as if we were on a date and I was sulking over my milk shake, "Why are you silent? Why don't you talk to me?" A Gastarbeiter in Zurich, Selver was on his way back to Kosovo to visit his family; I gave him my name and telephone number, more out of admiration for his stamina than any particular attraction.

Such human warmth, though, had to work hard to offset the physical bleakness of my adopted city. Everything in Niš seemed to be ugly or crumbling or both. The frowzy modernist bus station, styled as if for the Jetsons had they lived in the South Bronx, was peeling its plastic veneer. The most famous tourist attraction in town was a tower, erected by an invading Turkish army in the early nineteenth century, made from human skulls. Once, coming home from Belgrade, my bus caught fire. "What's that?" I yelped to my seatmate, as the black smoke began to swirl around our heads. "Oh, something's on fire," he replied, shrugging. I am ashamed to confess that I ran to the front of the bus and explained that I—an American!—could not sit back there and be expected to breathe in smoke. The gallant ticket-taker let me share his tiny jump seat for the rest of the trip, the price of his kindness being a cup of coffee at the station when we arrived, so that he could always tell of the time that he had coffee with the lady from New York. Though we talked of many things for those two hours, there was no talk of stopping the bus to put out the fire.

I came to nurture a perverse pride in Niš, coming to appreciate its rough charms, maybe even love it as its citizens did, for its very anti-loveliness. My home base was a shabby concrete hulk that, like most of the apartment blocks in Niš, had been put up in the '60s to house the influx of villagers who came to the city for jobs. Similar to dozens of others, perhaps a bit more salubrious because it sat near some woods, my housing development consisted of three towers, each fifteen stories high. Frequent power outages meant that I knew the grimy stairwells all too well. Climbing twelve flights in the dark was an experience I didn't need to have more than once, but Niš, in this respect, was over-generous.

Placed in a kind of rough triangle, the towers were cheaply built but at least not crowded together. From my two small but comfortable rooms, a bed/sitting room and a kitchen to which I had to add only a washing machine and a radio, I had an open, if fiercely polluted, view of distant hills, beyond the chimneys and fire-pots of town. There was close to an acre of open space at the foot of the towers, mostly unpaved, studded with trash and rubble. Though children played there, and people parked their cars there,

I avoided the area after seeing feral dogs and rats as big as raccoons nosing around the dumpsters.

It was rumored that every household in Niš had a gun, a token of the military service required of all young men, but—though I heeded warnings not to be out on New Year's Eve when those guns were shot off in celebration—the city had a low rate of street crime and felt quite safe to me. In all my solo wanderings through town, I never faced anything more unsettling than severe nosiness; even the beggars who came knocking at my door on the twelfth floor were annoying rather than threatening.

My one frightening encounter came in an unexpected form. Just off the late-night bus from Belgrade, loaded with shopping, I decided to take a taxi home. Robustly charming, as always, about my ability to tell him that my address, "*Chernojevicheva, broj deset,*" was "behind the supermarket near the cemetery," the driver dropped me off near the entrance of the building, where, as always, the lights were burned out. As I stepped around the corner, I came face-to-face with a large, if scrawny, dog. Each of us startled, we both bristled with fear: he bared his teeth and snarled, I bellowed, an instinctive, resonant "*Hah!*" that came from the depths of my lungs. It worked, and he slunk off into the darkness. Not thinking to worry whether the rest of the pack might be lurking in the lobby—the front doors stood open day and night—I ran inside and prayed that the elevator would be working.

Excepting this grim incident, I found my affection for the

place growing, steadily if not with abandon. I was an affectionate lover rather than a passionate one, but the cliché is true: your first foreign country speaks to you as no subsequent one can. Although you may come to prefer life in other places, first patterns persist, providing insistent, if faded, touchstones for everything to come. When I moved north for a second Fulbright year in Slovenia, I suffered the cultural shock of silence. The Slovenes were not the indefatigable talkers their southern brethren were and I was suddenly, conversationally, invisible. Though I came to love, for its own beauties, that small republic, which voted in its first free elections while I was there, I never became familiar enough with the contours of the spiky archaic language to enjoy the kind of easy meetings I had had in Serbia.

Being abroad for the first time brings one's unexamined assumptions into sharp focus. Having spent my first thirty years enjoying the inalienable rights of the American customer, I found the petty arbitrariness of socialist bureaucracy irritating and intriguing in equal measure, its childishness making me glad that I was only temporarily subject to it. A post-office clerk wouldn't mail an envelope I handed her because it was "dirty": I had crossed out one letter and written the correct character slightly above the smudge. Another one wouldn't sell me twenty sheets of airmail paper; the "rule" was that each customer could have only ten, a rule that the clerk in the post office down the street apparently had never heard of. An official at the motor vehicles department in Niš decided that I must be Greek. "You can't be

American," he declared, "you are not blond," and for a week insisted on speaking to me only in Greek. After realizing that I didn't understand a word he was saying, he conceded that I might be Polish, which explained why I seemed to understand some Serbo-Croatian. There was never a hint of apology or explanation for the fact that it took me more than a week to register a car I had bought, entirely legally, from a departing colleague.

Having come of age in the determinedly unisex America of the 1970s, I enjoyed the naive regendering I received one day. My friend Jana and I spent an afternoon visiting a friend of hers; I wore corduroy slacks and a button-down shirt, Jana wore her usual skirt and heels. A few days later, the friend's eight-year-old daughter asked Jana how her husband was. "My husband is away in the Army this month," Jana explained, wondering why the little girl was asking. "Oh," said the girl. "I thought the man who came with you the other day was your husband. Was it your brother?" My short straight hair and slacks (and perhaps my relative taciturnity in the women's conversation—my linguistic ability in Serbian was limited, and Jana's friend didn't speak English) had turned me into a man. It made sense in a place where even young women ravaged their hair with harsh colors and chemicals, and almost always wore skirts and high heels, even to walk the hills in Niška Banja, the nearby spa town famous for its clean air and radon baths.

And, like everyone who gives over a permanent piece of their hearts to a foreign land, I was not immune to the lazy thrill of simply having the exotic made commonplace. Street life in Niš was not exactly a carnival of variety, but the persistence of rural traditions in the city gave even a normal shopping Saturday a gloss of lyricism. It became quite normal, for example, to encounter a Gypsy wedding band, the procession passing me by as I did my daily errands. I always enjoyed the deafening wail and thump of the trumpets and drums that led the newlyweds, who walked—the bride's necklaces of coins jingling, the groom's embroidered hat awry—soberly but not unhappily in the midst of the small crowd of relatives decked out in swirling skirts and billowing knee pants. The wild music was both a celebration and a plea: giving money to a wedding party brought the giver good luck. In return, at Orthodox weddings, the grooms threw money to the children who crowded the front steps of the city hall, Gypsy urchins prominent among them.

Later, I might encounter a horse-cart bringing wood to a house in town, or follow a donkey hauling a private farmer's load of onions and carrots to the market square. At the market, I'd watch as shrewd head-scarved wives bargained for a few dinars profit, while the men gossiped in small groups, deftly balancing themselves on the low three-legged stools common to the region. Smoking a long Turkish pipe, taking slugs of fiery plum brandy between puffs, feet in open-backed slippers splayed for comfort, each man wore a peaked military cap atop a head of thick white hair.

Still, I liked the market for itself, not only for its picturesque scenes. Compared to the gray-stained palette of the town, it was a shabby riot of color: enormous burlap bags of red, orange, yellow, and green peppers sat in fragrant rows, brought in from the southerly climes of Macedonia, a four-hour car ride away. Socks and slippers, cheap nylon as well as thick local wool, were strung between the booths, while stashes of carrots, red cabbage, brilliant green lettuce, and local flowers competed for the pittance you would spend. Once I bought a huge bouquet of flowers for the equivalent of fifty cents. As I wandered around the market, flowers in hand, a woman mistook me for a flower-seller and asked me how much I would charge for the bouquet. Mixing up my denominations (inflation was in full swing, and what had cost hundreds last week might cost millions today), I told her five dollars. "That's much too expensive," she huffed, and turned sharply away.

In town, once past the gloomy state-owned *Beogradska* department store, I could enjoy a strange mirror image of home, homegrown capitalism with a Balkan twist. Yugoslavia's communism was never as exclusive as that of Stalin's states; private enterprise was allowed, and by the late '80s, nearly ten years after Tito's death, encouraged. A stroll down a side street brought the sight of a freshly painted sign inviting young people in for an "*americka kafa*" or a "*srpski hot dog*" at the "Tropikana Kafe," while at a corner fruit stand, I once found an amazing pineapple lurking among the apples and potatoes. For the most part, though, merchants did not lure their customers in with even the most rudimentary of marketing techniques: shops were called by what they sold, and in the "Electrics" shop window, drab electrical parts were laid out in a loving but dejected display, their sparseness suggesting the limited stock inside. In the "Folklore" shop, traditional weavings were haphazardly piled, rusty-gold kilim and heathered blue sweaters awaiting the infrequent tourist's interested glance. And in the supermarket, badly packaged spaghetti spilled from ripped cellophane packages, while dusty jars of spicy red-orange *ajvar*, a pepper relish, lined the shelves. Everybody who shopped there knew that the respectable Niš housewife made her own, just as her father-in-law distilled his own delicately colored, violently alcoholic fruit brandy at home. Commercially packaged food was for students, bachelor laborers, and foreign lecturers, rootless souls who passed through the city lightly, leaving no trace.

Though I was part of the city's life while I lived there, it closed behind me quickly. A few months after I left Niš for Slovenia, I drove back for a long weekend to stay with a few friends. They said nothing to me at the time, but when, the next year, I suggested a return visit, their refusal was reluctant but unmistakable: the police had interrogated every one of my hosts, reminding them that foreigners were not welcome to come and go so casually.

Still, stubborn as always, Serbia kept speaking to me: a year or so after I'd relocated to Slovenia, my phone rang. I picked it up, answered in English, then smiled when I heard the distant voice. It was Selver, the guy from the twelve-hour train ride. Was I free next week, and could we go to the seaside together? I told him, in my best rusty Serbo-Croatian, that I had a boyfriend now and that, anyway, I was busy next week.

"*Onda, do vidjenje,*" came the wistful but firm reply. ("Well then, good-bye.") For a while, the conversation was over.

Thirteen Ways of Looking at a Blackboard

Leza Lowitz

Many people have heard the maxim about the dangers of non-conformity in Japan, "the nail that sticks up gets pounded down." But few know what happens when no one's looking, when you're tucked away in your circle of friends in a college seminar. An old Japanese comic poem might have the answer. It goes:

> *Ecstatic at being*
> *set free*
> *the bird collides with a tree.*

When I first began teaching at a Japanese university, I might have believed it. I'd heard that Japanese universities were a playground for those who got in, those who studied their entire childhoods to make the grade—a party for those with reason to celebrate.

I'd heard that if the grade- and high-school rigidities are symbolic of the rigors of the Japanese company, the university is the wild, drunken night out on the town, the academic answer to the *matsuri* (festival) side of the culture. One of my Japanese friends described university as a "four-year Golden Week," referring to the one-week vacation in May when Japanese businessmen are practically forced to take a holiday. I wondered if this would be true, and how I would handle it if it was.

After all, I'd been raised in Berkeley in the 1970s and attended the utopian educational experiment called Malcolm X Elementary School, a fact that my interviewers—Chairman Katsura of the comparative literature department, and his cohort, the esteemed haiku poet Mr. Wada—were fully aware of and actually *liked*.

"Malcolm X, wow!" they nodded their heads, then sank into silence and deep thought.

I told them about my school days, how I'd been bussed; been visited in homeroom by the likes of the wiry James Baldwin, then living in Paris, coughing out invectives against America like an ailing carburetor; gone on field trips to Ho Chi Minh (People's) Park; listened, enraptured, to Maya Angelou dressed in a many-colored dashiki and singing out her poetry to an audience of sixth graders. And if that wasn't enough, I'd gone back to this same school later as a tutor, found one student with a loaded gun in his pocket, another with a hat full of crisp hundred-dollar bills. I found young girls smoking pot in the bathrooms, older girls who threatened to beat me up if I looked at them the "wrong way," and I had still managed to teach them something. I could survive anything in Japan.

"But you might be bored," they warned. "You see, students here, they don't . . ."

"What?" I asked nervously. I already knew that getting them to speak English would be difficult, perhaps impossible.

". . . study," the erudite department head said sheepishly, brushing his longish gray hair behind his ears. He leaned forward conspiratorially.

"It's officially sanctioned," Wada-san added, as if revealing a long-kept secret. "The elder generation tolerates four years of leisure at university. It leads to maximum production when it *really* counts."

At the time, I laughed it off. I'd been told about the partylike atmosphere, but I knew better. Didn't Japan have the best reputation in the world for its educational system, the highest literacy rate of all industrialized nations? What did a haiku poet care about corporate productivity, anyway?

"If they don't come here to study, what do they come here to do?" I said, looking out the window at the campus quad, where students were standing in groups, talking, smoking, handing out pamphlets for sports clubs or parties.

Katsura-san leaned back, lit his pipe, puffed on it in exaggerated Kabuki style, and explained that since the age of eight, many Japanese students had been shuttled to cram schools, called *juku*, by their mothers, who waited dutifully in cars parked outside, cooked them hot dinners, and even reportedly relieved their sons of amorous tension if it got in the way of their studying! Seventy-five percent of a kid's life from the age of twelve was spent at the desk, either studying or keeping up appearances. Competition for the top universities was fierce. Indeed, these students had proven themselves quite well by getting in, so the system tried to make getting out easy. On the other side of graduation, they'd be working very long hours in boring jobs for big companies.

"Oh, and don't forget. You must start ten minutes late and end ten minutes early," Katsura-san laughed. "Otherwise, the students will be mad."

"Mad?" I repeated, feeling like Alice in Tokyoland. Things were suddenly not what they seemed.

He nodded, told me not to expect too much or demand too much, and to give only one exam per semester, one paper per school year.

"Mission accepted?" Wada-san asked in a billow of Sir Walter Raleigh smoke.

I signed the contract, happy that my English degree and Master's in creative writing had finally gotten me something other than inquiries about my lack of vocational ambition.

We shook hands and went out for a ceremonial beer.

One

On the first day of school, the cherry blossoms were in full bloom and the wind was pulling the petals off the trees, sending them floating down to the ground in a rush of soft white. I made my way across campus, enchanted by this most classical of Japanese symbols.

Spring had arrived, and school had begun. It had taken a while to adjust to this seasonal shift, but it made sense to start school when the blossoms were blooming, rebirthed from a dormant winter.

Though I'd been briefed on the party towns that Japan called institutions of higher learning, the university's legacy was anything but wild. First built by an American missionary in 1874 in a ramshackle wooden building near Tokyo's bustling wholesale fish market, in 1918 it was moved to Ikebukuro, home to the city's central black market until the late 1950s and now the site of blocks of high-tech department stores offering everything from Russian caviar to Australian sheepskins. School, too, was expensive—about $17,000 a year, including room and board.

Before planning my course, I had looked at the catalog of the previous years' offerings in English literature. One professor had taught Virginia Woolf's *To the Lighthouse*. Only. Another had used *The Letters of Vincent van Gogh* and had described the work thusly: "Van Gogh Meeting and Marrying a Slovenly Woman." A class on contemporary American culture featured videos of *Twin Peaks*. No wonder Japan has skewed views of the West, and vice versa. I opted for an anthology of short-short fiction by international writers, placed my order, and waited for school to start.

While the quad was littered with the petals of cherry blossoms and leaflets, the classroom was the epitome of order. The blackboards were completely free of chalk marks and, to my surprise, there were small caddies in which chalk was arranged by color: baby blue, yellow, pink, and white, all unbroken.

Almost all of the students were there before me, waiting for class to begin!

They sat quietly in their seats, their thin notebooks opened, pencil cases placed on the desks in front of them the way samurai might have disentangled their swords from their kimonos and lain them down on the floor in front of them to demonstrate the benevolence of their intentions.

I took a quick count. I had thirty-five students, about thirty women and five men.

I said "good morning" in Japanese. They giggled appreciatively, then repeated my exact words.

I introduced myself. I said I was from Berkeley. They nodded their heads in recognition, but had mistaken the name for Barclay, the popular cigarette. I let it pass.

I asked them why they were there. They appeared shocked by the question. What about roll call? What about the professor's first lecture detailing the coursework, assignments, expectations. I waited for their answers. No one said a word. I asked again, this time more enthusiastically, prompting them to talk.

"I went to San Francisco once on a home stay," one of them said shyly. "I heard you were from Frisco, and I figured this class would remind me of that time," he said and sat down.

A girl in a business suit said she wanted to learn women's pronunciation, something I do not believe exists in the English language. Many wanted to study with a native speaker, to improve their English. But most, it seemed, wanted something new and easy in a relaxed, "American atmosphere" where they could be themselves.

Only a handful had taken classes taught by *gaijin* (foreigners).

Another student was more practical. "I thought you'd like the Grateful Dead," she said hopefully, "like me." She played air guitar and rolled her head from side to side.

Everyone laughed, a sign that they were comfortable. I laughed too. We were off to a good start. I tried to recall my freshman English class at U.C. Berkeley, where I had been terrified to talk. Why weren't they?

"It's freedom to speak in English," one girl said after class. "I don't have to be constrained by Japanese thought."

"Very well," I said. "Then neither do I."

Two

The next class, they were decked out in Sonia Rykiel miniskirts or dressed down in jeans and sweatshirts. The clean-scrubbed boys wore jeans and Shetland cardigans under faded leather aviator jackets. As I surveyed them, they surveyed me right back, and the questions soon began with a flurry, like the falling cherry blossoms.

Where do you get your hair cut? Can you eat Japanese food? How old are you? Do you like Japanese designers? Why did you come to Japan?

The last question was simple. I came for love, to accompany a man who did research at the University of Tokyo, the prestigious

Todai which graduated one-third of all major Japanese company presidents. I didn't tell them we'd broken up, and that one of the causes of the breakup was my teaching job. The balance of power in our relationship had shifted too far for me to continue my Pygmalion routine, and, frankly, I had outgrown it. But what had I grown into? I had stayed here to find out. From my ex-boyfriend's office window, I'd seen small seminars with *sensei* in the front and the first row of students eight rows back, asleep. These were not the surreptitious open-eyed lizard naps we'd perfected in our college days; they slept unabashedly, heads on arms folded on tables. Down. Snoring, even. I myself had no idea how I had ended up there.

When I told them that part, they laughed appreciatively.

With still an hour left of class, I asked them what they thought an "American-style class" was. They said one in which students can speak out, where they have a more open relationship with professors, where they like to debate and discuss cultural affairs.

Pleased, I started with a short story by Amy Tan about growing up in San Francisco's Chinatown. They read aloud, one paragraph per student, round robin-style. I corrected their pronunciation, judged their fluency. The story was about Mei Mei, a young girl with a stubborn mother who holds onto the old Chinese ways. The girl receives a chess set and learns the strategy of invisible strength (what we call not showing your full hand) in order to win the game. Chess is used as a metaphor for life, for adjusting.

They read well, and when we finished going over the vocabulary, I opened up a discussion of the story, hoping to debate the
difficulties of cross-cultural adjustment, assimilation, the generation gap, finding one's own strength.

No one made a move.

I went over the story briefly, then opened up the floor again.
Silence.

Then, I did what I hated to do and called on the girl who
made the mistake of making eye contact first. She turned red and
stammered before she finally spoke a single word.

"Pass," she said meekly.

Pass? The word echoed in my brain like a bad joke.

I fed her hints, goaded her on, went over the story line by
line, cajoling her.

Still nothing.

I knew she had read the story, understood the vocabulary. I
was completely stumped. I called on the next student, and the next.

"Pass," they all said.

Frustrated, I suggested a written summary. Without hesitation, their pencils began to move across their papers.

I sat and watched them, utterly confused. Why had they been
so eager to talk before?

And if their English was good enough to ask a wide range of
questions, and the vocabulary was sitting right in front of them,
why couldn't they summarize a story they'd just read? Despite
their talk about wanting an American-style class, they seemed

reluctant to offer their own opinions. Perhaps they were being shy. Or was it something else?

I thought of the popular Japanese proverb, *neko o kaburu,* which means "to wear a cat on your head." Translation: to hide your talents.

The wonderful proverbial bell rang and they filed out of the room.

"Invisible strength?" I wondered if I was seeing it in action.

Three

Before class one day, I ran into the professor across the hall, asked him what he was teaching to his seminar. The answer came back: Wallace Stevens, "Thirteen Ways of Looking at a Blackbird."

"Do they get it?" I asked.

"How would I know? So far, they haven't said anything," he replied.

I read my students' papers only to learn that they had followed the story perfectly. Save a few grammatical mistakes, their summaries were flawless.

I went to ask Katsura-san's advice.

"I told you they wouldn't study," he said sympathetically.

"It's not a question of studying. It's about abstractions. What about forming their own opinions?" I ventured.

"That's your job. Of course, if it's too difficult, you could give them tests. They're good at tests. Give them little quizzes," he smiled.

"No," I said firmly, smelling the challenge. They'd been tested since birth. Their *tests* had been tested.

My class would be 100 percent abstract ideas, extrapolation, discussion. There would be absolutely nothing to memorize. If they wanted American-style, they were going to have to work at it.

"Just give them time. They aren't used to giving their opinions. They don't want to make mistakes. They're *mortified* by it, in fact. Be patient. In feudalistic times, offering one's opinion was tantamount to death. Stepping out of line in such strict vertical castes could cost one his head," he explained.

"But it's the '90s," I protested. "No one's walking around with swords anymore."

"You'd be surprised," he said with a wry smile in a puff of smoke.

Four

The Japanese educational system dates back to when the country was made up of semiautonomous districts controlled by the *daimyō*. The districts, or *han*, had schools called *hanko*, where pupils learned literary and military arts suitable to the samurai's lifestyle. Schools in Buddhist temples, *terakoya*, were set up to teach reading, writing, and abacus. This Edo era system was reformed—westernized, really—in the Meiji era, but some allegiance to it lingered, it seemed.

An American missionary wrote as far back as 1874 that "the sole duty of Japanese teachers was to stuff and cram the minds of pupils. To expand or develop the mental powers of a boy, to enlarge his mental visions, to teach him to think for himself, would have been doing precisely what it was the teacher's business to prevent."

Hadn't anything changed?

As true to their cultural heritage as they were, I was bound to mine as well. If theirs necessitated that professor or *sensei* was high up on the ladder they were just learning how to navigate, mine was a heritage of obstinacy, where the squeaky wheel got the grease. The student who talked in class got noticed by the teacher. He or she earned respect.

If I wanted them to break out of their forms, I knew I'd have to break out of mine first.

I had to stop being Professor and become more *Sensei*.

Striking the balance became the hard part.

Tree number one had been bumped into, not by them, but by me. The bruise on my head was invisible, but it hurt.

Five

Walking through the school's ivy-covered quad, I spoke with one of my students, Hiroko, who was already employed as an interpreter.

I asked her what she and the other students thought of the class so far.

"Well, they enjoy it. But the truth is, most students in your class don't care about literature. They want to know about you," she said.

"Me? Why?"

"Because you're twenty-eight and not yet married. And you're here. That's far more interesting than any literature," she said boldly.

I begged to differ.

"Anyway, aren't Japanese women changing, waiting a little longer?"

"Yes, but you're not Japanese. You don't seem nervous. They want to know how you do it. Live your life freely."

"I don't know if it's free. It's just what I have grown up with. But we can talk about that, too," I said. "So what about class? I want to know what you think of what you've read."

"What could we think?" She lit a cigarette.

I was puzzled.

"Well, for starters, do you *like* the writings?"

"Sure," she said, "but how could we have anything to say about those stories by famous writers? How could we possibly criticize them?"

"We can talk about things the stories remind us of in our lives," I said.

"It's out of form to talk about one's personal feelings like that," she explained.

This was the famous *kata* factor I'd read about. Form.

"It's part of our history. No one can change it. *Sho ga nai.* It can't be helped," she said.

"What happened to wanting to do it the American way?"

"We're taught as women that not having an opinion is ladylike. Even if you have one, you are not supposed to express it. It's immodest!"

When I asked her why no one could summarize the Amy Tan story aloud, why no one spoke up, she laughed and explained that the first girl I'd called on was a kind of "leader," and that competition was out of the question. No one wanted to show up the leader, so if she didn't know, no one else could know, either.

I nodded in understanding. Harmony and consensus. Most teachers want their students to succeed, if not to become shining stars of pointed insights, at least to have the right answers. But I wanted my students to fail, fail in a system that asked only that their thinking be speculative rather than convicted, safe rather than original. I wanted them to take risks, to step out into that void. To crash like I had.

As I was wondering how I might encourage this, she waved good-bye, ducked into the old wooden building for her next class, and left me to think about creating a new form for a cross-cultural classroom.

Six

The accepted form was that the teacher stood in front of the room lecturing while those students who had bothered to come fell asleep. The hot summer was approaching, and we were all getting restless.

I brought in coffee as we'd done in California, sat on the edge of the desk as I lectured, and began making eye contact with the students. Fiercely. My legs dangled like loose fishing lines. I put down my notes, punctuated my speech with gestures. They thought I'd gone crazy.

"American-style," I assured them.

Soon, it was their turn.

I held the Aristotelian view that education could be pulled out of everyone from a chain if you could find the chain. But they were all tied together, and a chain is only as strong as its weakest link.

So I found the weakest students and put my plan in motion.

Understanding their reluctance to be singled out, I asked them to put their chairs in a circle—all the tricks cooperative education and alternative schooling had used on me. They would come up with the answers together, and a leader would be chosen randomly—the person with the longest hair or the most books in her backpack—to take notes on the group's responses, and offer them to the class.

"Just close your eyes and pretend you're in America," I said, trying to be patient.

We read a story from Italy, a country whose citizens are not known for their reserve. The groups worked well enough, but the response came directly from the fiction. If they didn't quote the writer verbatim, they quoted what I had said.

Tree number two had been covered with snow.

❁ ❁ ❁

Seven

A 1991 poll by the *Asahi Monthly* magazine asked fifth graders the question "Are you good at school?" Seventy-five percent of U.S. students said yes, thirty-three percent of Koreans said yes, while only sixteen percent of Japanese answered affirmatively. If grade schoolers lacked confidence, what about college kids in a new environment?

Mental training has a rigorous legacy in Japan. Thirteenth-century Zen priests taught their disciples that the object of learning was to become one with the materials one used—the calligrapher with his brush, the archer with his arrow, the potter with his clay. Where did that leave the study of foreign literature? Just as many Japanese believed that foreigners could never understand their souls, so, likewise, did they believe they could never touch the heart of another culture.

I realized I had to emphasize the universal themes and, before the students could be expected to analyze a short story, they needed to have some tools, such as metaphor, simile, plot, point of view, theme.

So the next class, we studied similes. A simile diffused the comparison, watered it down, I explained.

"Like adding lemon to your *shochu?*" one of the students asked, referring to the cheap but highly alcoholic drink similar to vodka that was popular among the working classes and the college crowd. They put lemon soda in it to make "high sours," which they drank with impunity.

"Correct," I said.

"Madonna is like a virgin," someone said.

"This school is hell," the class broke out in titters.

"If you think this school is hell, try an American college," I said, happy they were participating so enthusiastically at last.

When it came to discussions on culture, they were open and free. But when it came to literature, it seemed, they felt "unqualified" to respond. How could I teach them that literature comes from life, reflects life, is an integral part of life, and not just words on a page?

Eight

As time went on, they made up their own metaphors and similes in English.

"Dogs and cats are as different as Americans and Japanese."

"The loss of him was like a baseball game without the audience."

Still, they whispered, shyly, afraid to make mistakes in English. But they invited me to lunches, where they showed me photos of their trips to Hong Kong, Paris, New York, taken with their girlfriends, paid for by their parents. At their request, we ate ethnic food, spicy Indian and Thai curries. Never *sushi* or *soba*. Those were not nearly exotic enough, and, unlike me, they could have them anytime.

I asked a friend who worked as a top-ranking bureaucrat at one of the government ministries to comment on the nature of university education in Japan. "If you compare American universities to Japanese ones, clearly America creates the 'best people' in limited numbers, like scholars, leaders, presidents. But if you look at industrial capacity, it's clear that the Japanese education system creates extremely capable people in vast numbers."

"Yes," I said, holding out for the gist. Japanese conversations, like Japanese literature, are often concentric rather than linear. One has to wait, and listen.

"The whole history is like the theory of rice growing," he continued. "Japanese people are an agricultural people. Over the centuries, we concentrated on growing rice. We have to consider the unchanging circumstances. The seasons, for example. There will be a rainy season in June, therein you should plant rice. Summer will be very hot, so you should water greatly. Autumn typhoons will come, so you must harvest the rice before that. So, basically there are ten days to do the optimum job. Consensus is highly appreciated, more so than individual opinion. The goal is to get the best crops. Period. Ten days is a short time in which to ensure a country's survival for another year. Organization and efficiency are key."

I asked him how this related to education.

"Jobs must be done in short times, so we need to have our workers prepared," he replied.

"But what about individual education? You're talking about technique. What if someone comes up with a better technique, or a different schedule?"

"There is value in learning things like mathematics through

standardized tests. It's not just memorization. When faced with a math problem, you have to determine whether to multiply, divide, use geometry to solve it. This is an intellectual process," he insisted.

Wrong or right, each view had its truths. I decided there was room for both.

Nine

When the maple leaves were turning orange and red in the autumn glow, we read a Chinese story called "The Explosion in the Parlor" by Bai Xiaoyia about a father and daughter who visit the home of a person of high social standing. While they are waiting in the parlor, a thermos at a nearby table falls.

The host comes back into the room, and the father says he made the thermos fall. The daughter doesn't understand why her father has lied. The story illustrates the classic dichotomy between appearance and reality, *tatemae* (public façade) and *honne* (personal feelings). The students seemed to understand this well, and liked the fact that it existed all around the world— and not just in Japan.

Soon, they were raising their hands, jumping into the discussion. One said, "Telling a lie is bad, you know, but sometimes it is a good way to make things go well or get people not to hurt others."

"The story shows that you must defend yourself more than necessary when you want to be accepted, so you will be accepted with a better feeling," someone else added.

Though I'd noticed great changes in their confidence and interest, still they whispered, afraid. Could I let go of my expectations and allow them to be the way they were? I had learned from them how to allow an answer to unfold over time, how not to impose my expectations on others. I had changed as much as they had. Was it enough?

Ten

Then one day it happened. The building next door was being torn down, so our normally quiet discussions were obliterated by the din of a jackhammer and the crunch of the wrecking ball. If I had to shout, my students would have needed a karaoke microphone to make themselves heard. So shout they did. And finally, I heard them.

Katsura-san sat in on my class.

While we drank our coffee, we read a story by Heinrich Böll about a professional laugher who has never heard the sound of his own laughter—except on command.

Then I sat back and waited, patiently, for them to talk. After a while, they told me about the *nakionna,* women who are paid to cry at Japanese funerals. They talked amongst themselves.

"I wonder if they are really cheerful girls and have not cried in their private lives?" a student asked.

"Laughter is necessary in human life. But the laugher doesn't do it naturally. If he comes to have imitation laughter in his private life, he will lose himself," another pointed out.

"I think he works too hard. In our society, people work so hard that they lose the important things, like health and communication with their families. This story is meaningful for us in that way," a very soft-spoken girl commented for the first time.

"In modern Japan, this tendency is strong. Many Japanese devote themselves to their jobs and lose themselves and their enjoyment of life. To do something purely for money is good and important, but doing only that will make one's life vacant," another said with confidence.

I just shook my head, grinning from ear to ear. Literature had met life.

"It's more American-style than America!" Katsura-san said when it was over. "And you've learned that silence is a gate to deeper understanding. You've become almost Japanese!"

The funny thing was, I didn't know what those two distinctions meant anymore. I didn't want to think of American and Japanese as opposite or even conflicting. I was starting to see things as more multiplicitous. Anything could be included in a worldview, and not at the exclusion of something else.

Eleven

I called my friend at the ministry to tell him how things were going. He told me that teaching literature to Japanese students was a bit like shooting arrows at a moving target.

"Where does that leave foreign teachers? How can we teach Japanese students? What can we teach them?"

"You can teach them values," he said frankly. "Foreign teachers appreciate individual values more than Japanese teachers. If you could guide Japanese students in developing personal values, it would help them immensely."

"But my values are different than theirs. I have American values, whatever those are."

"Exactly," he said, "but differences are good."

"I'm not sure if they are good or bad. They just are. That's one thing I have learned from my students. We don't always have to judge something. Just let it be."

Twelve

I wondered if the testing system hadn't so irrevocably ingrained its values of diligence and conformity into the students that teaching different ones was a losing proposition. It was ironic that it was left up to foreigners to teach Japanese students the value of individual thought in a brief six-month course. Still, we were all learning, and, as time went on, they did study and learn, and so did I.

Thirteen

The last day of the year we had a spirited party. Most of the students brought cameras. We lined up in neat rows, smiling broadly. I brought hand-rolled sushi. They brought Oreo cookies and Doritos. They liked Jay McInerney and Andy Warhol. I liked Haruki Murakami and *ukiyo-e* prints.

Some of them gave me presents and cards. One of the cards

said, "It is not a special expression, but I would like to suggest that humanity's spirit is its own brightest ornament."

We clinked our glasses, flashed our cameras, downed our drinks, and made a toast to all the trees we would plant next year to replace the ones we'd crashed into.

Jean-Claude Van Damn That Was a Good Movie!

Emily Wise Miller

I admit it, I am a film snob. I can't get excited about most of the fluff that Hollywood excretes each year: lame teenage-sex fantasies; sugarific romantic comedies starring Meg Ryan or one of her clones; macho action flicks whose bad guys alternate between Russian mobsters, scary Arabs, or pharmaceutical executives, depending on who finances them. I still like to go see "independent" films, but now, what with Miramax's stranglehold on the genre, independents are just Hollywood movies with facial hair: the same paper-thin plots, the same guy-gets-girl formula, only the actors are less good-looking and you've never heard of them. Sometimes I'll go for months without seeing anything rather than waste my time.

But put me across an ocean, where I have few friends, no TV, and precious little to do in the evening, and suddenly I'm a changed woman, starved for American-style entertainment. I'll gladly see anything, *anything* they can throw my way. Stallone? Hey, *Cliffhanger* wasn't half bad. Ryan? Wasn't her latest movie filmed in my hometown? Schwarzenegger? Yes, *bitte!* Far from being a snob, I quickly become what can only be described as a film SLOB: a Sucka Living O'Broad.

This transformation, this evolution of character and taste, has several underlying causes. When I've lived abroad, I've always been reasonably happy with the situation, and yet I can't help but feel nostalgic from time to time. American movies provide a glimpse of home without the plane ticket—often with recognizable landmarks or cityscapes of L.A., New York, or San Francisco. And they bring a taste of American life, American people interacting with one another, being very American and speaking English. You never feel more "American," for better or for worse, than when living abroad. You start daydreaming about gas dryers and twenty-four-hour Safeways. You find yourself in arguments defending Kraft American cheese (it tastes good on a burger). I even know a grown man who cried all the way through *Dances With Wolves,* which he saw in Prague in 1991, just because it was filmed in South Dakota, his home state.

I first noticed the SLOB phenomenon ten years ago, the first time I lived abroad. A friend and I were stuck in the rain in Budapest, tired, wet, and bereft of ideas. We decided to see a movie—any movie—and the closest theater was showing *Kickboxer,* starring Jean-Claude Van Damme. Had we really sunk that low? Indeed we had. Maybe it's because our expectations were subterranean, but we sheepishly admitted on the way out, "hey, that was pretty good." We fell for it all: the sappy love story, the tried-and-true final Rocky-style fight (only with crushed glass glued to their gloves—ouch). Out of the rain and reasonably entertained for two hours, we knew we'd hit on a winning formula. What more could we have asked for?

Moving abroad necessarily causes a change in routine. In my old life in San Francisco, a fun night was eating take-out from the Pakistani place across the street and then watching a video with my husband and assorted friends. You could set your clock by when Tom's snoring would overtake the volume of the soundtrack and when Sean would start drooling into the upholstery. (We're over thirty, okay? It can be hard to stay up late on a weeknight.) One of the things I really miss in Italy is being able to hang out with old friends and just relax and do nothing. It takes years to develop the kind of relationship in which you can comfortably sit around with your socks up, tell fart jokes, and insult each other's bathing habits.

In Florence, we are still on the tenuous cusp of new friendship with several people. We invite them over for dinner and serve the good wine. We are polite, conversational, and maybe not all that funny and fabulous in a foreign language. Going out with Italians often means hanging around while they take and make calls on their *telefoninos,* endlessly planning other meetings with friends where they will do the same thing. Sometimes speaking in a foreign language for a whole day or night can feel more like work than play: I try but usually fail to engage in the patter and wordplay, much of which goes straight over my head. At a table full of people from all over Italy, I strain and struggle to catch the puns, the words in dialect, the use of the remote-past verb conjugation (hey!) over the music or noise of a loud bar or restaurant.

Bring your crowbar if you're planning to penetrate the inner sanctum of Florentine social life, whether you are from San Francisco or Sicily. Real locals have known one another since elementary school; they go hunting for wild boar together in the Maremma section of Tuscany and head to the beach at Viareggio in summer. So many foreigners traipse through their city every year that they hardly have reason to get excited about meeting another one. Once you're introduced, plucked from anonymity, Italians, even Florentines, are often extremely warm, talkative, generous—and, as one friend who lives in Paris said, it could be a lot worse: they could be French. She has a point there, and clearly it's our own social retardation and not any lack on the Italians' part that's causing our isolation. But nonetheless, we have plenty of free evenings, and shivering in a church listening to early choral music is often trumped by whatever movie is playing at the Odeon cinema.

In many ways I welcome the challenge of starting from scratch, living in a foreign place, speaking the language, and making new friends. I've adjusted (a little too easily) to the slower rhythms of life, where stores close every day between 12:30 and 5:30, and also on Monday mornings and Wednesday afternoons, because *five hours a day* didn't seem like quite enough time to relax. I'm getting to know and understand Italy, a place where you often have to sit down to shower and stand up to pee (Turkish toilets). What with Bush in the White House and the economy down the tubes, this does seem like the perfect time to be an expatriate. We had been living in San Francisco for so long, hanging out with many of the same people we went to college with—it was all a little too easy, a little too comfortable. Nothing is too easy when you first move abroad. Normal things like finding an apartment or putting gas in a rental car become complex tangles of language, cultural difference, and the pure unknown. But when you watch an American movie in English, for those two hours, you escape from 500-year-old bathroom pipes and rodent trail-sized sidewalks. For those two hours you are back in your comfort zone, chasing bad guys with Nicolas Cage or running numbers with Robert De Niro.

I've lived in Italy twice in my life, once as an exchange student during college, and now, on a more extended stay. Over time I've learned several sure-fire conversation starters between Americans and Italians: 1) Is it true that Americans eat food from a can and drink beer from the bottle? 2) Dubbing. Any Italian, from a gelato-maker to a graduate student, will proudly extol the virtues of dubbing and illuminate for you the fact that Italians are the best dubbers in the world! They dub *everything*. No film is safe from their expert ventriloquism.

In Paris, I understand they show most films in their original languages, but the Italians have made an art of dubbing. One man has been doing Woody Allen's films for about thirty years. He has a distinctive high, comedic Italian voice. Only one problem: he sounds nothing like Woody Allen. One Italian friend finally saw a Woody Allen movie in English and was terribly disappointed. "His voice is all wrong," he explained. "He wasn't as funny."

Impressively, they found someone who could speak Italian with a low, slight Scottish brogue to do Sean Connery. And on TV, the Simpsons' voices are an amazing match. But in general, the Italians don't realize how much they are missing in terms of intonation and live sound. For one thing, there aren't too many dubbers of non-white ethnicities, and so Denzel Washington and Benicio Del Toro might get the same generic voice as John Travolta or Brad Pitt. Some actors' voices that we simply take for granted—like Kevin Costner's or Sean Penn's—are actually full of character and subtlety if you stop to listen. The soap-commercial voices that emanate from 90 percent of the actors' mouths are maddening.

I do speak and understand Italian, and seeing movies in Italian can be a great way to pick up more vocabulary and turns of speech, but after a while you get tired of missing key plot points because the Italian figure of speech for "torrid affair with your sister" or "I squirreled it away in a Swiss bank account" is beyond your grasp. It took me weeks, back in 1990, to figure out what demonic *thing* was haunting Twin Peaks because I had no idea that the word *gufo* meant owl. More recently, I sat through all of Wong Kar-wai's *In the Mood for Love,* set in Hong Kong but dubbed into Italian, without realizing that the two main characters' spouses were having an affair *with each other.* (And yes, Chinese, French, Iranian—all films get the same monolingual treatment. It seemed strange for Chinese people to be speaking Italian in the movie, though afterwards, tempted by all the film's eating scenes, we went out for Florence's best Chinese food, where it didn't seem quite as strange.) So, I find myself—standards cast to the wind—at the front of the line on English-language Mondays at the movies.

I had heard a lot about *You Can Count on Me* from friends, and jumped when I read it was playing for one night at the "arty" cinema in the town center—dubbed, of course, but this would be my only chance. I liked it, but it was clear that I had missed something. For some reason the brother character came across as more destructive and less tolerable in Italian, and the reverend from Linney's church was much more likable—the first positive representation of Christianity I had ever seen in a movie, or at least an "independent" one. With this kind of film, where characters are actually developed and the dialogue carries nuances and subtleties, dubbing rubs out the edges and robs you of the original, intended experience. Mark Ruffalo's whiny, hesitating voice; Laura Linney's laugh—I had missed these, as well as some minor plot points, and wouldn't have known what all the fuss was about if I hadn't rented it in English back in the States.

The one night that *Traffic* played in Florence in *lingua originale,* the entire expat community of Florence came out for the show, packing the Odeon up to the balcony. It was *the* anglophone event of the season. And here is one movie you do not want to see dubbed. First, the Spanish spoken in the Tijuana parts is an important (and colorful) aspect of the movie, and second, I could barely follow what was going on in English. At the end I actually thought Benicio Del Toro's character had manipulated things so that he would be the next drug kingpin, until someone filled me in. Afterward it took half an hour to try to explain the plot to a German friend: "Okay, remember those two guys with dark hair, they're federal agents. No, the other two guys. . . ."

When you live abroad, typical, cheesy Hollywood films start to take on a magic glow—of home; of the English language; of life, liberty, and the pursuit of silly happy endings. Suddenly a middle-brow film like *What Lies Beneath* has me hiding inside my sweater. I completely forgive its ridiculous supernatural subplot just for the joy of being genuinely scared and seeing Michelle Pfeiffer wander around a typical New England mansion in her J. Crew casuals. I caught *Cast Away* with Tom Hanks on one Monday night, and it brought a tear to my eye. Look how he makes fire and builds a little boat all by himself! Look at that Eagle Scout ingenuity! Even the heart-tugging beginning and ending didn't bother me much. Maybe it's my instinct for survival, an innate willingness to adapt to new situations (I can dry my laundry on the line and dodge speeding scooters when I cross the street); for the time I live abroad, I am just as happy to put my critical faculties on occasional pause for a dose of home on the big screen.

A Mediterranean
Thanksgiving, Take Two

Mandy Dowd

One languid autumn afternoon, on my friend's terrace that looked down through a wooded valley to the Mediterranean, Murielle amused us with stories about the year she lived in Boston. "*Et alors,*" she leaned forward, "And so, *le Tanksgiving.* I never understood. Everyone, but everyone, tells me everything there is to know about this very important American feast. The turkey, the pilgrims, everything. All of Boston, all of America is going to eat this great feast. And then? No one invites me. One day, the office is closed, everyone is gone away to their family to feast and *voilà.* I find myself all alone at a twenty-four-hour supermarket on Tanksgiving, and I buy a turkey on sale. I go home to my apartment and I eat it alone. There is my American Tanksgiving."

Born and raised in Cambridge, Massachusetts, I listened uncomfortably to Murielle's account of poor Bostonian hospitality. Too well I recognized the stuffy family tensions that can surround that particular holiday in New England. I could easily picture how Murielle was overlooked, and as the representative

American, I felt indirectly accountable for her disappointment. I determined to make it up to her and offered to cook a classic Thanksgiving dinner. She thrilled at the idea and I was delighted. We checked the calendar, found the date, and agreed that she should bring a friend.

I had lived a year in France and often, but especially in the kitchen, I felt like a useless bystander clumsily trying to participate in a culture riddled with secrets hidden from my ken. I had come to France for a few months of repose after years of chronic illness, fallen in love and decided to stay. Now I was in the awkward phase of transition between visitor and inhabitant. As a visitor, gliding or bumping over the surface of a foreign culture, it was easy to be amused at cultural misunderstandings. The gross faux pas inspired peals of laughter or, at worst, kind smiles and explanations. But as I settled in I didn't care to be viewed as a joke any more than the French care to be laughed at by Americans. What had been funny before was now a more delicate matter.

In my new home I was scarcely competent at even the simplest tasks, such as using the telephone directory, which has its own French logic of organization but remained a mystery to me. It was little help to call information, for telephone operators would whip out a trick math quiz faster than I could write the problem down. "It is the zero four four twenty thirteen sixty two sixty seven four twenty four." If I could get the numbers down fast enough, I could then decode the translation, "zero; four; four times twenty, plus thirteen, equals ninety-three; sixty-two; sixty plus seventeen equals seventy-seven; four times twenty, plus four, equals eighty-four," to obtain my number. One of the earliest expressions I learned to articulate clearly was "Excuse me, I have dialed a wrong number."

In the U.S. I had been an English teacher, was a published poet; language was my medium. In France, five-year-olds had a better command of the language than I. Thus in France, finding means to demonstrate to my new French friends that I wasn't actually stupid did not come fast or easily.

In the U.S. I had thought of myself as a good cook. I had even been hired as a chef and caterer in some not-so-shabby settings. Here, my cookbooks and culinary impulses were left on the shelf because the French maintain a mistrust of food other than their own. Everybody knows that when it comes to fine cuisine, the French know best. Or, anyway, if you don't know it, the French do. Yet now, at last, I would not be the aberration on the sidelines; an American meal was in order, and an American meal I knew I could cook.

Excitedly, then, I buried myself in recipes and began to plan the feast. I lay in bed where the late morning sun glanced off cookbooks spread open around me, and, submitting to a creative fervor, I temporarily ignored the challenge that such an endeavor posed to my uncertain health. Still hampered by systemic arthritis, sudden fevers, and bouts of insurmountable exhaustion, a project of the scope I was now planning presented the risk of driving me to bed for weeks. But while I had come to France for repose, I was enticed by this chance to offer my friends some palpable part of myself.

I got out of bed and set out to town afoot to search at length for ingredients that are very hard to come by in southern France, such as cranberries, molasses, yams, brown sugar, and a decent pumpkin. Turkeys are available at Christmas, but in November must be especially requested at the butcher. And they are expensive. Over the course of two weeks, I gathered together my ingredients, and as I sat my achy bones down with a cup of tea and surveyed my rare provisions I was very pleased.

On the Wednesday before the holiday I rose early and started cooking. I had foreseen to parcel out the tasks through the day, allowing for naps and conserving sufficient energy to enjoy the turkey on the evening to follow. Meanwhile, I had to cook as many dishes as I could put outdoors in the evening air, to make room for the turkey in the fridge. Our refrigerator is about the size of your television set. Or smaller.

The pumpkin pie was perhaps the most challenging because the pumpkins here are not grown for pies but for soups. They are not fleshy, but stringy and wet. Then too, I have yet to meet a French oven that will allow you to select oven temperature. Your choices are Hot or Less Hot. The longer I baked it, the more water and tough strands it produced. The first pie failed, so I had to start over with butternut squash and skip the nap. By Wednesday evening I had accomplished the pie and a passable facsimile of cranberry sauce, prepared a walnut-and-liver stuffing with sherry and sage and parboiled the yams to be baked the following day. I was exhausted, but proud, and was decorating the pie with walnuts when the phone rang. It was my Thanksgiving guest; she was calling to ask if I would mind if she and her friend didn't come after all.

"Uh," I paused somewhere between my dismay and my ignorance of protocol. "Well, I've already got the turkey," I told her, "and I've made the pie."

"It will keep, though, the turkey, yes? Can we eat it another day?" She went on to explain in a most friendly tone that she and her friend had an unusual invitation (more unusual than mine, it seemed) and that really she was very touched for the Tanksgiving but we will have a nice big dinner again sometime soon, OK?

"OK," I echoed, recognizing I had no choice in the matter. "*Je suis un peu déçue,*" I said, admitting my disappointment (very un-French) but I patched it up with "*Je comprends,*" which was a lie. I did not understand at all.

I would have told an American friend that I didn't understand. And I would have been awfully sore. But alone in France I felt sad and defeated, like an irrelevant adjunct to my new social circle. I had invested weeks' worth of grocery money, time, energy, and eager anticipation in the feast, but neither could I speak French fast enough to muster a friendly dialogue about the details, nor could I fathom the lightheartedness with which she was changing the plans. There was a gulf I could not cross.

My girlfriend came home and found me slumped on the

couch, looking across the room at a pale and hollow turkey spread-eagle on the counter. I told Corinne that our friends had cancelled.

"It is not you," she tried to explain in English, "It is Thanksgiving. It means nothing to them."

"So they don't understand the holiday. But all the work! Look," I waved my arms around the kitchen. "I've been cooking all day. I've been shopping for weeks . . ."

"But they don't know what this means to you. We will invite somebody else," she tried to console me.

"Someone else," I grumbled, "to whom this labor of love represents what? Suspicious American Cuisine?"

"No, but, you are taking this too hard." She searched cautiously for her words. "It is only one meal."

I stared at her, mute with consternation.

"I mean it is very important for you, yes, but for her? She doesn't understand." I could see my girlfriend felt cornered. Her dark eyes searched the room for help. We were at a place in our relationship where some things were said in French, and others in English, but neither of us yet spoke the other's language well enough to fluidly navigate the sticky spots. Now, she sensed it was up to her to account for Murielle's lighthearted change of plans because I wanted somebody French to tell me what was going on. Corinne wasn't entirely up to the task of understanding the scope of my disappointment and accounting once again for our cultural differences. She shifted her weight as she leaned on the counter beside the turkey.

"No, anyway, she is sometimes like this. One day we had plans to make a party and I waited and waited. Then she called me to say that finally she will do something else. That is Mumu," she shrugged.

But that is you too, I thought to myself. And pretty much everyone else I've met since I've lived here! Because plans along this stretch of the Mediterranean, I now saw with despairing clarity, are never really more than interesting ideas that may or may not come to fruition. Plans depend on one's mood, the weather, or whoever else may saunter by on a given day.

"Mmm, *ma chérie*, it smells good!" She cooed, trying to shift the tide with the pull of a single oar. "But what is this?" she asked, affecting candor, as she looked at the pumpkin pie. "The tarte of Pumpkin?"

"Yes, I was just decorating it," I sighed.

"It is very pretty. It was in the oven too long?" The French don't have brown pies. I guessed it looked a little like mud to her. I explained the color comes from the molasses and the brown sugar and the spices.

"*Ah. Bon!* (Oh Good!)" she exclaimed as if she'd been let in on an important secret. She was trying so hard to obviate a melt-down, which was almost inevitable given my fatigue and disappointment, that I felt it only fair to try to cheer up.

"Well, too bad for those girls," I said. "We'll eat the pie ourselves tonight!"

❀ ❀ ❀

Corinne made good on her promise and invited some recent acquaintances to join us for a Thanksgiving feast that was postponed till Friday night. Though I was hesitant to undergo another humiliation—I really wasn't up for a lot of *amusement* and *pleasantries* about American cooking—someone had to help us eat all this food, which wouldn't fit into the refrigerator.

That night we planted ourselves in front of the television set, where I generally understood about half of the stories unfolding but was satisfied to watch all manner of gesticulations and learn one or two new French expressions. I put the pie on a tray, with plates and dark black tea, and carried it up the ladder to our nest. Just then, an old friend of Corinne's wandered by, in search of a diversion. He climbed up into the loft and scootched onto the bed with us in front of the television.

"Would you like some pie and tea?" I offered, quietly pleased that someone else would share the pleasure of my long labor. I started down the ladder to put the kettle back on.

Marc looked curiously at the vaguely rumpled tawny surface of the pie. "*C'est quoi ça?*" (What is this?)

"It's a pumpkin pie—*tarte au potiron*," I said.

"*Une tarte Americaine,*" Coco quickly added.

"Ah bon." "Oh good" is an expression in French that means many, many things, all depending on the context. Here again, a strange secret had been explained. But there was a hint of a question mark punctuating "good", suggesting doubt.

I returned with tea and a plate and cut him a slice.

"And, what happened to the pumpkin?" he asked, holding the plate up to take a better view of its color.

"It was cooked in the oven," I said, "and then mixed with molasses and brown sugar." But, mispronouncing "molasses," I unfortunately said "malaise," which means discomfort or disease. Faltering to explain to him the difference between unrefined sugar and brown sugar, I said that that, too, had been "mixed with 'malaise,' which is the crude, if you will, of sugar."

He looked at me with polite confusion, confessing to have understood nothing. "American ingredients," I asserted, only to create further doubt where I'd hoped to enlighten.

"*Allez!*" he cheered, sportingly, "let us taste the American tarte," and so we ate. And while the pie was a skinnier version of what I'd hoped for, it was just as tasty and very pleasing to my tongue.

"It is very good, ma cherie," said Corinne, because she is kind and she loves me and she saw me working two days for this result.

"What did you say is in this pie?" asked Marc, swallowing some tea.

"Molasses," Coco quickly offered, "It is a kind of brown sauce . . ."

"It is what is left over," I tried, determined to explain something that I thought I understood, "after the sugar is crystallized off the cane. It is the crude, the base that remains."

"Ah, well, it is special." he said, putting the plate down, pie half-eaten. "But really, I have already eaten. I would eat it, but I have eaten too much tonight already, really." He rubbed his belly with an air of discomfort as if to insist on the sad consequence of his gluttony.

Perhaps I shouldn't have said "crude," I considered, savoring the dark flavors of clove and allspice and molasses and squash. This is a country that prides itself on its refinement, especially of its foods; the whiter the sugar, the finer the flour, the prouder the baker with his results. All vegetables in France are peeled of their edible skins, potatoes, carrots, and mushrooms alike; not to do so, I had long since learned, is considered sloppy and, well, crude. To argue for the nutritional value of the skins of new potatoes is almost as good as arguing that we should throw the pelt into the pot with the rabbit. So, to say that something is "special" in France is not to pay it a compliment. In short, "special" means "strange." And what is strange to the French palate is on the whole unwelcome.

On Thanksgiving Friday, our new friends Sylvain and Ferial descended the steeply terraced hillside to our door for the first time with their two-year-old tot, Meldwyn, in tow, and their arms laden with wine. We ushered them into our small house—one long open room of which the kitchen was part—and seated them on a large old couch and a chair angling around a wood-stove in the corner.

Since much of successful cooking is a function of timing, I had worked myself into a dither juggling pots over three burners and one small oven. And somewhere in the middle of production we had run out of fuel and I had had to get under the sink with a wrench to detach the gas can, carry it up the hill and drive it halfway down the mountain to the gas station for a refill, an interruption I might have foreseen had I not been raised in North America. Nevertheless, I managed to get the whole meal on the table at once—the turkey hot and moist, the cranberry sauce cool, brussel sprouts, and candied yams steaming, wild rice with walnuts of which I was quite proud (because the French have *no idea* how to cook rice), a salad of endive and watercress and, of course, one more time, a pumpkin pie.

To say I got the meal on the table is misleading. We did not have, in fact, a table at which to eat, which somewhat altered the Thanksgiving atmosphere I'd hoped to achieve. Near the center of the room, around a perpendicular wooden beam supporting the loft in which we slept, the landlord had built a tiny mosaicked table at which no more than two could eat without banging elbows and struggling to see one's fellow diners around the wide beam. Permanently fixed in place, it also obstructed one's path in almost any direction in the otherwise open space of the room. I had come to dislike it with exaggerated annoyance, as if it represented every obstacle that hindered my easy entry into French culture. It was onto this table that I delivered the feast, or as much of it as I could.

My guests were overwhelmed. "So much food!" they remarked.

"That's as it should be," I explained. "That is Thanksgiving."

Sylvain, with his mischievous grin and twinkling squint, truly resembles an elf under a tousle of curly black hair, while blue-eyed Ferial, of almost porcelain complexion and pale red hair, could be the translucent fairy keeping watch from the wicker chair by the wood-stove in the corner. Now, Sylvain, rather short and with a proud chest, stood up and examined dishes while Corinne arranged assorted wooden dining chairs around the room to double as eating trays.

"So what is this?" He nodded over the yams. "And this?" He cocked his head toward the rice.

I, at full American throttle, and far from the languorous Mediterranean pace that is in the bones of the locals, turned to and fro grabbing for plates, forks, and napkins. What gastronomic vocabulary I'd recently acquired vanished in the bustle.

"And this," he grinned, "is the famous turkey."

"Yes," I said, stopped by his smile. "This is the turkey."

"And is it always a turkey for this feast?"

"Yes, always. Turkey represents the food that the pilgrims ate."

"And why is it not a duck or a deer? Did they not have those?"

I wanted to say that maybe the English ducks had frozen to death and that deer had outsmarted their hunters, while the pilgrims seem to have been overrun by wild turkey, but I lacked the vocabulary. I said, "They didn't tell us that in school," because I could construct the sentence.

"Ah." He paused, looking over the spread, which was more of a clutter, "And where do we start?"

"I will serve you a plate. Just sit down." I was feeling very hostessy, at once eager to please and a little awkward.

Sylvain sat back down on the couch and relieved Ferial of their bulky toddler Meldwyn, who was wriggling with vigorous anticipation.

"What do you like?" I asked, holding my carving knife over the turkey.

"But I will try everything. Tell me, what does one eat first?"

I paused. "Why, whatever you like." I said. "Do you prefer the breast or the leg?" I had described human parts, something like the bosom or the thigh. Sylvain twinkled at Ferial, who smiled. In France they ask, more discreetly, "The white or the foot?"

Corinne chimed in, gaily explained my meaning, and refilled the glasses of wine.

"I like everything," he assured me.

Ferial liked white meat, as I would have guessed, "but only a little bit," she said, intimidated by the quantity that faced her.

"We start, then, with the turkey?"

"Ah, I see. Well, in the United States, we eat it all at once—I mean, forkful by forkful, but there isn't really a starting place the way there is here in France. But of course, we will have the pie after."

"Ah bon. Then all at once," he agreed.

Ferial laughed pleasantly and suggested that due to the size of the plates she would start with the turkey and brussel sprouts.

It was hard for me to imagine separating the flavor of the yams and the rice and the nuts from that of the turkey, but I solved my dilemma by adding a fair dose of stuffing to her plate.

Sylvain stood up again to watch the proceedings. "*C'est la farce?* " he asked. "Farce" means, as it sounds, "farce, joke."

"No, no," I said, "This is how it is done."

Corinne, meaning to let me run my show, quietly passed the plate to Ferial.

"I mean that," Sylvain pointed as I plunged the spoon back into the turkey, "*c'est farcie?* "

Now, I had heard this word before in reference to tomatoes and zucchini when they are hollowed out and heaped with ground pork and herbs. But there wasn't any pork in this turkey.

"Not really," I said, "but a little the same. *C'est etouffée.*"

Since much of English is born of French roots, I could often pronounce a word I did not know as it would sound in French and expand my vocabulary with the blink of an eye. Equally often this did not work. I had just explained that the turkey was suffocated.

Sylvain looked to Corinne.

"*Oui, c'est farcie,*" she offered. (It is stuffed.) "*C'est une farce Américaine.*" Everyone enjoyed the double-entendre, and we sat down to eat with plates perched on chairs and knees.

They turned out to be the perfect guests for the occasion, especially Meldwyn. One of the curiosities of French gastronomy is that, unlike the adults, French children never complain about food. It also happened that young Meldwyn was a veritable glutton, who wanted more and more, and while his parents tried politely to restrain him from grabbing at the turkey and the brussel sprouts, I allowed myself to be endlessly flattered. Someone, anyway, appreciated my cooking.

Sylvain and Ferial were also delightful guests because, regardless of how strange they might have found the food or circumstances, they dined with a genuine curiosity. Questions ensued as to ingredients, manner of cooking, and American tradition. I stumbled through my explanations and they listened with diligence to my vague replies. It is terribly frustrating not to be able to express oneself. But here, as the subject matter was concrete, rather than conceptual, the matter of making myself understood was a simple problem to solve. I still haven't found the word for cranberries, for instance, but was able to describe the importance of the sour fruit to the New England whalers in preventing scurvy at sea. And because Thanksgiving was the subject, and I the authority, our guests showed special patience in lending their ears, and a word or two where I fell short. In this I was very satisfied, for, at last, a whole evening of conversation allowed my full, if fumbling, participation.

The conversation turned to the subject of feasts. As my friends recounted feasts they had eaten, feasts that had started at noon and endured till one in the morning, I realized that despite my guests' protests at all the food I had served, I had actually served about half the amount of food one might eat in France for Christmas or the New Year. It was the timing that overwhelmed them.

What is notable about a French feast, and distinguishes it from our American Thanksgiving, is that the object of the meal is as much the social interludes as the exquisite food. It is not a get-together, but a careful braid of three equally important elements: wine, food, and conversational pauses between many modest courses. Each aspect is timed to enhance the quality of the other aspects. Portions are slipped before you, one by one, from somewhere out of view. As one plate is taken away, glasses of wine are filled to animate a little interlude before the next dish appears. And thus the appearance of gluttony is replaced with an idea of civilized dining.

While we enjoy Thanksgiving as an occasion for family reunions, it would be fair to say that the object of the feast itself is a hardy quantity of good food, with some gratitude for a full stomach if there is religion or hunger in the family. My aunt, a cultured and worldly woman, once commenced the feast with the simple prayer, "On your marks, get set, go."

Upon serving my meal, I had not thought about these differences. So far I had mostly noticed that the French—or at least these Mediterranean French—eat nibble by nibble at a very late hour. They don't employ expressions like "low blood sugar," perhaps because they are always nibbling. They nibble for breakfast, then nibble for a solid two hours at lunch, nibble a bit at four and then when it cools down enough to consider the big long nibble, they start again until it is, by my clock, well past bedtime. Not a nibbler myself, I had learned this the hard way. I used to save my appetite when I was invited to dinner, only to find myself teary-eyed with hunger and uncontrollably scarfing all the olives served with the

drinks at 10:00 P.M., while dinner was still an afterthought somewhere in the back of our host's mind.

But, I had not yet put the pieces together, and what I had
deemed the crowning accomplishment of my performance—
having successfully delivered the whole steaming meal onto the
table at once—was exactly what my guests found most confusing.
It had not occurred to me that the timing of my meal was in itself
shapeless and, to my guests, vague.

Thus, when we got to the pie, they awkwardly admitted surprise. They thought that the yams were dessert, and that I had
simply served it up with dinner. "All at once," *à L'Americaine*. I
now understood why Ferial had eaten her yams as a separate
serving alone, and last.

"Oh no," I said, "those were—sweet, yes, but they were of
the vegetable group."

They laughed and asked about the brussel sprouts, "Were
they not of the vegetable group?"

"Yes, the brussel sprouts, too. But they are green."

"Ah," Sylvain giggled, "I see you are making a painting."

"Yes. And the pie is brown." *Marron,* I meant to say, for
"brown," pronouncing instead *"marrant,"* which means in slang,
"funny." "Actually, it is rather burnt sienna," I corrected, holding
it up from the counter for show. On this, the third time round, I
had slightly overcooked the pie, and the heat of the oven had
cracked its surface as the sun will crack the silt at the bottom of an
evaporated puddle. "This pie," I warned them, "is special."

Corinne, who throughout the evening had labored to restrain her urges to finish my sentences, improve on my explanations or offer any comment that might hurt my feelings, now let loose a gale of laughter. She gasped for air, and the whole story tumbled out. *"Alors la!* (Now here!) The story of a special pie!" she howled. She revealed the soupy catastrophe of the first pie and how it had fallen on the floor and been rescued only for the dog to find and eat it. She recounted my pride with the second pie, my disappointment when dinner was cancelled, and its short success with Marc. "And you see," she concluded, waving an arm at my last attempt, with tears rolling down her cheeks, "three is not the lucky number!"

I wasn't sure if this preface was meant to advise my friends to be delicate about the pie, or was simply an inevitable outburst after trying to keep me from a meltdown for two days, but the truth was out, and all in good sport.

"And for that matter," I added, "it is very much like the candied yams, which I did not overcook, so you may forget the pie, if you wish."

But they did not wish. And so I insisted that we be truly American and serve the coffee with the dessert instead of waiting till after. The French custom is to serve the coffee as one tiny final liquid course, a custom which, after four years, I still find nonsensical.

"Coffee with the pie?"

"Yes," I said, assuming a French air of culinary authority, "coffee and pie go together."

When the Skinheads Start to Grow Hair, It's Time to Leave Town

Angeli Primlani

It's hard ending an abusive relationship in a small southern town. Chapel Hill, for all its hippie pretensions, is a Small Southern Town. Everyone gossips so much that they think they know the real story, and, what's worse, they think you "deserve" to hear the "truth" when a real friend would just shut up and make you tea.

In fact, I didn't end the relationship at all. Napoleon Bonaparte ended it for me. It was the greatest favor anyone dead for a century had ever done me. But I didn't appreciate it at the time, when my long-term live-in lover decided to start a cult of people looking for the reincarnation of Napoleon Bonaparte.

I was traded in for a younger, more tractable girlfriend . . . one who Understood. I, after all, Just Didn't Understand.

Unfortunately the new girlfriend was one of my best friends.

All our mutual friends felt enormously pressured. They went through exotic gyrations to justify taking a side, or not taking a side, or their guest list for New Year's. And nobody wanted to hear about the violence, or the cheating, or the insane paranoid rants that had been my daily fare for seven years. Some people decided to avoid both of us. I didn't like this, but it was bearable. I couldn't handle the "friends" who took me aside and gave me lectures on how I should be more mature. I couldn't handle the "friends" who acted like the bad part was how inconvenient their social schedule became. I have never been more alone in my life.

In addition, I had a Really Evil Job. It wasn't a *bad* job, although it had its unpleasant moments. I liked the people and I did make enough to pay off my debts. I got to travel. But I made the world a little worse every day.

I gave away free benchmark software for a major computer publishing company that puts out magazines you would recognize on the newsstand. The benchmarks measure processor speed. They performed the same tests that the magazines ran when they reviewed computer hardware. In exchange for the free software, I took addresses and maintained a database. The company sold the database to telemarketers. Most of our customers failed to make the connection between the smiling girls at the trade show and the annoying phone calls at dinner.

We hawked benchmarks at trade shows in wonderful cities we were too exhausted to enjoy. It wasn't enough to give the things away, oh no! We had a sales patter, and we kept going like manic little Muppets in black polyester smocks. One afternoon I was in sort of a wheezy benchmark coma at the Boston Macworld Conference and

Exposition when a perfectly delightful hippie couple appeared. I'm not sure I remember them right. I now imagine that they had a baby in a stroller, that they walked hand in hand, that they looked at each other with radiant devotion. But to tell the truth, it was just before my afternoon break, long after I had ceased to really see anyone. So I did my little spiel and almost didn't hear the hippie say, "Oh, I don't need that."

"But it tests your processor speed," I persisted. "It works on Macs, PCs, and servers, and shows you how your system. . . ."

"I know," he said. "I don't need that."

"But—" I sputtered. "But it's . . . free!"

He said, slowly, as if to a non-native English speaker, "I don't . . . need that."

Because, of course, nobody really needed the stupid benchmarks. Oh, maybe some people did, but most just got going on the trade-show-free-stuff trail. They would take anything: stress beanbags, ugly yellow visors, key chains, Frisbees, shirts that said "blood, sweat and code." Anything. As long as it was free.

So my break came and I looked out on Boston Harbor and I knew that I had reached the end of my rope. My entire life had narrowed. I was wasting my youth by giving away little pieces of plastic that nobody actually needed.

When I got home from that trip, I went out and bought a ticket to Prague.

People later asked me "why Prague?" To tell the truth I knew very little about Prague, but I knew I wanted out of Chapel Hill.

Prague sounded terribly romantic. There were a lot of writers there. They have a dissident playwright for president. It was easy to get work even if you didn't speak the language. I had the vague impression that it was cheap. I was so ignorant that I didn't yet know they make the best beer in the world.

But I delighted in my ignorance. Prague was my great frontier. Prague was in that long pink stretch of globe that nobody would talk about in grade school, where, if you ventured, you'd encounter Communists. In the Bible belt during the Reagan era, communism may as well have been Satanism. We hoped the Russians loved their children too, but nosy questions were not welcome in social studies class.

I wanted to see who I was outside of this very small place. I wanted to know how I would think if nobody stood next to me. I was sure that Prague was going to solve everything. I would meet my soulmate and have wonderful, romantic experiences, and write a great novel and come home, if not famous, at least secure and peaceful. Bigger than these small town people, with the fairy dust of the "Left Bank of the '90s" in my train.

It all fell apart the first day.

I had booked a room in an HI-recommended youth hostel in the industrial, communist-era neighborhood of Krc, pronounced KUR-ch . . . um, well, almost like that, anyway. That first morning in Prague, I saw the confused look on the face of the woman who gave me my room key. But I didn't give it much thought. I was groggy, first of all. I hadn't slept the entire flight.

And I was distracted by the incredible morning sunlight. I didn't yet know that February mornings in Prague are rarely that bright, that they were having an unusually mild winter. At the time, the air seemed painfully cold to me, given that I'm from North Carolina, where it seldom gets below freezing.

The other thing was, everyone was speaking this strange language. People had said that a lot of people spoke English, but I wouldn't find them for days. Instead, I found myself surrounded by consonants, written and spoken. I couldn't believe they formed actual words. I had thought that Czech wouldn't be too much of a challenge because it uses the Roman alphabet, but I was wrong. Some witty Czech students suggest that the Czech nationalists who revived the language in 1848 deliberately and with malice aforethought made it into the most complicated language on Earth. All I knew then was that my few Berlitz tapes were no match for this sea of unpronounceable sound.

I figured out what *"ukončete prosim, vystup a nastup: dvere se zaviraji"* meant when the doors on the metro slammed shut. But *veprove, zmrzlina, mleko, syr, gulašove polevka* and *chleb* were all mysteries to me. I had beer for breakfast one morning that week because that's all I knew how to order. German, French, Spanish, and Italian all have some words in common with English, cognates and Latin roots to give you clues. Czech has darned few.

So there I was, sleep-deprived and blinking, feeling like a groundhog looking for his shadow and trying to take in the tall '70s-looking cinderblock hostel. I didn't understand the hostile sneer of the lady behind the desk, who demanded to see my passport, but I didn't care—I just wanted to sleep.

When I came out that afternoon, I saw that I was going to have to learn this language fast or I was going to starve to death. Absolutely nothing was in English. None of the people in the restaurants spoke English. And nobody was the slightest bit friendly. The woman who pushed a broom around the lobby actually spit whenever I walked by, fixing me with a look that made me wonder what horror comic she'd crawled out from.

I went to the desk to find out how many days I could stay. "You have to leave tomorrow," the girl at the desk said. "We don't have any rooms."

"It's February," I said. "The place is half-empty."

"You have to leave tomorrow," she said, and turned her back on me.

So, there I was, in this strange country, alone and homeless. I took the metro into the city and hunted for some sign of apartments or rooms to let.

I finally stumbled into the basement of a crumbling Victorian in the filthy but cobblestoned neighborhood of Zizkov, where an anxious girl said, in perfect English, "Are you looking for a room?"

"Am I!" I said. "How long can I stay?"

"Don't you want to see the room?" she said.

"I'll take it."

"No," she insisted. "Come look." The room was beautiful,

bright and sunny with cheerful colored curtains. And it was cheaper than the big Krc monstrosity. *Finally, Czech hospitality,* I thought, but I was wrong. Ivana was Croatian. The hostel had just opened and the Croatian owners were as desperate for business as I was for a room.

"They thought you were a Gypsy," said the manager, a twenty-one-year-old Ziggy Stardust look-alike from Liverpool named David. "You'd better watch out for skinheads. Most Czechs won't do anything, but just watch out."

It was my first hint that Prague in the '90s was more Christopher Isherwood's Berlin than Hemingway's Paris. Complete with Nazis.

Czechs don't like Gypsies, or Romanies. To be fair, Czechs don't like much of anyone. For about 500 years, the Austrians, Germans, and Russians have stomped on the Czech people. Czech culture has survived by being very insular. "Foreigner" and "stranger" are represented by the same word in their language. Especial hatred is reserved for the Romanies. This is remarkable considering how few there are. Ninety percent of the Czech Romanies died in Auschwitz, and some of those left have been denied statehood during the Velvet Divorce. The Czechs claim that they are Slovak and the Slovaks claim they are Czech.

Even the actual Romanies mistook me for Romany! Meanwhile, I was shoved off buses, yelled at, spit on, denied service in restaurants and ejected from buildings where friends lived.

Now, understand that in the American South I am white.

South Asians in England or California might be a recognized minority, but where I'm from you have African Americans and you have everybody else. I was so incredibly assimilated that I was offended to see the neo-Nazi skinheads sporting the Confederate flag. (Like many white Southerners, I used to see the Confederate flag as a symbol of regional identity, not racism.)

Suddenly I was not only "not white," but I was constantly being mistaken for "subhuman." I was bewildered. I was appalled. I would look in the mirror wondering what on Earth they were seeing that was so offensive. I wondered if I was in actual danger. I'd see a swastika chalked on a wall and realize, with cold, sick shock, *hey, they mean me!*

I might have gone home, but I was more afraid of the Small Southern Town than I was of the skinheads. That sounds absurd, but it was true. The skinheads were easy to spot. They had, well, no hair. Back in North Carolina, the bad guys didn't wear little armbands that said "I Am a Bad Guy." They were my lovers, my roommates, my former friends.

Some Czechs, when they heard I was Indian, promptly bought me drinks. "Do you really worship cows?" people would ask, and they actually wanted to know. Americans had outstayed their exoticism. Indians hadn't.

Over time, the people I became closest to in Prague were Czechs. My very best friend was Pani Brodilova, the ninety-year-old lady whose apartment I shared. When I moved in she spoke no English and I spoke no Czech. In time we developed our own language, a mixture of English, Czech, German, and French. Nobody else could understand what we were saying but we made perfect sense to each other. Pani Brodilova taught me to cook without convenience foods and microwaves. I learned how to make things from scratch and how to make do when the only vegetables in the stores were carrots and garlic. I made Indian food, and she tried it with great enthusiasm; it was too spicy for her and she pushed the plate back, shaking her head with tears in her eyes. Pani Brodilova still remembers World War I. She had no patience with my angst on my thirtieth birthday. "I am three times as old as you are," she said, "So don't tell me your life is over. Your thirties are your best years!" As she spent her thirties in the Nazi-occupied Protectorate of Bohemia and Moravia, I'm not sure what made them her best years. But I did stop feeling sorry for myself.

It never crossed my mind that I could actually be in danger. In 1996, the stardust of post-communism still covered everything. I was giddy. I was young and drunk on freedom and good beer. And so were all my Czech friends and Russian friends and Yugoslavian friends.

This was the year I found people singing "Let the Sun Shine In" and dancing in Wenceslas Square. I was coming out of Dunkin' Donuts and ran into my friend Pavel from Moscow and we threw our arms around each other and gloried that we were there and that we were doing this. I sang peacenik songs in a basement bar in Zizkov, with a Croatian boy who eventually got drafted and drove off into a rainstorm yelling "Good-bye groovy chicken!" I lived three blocks from a real ninth-century castle. I was playing with clichés, I was making them new. It wasn't the happily-ever-after I'd imagined. It was better, crazier, full of impossibilities come true.

And nobody knew me! I could be anything or anyone I wanted to be. In Chapel Hill, in part because so much of my time and energy had gone into disguising my abusive relationship, everyone thought I was a flake. In Prague, people took me for who I was in the present. They respected me and, seeing myself reflected in their eyes, I started to respect myself again. I planned to stay in Prague for a year. I stayed nearly four. I had all this new-found energy and I poured it into my new job at the *Prague Post*. By 1999, I was editor and manager of the online version, and a culture and features reporter.

I started writing about the Romanies. Perhaps it was because the things people said about them were so outrageous. After Chapel Hill, I couldn't help but sympathize with people whom everyone talked trash about. It was also a way to manage my anger at being the target of race hatred. (Westerners in Prague seemed to go out of their way to be "understanding" about the Czech attitude toward race, out of a warped sense of political correctness or cultural relativism.) I kept writing about the Romanies because of the way a lot of the Roma children reacted to me. "You mean you're a journalist?" they would ask. Most of them had never seen an adult who looked like them working as a professional. One boy touched my nice black British wool coat and said, "I know there is no racism in America."

Just before the Czech Republic joined NATO in 1999, the Czech economy entered its first recession. Just after it joined NATO, the Czech nation entered its first NATO war. And then everything got really weird.

Most Americans don't realize how unpopular the Kosovo war was in Europe. Officially the Czech Republic adopted a good-sport policy. Inwardly Czechs were seething. There were threats on American businesses and everyone went around laying bets on what restaurants were safe to eat lunch in. (I ate in the Chinese-mafia restaurant until the U.S. bombed the Chinese embassy, and then I stopped eating out.) Still, I'd have stayed in Europe if the neo-Nazis hadn't decided to form a political party.

When the skinheads start growing their hair it's time to leave town. For one thing, they suddenly became a lot harder to spot. They would wear designer sweatshirts or shirts and ties and stand in the very same square that three years earlier saw spontaneous outbursts of public singing. They would pass out their tracts and talk to passersby, for all the world like pit-preachers back home. They were very slick. Tourists probably didn't realize they weren't Jehovah's Witnesses.

They started standing next to me on the tram. At first I wasn't certain they intended to threaten me. They were very careful never to cross the line where I could accuse them of doing anything illegal. They never touched me. They just stood next to me and stared. For a long time I didn't really pay them much attention. After all, there had always been skinheads. Then, one day they followed me while I was walking in the park. A small group of them started throwing apples and rocks and yelling "Heil Hitler." They had two little kids with them, a boy and a girl. There were other people in the park, but they just looked away.

After that I started taking the neo-Nazis seriously. I don't really know why they started following me. I'm not even sure they were following me in particular. Maybe they were harassing every foreigner who looked kind of dark. I wouldn't know, because the *Post* didn't investigate. The editors knew I had written pro-Romany pieces. They assumed that this was just happening to me.

My Czech friends took the threat a lot more seriously. One friend tried to help me talk to the police, but hung up in the middle of the conversation. "Go to the embassy," she said. "They want to know all about who I am and why I'm calling." I knew quite well, from journalistic research, that there were skinheads in the police. I got no help from the embassy. The chief security officer said that without a police report, nothing had officially happened. "If we helped you we'd have to help everyone who lost their passport."

One night I was buying toilet paper after an evening at the opera. I came out of the *vecerka* and my way was blocked by a man on a motorcycle. He was dressed in black leather. On his shoulder was a well-sculpted neo-Nazi symbol, in red on a white circle. I couldn't get past him. He didn't say a word. He didn't have to. I knew that I could get killed here in front of the *vecekra,* and the patrons would pretend not to notice. And so would the newspaper. And so would the embassy.

A theater group I performed with did a show at Bohenice Mental Hospital and we all got very drunk. They locked us in for the night. We climbed over a fence and escaped. I suppose that was a metaphor for what I was about to do, climb back over the fence, out of the madhouse, back into the west. But the west as I knew it hadn't been very sane. I didn't want to leave. I was still reveling in the fact that I could move the dining-room table anywhere I wanted to.

I should be able to come up with some tidy conclusion about how I've changed, but I can't. The story isn't over. I went to Prague to escape from violence, only to find more. I came back to America, and trouble reared its ugly head here. Following the attack on the World Trade Center on September 11, I have exchanged being mistaken for Romany with being mistaken for Arab. I crawled back over into the "civilized west" only to have it turn into a war zone.

But I learned how to handle fear in Prague. I'm a writer, swimming through a dark and broken world, trying to make sense of it, as writers do. In Prague I learned that there are more decent people in the world than there are thugs. And I learned that the best way to deal with fear is to find something useful to do.

So here I am, in the middle of my story.

Watching Them Grow Up

Laura Fokkena

Al tufle taht al siara. The baby is under the car.

It was the first sentence I learned in Arabic. I was in Egypt taking classes at the American University in Cairo, where my instructor was teaching us prepositions. As first-semester students we had to make do with the limited number of nouns we'd already learned, ergo the creation of improbable constructions such as "the elephant is on top of the sink" and "the rose is next to the airplane." I have always loved and remembered "al tufle taht al siara," because the monotone in which my instructor chanted it was a perfect reflection of Egypt's total inattention to the myriad dangers faced by young children. This was a country that raised its kids haphazardly, nonchalantly; heavy on trust, low on panic.

Egypt is not a society that has safety boards just for elevators, nor one particularly concerned about catching bilharzia from the water. In contrast to the United States, a country in which the phrase "but it's for the children!" is used to justify every inane political agenda, Egyptians don't even enforce drunk-driving laws, much less regulate bumper cars at the amusement park. Infant car seats are considered to be more hassle than they are worth, and precautions on the underside of buckets warning that a two-year-old could tip them over and drown—well, that is just out of the question. "The baby is under the car. Repeat. The baby is under the car. Repeat."

Flash forward four years and I am returning to Egypt, this time as a mother. Since I'd been there before, the thrill of arriving on uncharted territory had worn off, but this trip was different from my earlier extended visits. My role before had always been that of the visiting American, going abroad to study, travel, undertake research or engage in some other ultimately self-serving mission. Despite my marriage to Bassel, an Egyptian I'd met during my first trip, my status as a *khawagayya* (a foreigner) had always superseded any other claim I might make about my identity.

This time, my American passport was secondary. My main role was that of wife, young mother, and grieving daughter-in-law. The raison d'être of this particular journey, hastily thrown together in a daze of shock and confusion, was that my husband's father had just died of a heart attack.

Whenever I speak of this event it somehow sounds as though I'm referring to an aging patriarch who had been ill for years. In our case the news was completely unexpected, handed down with one grave thump from my sister-in-law almost 5,000 miles away. The phone fell from my hand and I slumped to the floor. Luckily my mother was there to pick me up and she drove me from her house to my own, two hours away in the middle of a hot August night, to deliver the worst imaginable message to my husband.

In accordance with Muslim custom the funeral was held within twenty-four hours of the death, so there was no point in our trying to race to Egypt to attend it. But Bassel wanted to return as quickly as possible to take care of the endless paperwork that needed his attention, to ease his mother's and sisters' relocation to Egypt (they had to leave their home in Kuwait now that the major breadwinner was gone) and, of course, to be with his family. It would be the first time that they would meet our eighteen-month-old daughter, Rakaya.

The change that motherhood brought to my standing in Egyptian society was apparent before we'd even made it out of the airport. We'd traveled with a suitcase full of computer equipment, knowing that we'd have to pay import taxes on all of it. We couldn't afford this and as usual had no plan to deal with this or any other uncertainty. Fate was on our side, however, in the form of an airline official who examined our passports and waived the fees when he learned we'd given our daughter an Arabic name. "Most Egyptian men who marry foreigners come back with kids named Jennifer," he noted ruefully. Rakaya, however—by virtue of her name, if not her passport—was considered an insider to this country she'd not yet seen, and as her parent I was granted privileges I'd not had on earlier trips when my loyalties were less certain.

For the next few months we lived with my husband's three younger sisters and two of his paternal aunts, Auntie Abla and Auntie Zuzu. Auntie Abla was almost eighty years old, the retired headmistress of a girls' school in Cairo who had, I was told, spent her youth driving by Jeep through the Saudi Arabian desert, teaching in various Bedouin schools. She was a devout Muslim who'd made the pilgrimage to Mecca more than a dozen times and the only woman in the family who veiled. Like any good head-mistress she was stern and strict; whatever reserve of affection she had she saved for Rakaya alone. When she prayed, Rakaya would climb on her back or lean next to her and imitate her, dropping a hand towel over her head as a makeshift scarf. Whenever I saw this I would assume Rakaya was interrupting and try to usher her away, but Auntie Abla enjoyed it immensely. She was less forgiving, however, with the older girls in the family when they balked at chores or expressed a desire to study art instead of law or engi-neering. Indulging little children was one thing, but accommo-dating the whims of teenagers was plain nonsense. She'd reluctantly accepted me—she was not given to outbursts on any matter, including her only nephew's choice of spouse—though she did mutter about my lackluster Arabic abilities "after all this time." (She was delighted when she overheard me call Rakaya "Ru'iya," assimilating the hard "k" sound as is common in the Cairene dialect.)

Auntie Zuzu was ten years younger, a distinguished professor, soft-spoken and impossibly polite. When I left the doors to the garden open, she told me that I should remember to close them because mice could get into the apartment. When I did it again, she gently reminded me again. When I did it a third time and one fat mouse did, in fact, meander inside and proceed to give birth to eight or nine baby mice behind my dresser, she gently reminded me a third time.

Within a few weeks Auntie Zuzu and Bassel developed a good-cop/bad-cop routine with regard to Rakaya. Rakaya used to wake up every night to nurse, but soon learned that a more elaborate feast could be had by sneaking out of bed altogether and toddling into Auntie Zuzu's room, pushing her eyes open and whispering, "*ruzz, ruzz, baid, baid!*" (rice, rice, eggs, eggs!) Auntie Zuzu, unbelievably, would actually get out of bed at 3:00 A.M. and prepare such a meal, then send Rakaya back to bed and never mention it the next day.

When we discovered this nightly ritual, Bassel threatened both of them with all manner of drastic consequences. Rakaya was interrupting Auntie Zuzu's sleep! Auntie Zuzu was spoiling the child! This one-year-old was getting too demanding for her own good! Beatings would ensue at any moment! This last statement was a notoriously idle threat that never materialized, but it was interesting to me because it was something he never said in America, either before that trip or since. Rakaya cried and Auntie Zuzu tsk-tsked at such a display, though not so much as to cast doubt on his right to engage in it in the first place. Accustomed as I was to the American maxim that parents must appear as a united front, even if it means privately discussing parenting tactics for hours until absolute agreement is reached on every single issue, I was surprised that Auntie Zuzu would question his judgment right in front of Rakaya. But I soon realized that he expected her to be soft, so he responded to minor infractions with an extra dose of bravado. Auntie Zuzu in turn knew that discipline was someone else's territory. Bassel could be overly strict because he knew she would be overly forgiving and it would all even out in the end.

The larger backdrop, however, was one of lamentation. The piano had been closed, the radio locked up. The aunties' anguish over losing their brother was palpable every minute of our stay. Both wore black even beyond the traditional forty-day mourning period. When we arrived we'd dressed Rakaya in a black dress as well, quickly hand-sewn the week before by my mother and grandmother, but Auntie Zuzu found it too somber for a child and softened it by adding a white lace collar. Children shouldn't have to think about death, though it was hard to avoid under the circumstances.

My own role during that time was somewhat enigmatic and I never properly came to terms with it. Because I was American, non-Muslim and, perhaps most significantly, did not have family in Egypt, I was often politely ignored, excused from what would have been my responsibilities had I been more thoroughly inte-grated into the culture. They didn't expect me to cook, for example, despite my unparalleled ability to heat up SpaghettiOs, and things like buying bridal gifts for the maid and bribing gov-ernment officials required a more nuanced understanding of Egyptian culture and the Arabic language than I possessed. In the end I thought it best simply to stay out of the way, terrified as I was of inadvertently embarrassing myself or the family in front of the many visitors who had come, often traveling long distances, to share food and news and grief.

Those days in Egypt fell into a regular pattern. Bassel, previously a round-the-clock companion, disappeared into the Cairo heat each morning. I lost track of his comings and goings, something I had never done back in America when we had only each other to count on. He came, he went, I barely noticed, for a seven-hour absence on his part no longer meant I was home alone with a demanding child. Each morning I awoke to find Rakaya happily playing in the garden, already fed and dressed by someone who wasn't me. I wasn't used to this. Parenting in the U.S. meant sleep deprivation and a laundry pile as high as my chest. If I engaged help I had to pay for it, first in cash, and then in the blow to my image as someone capable of doing it all. In Egypt, taking care of the baby was a shared endeavor.

Auntie Zuzu encouraged me to use my newfound free time to study, and I did. Despite all the upheaval, I managed to finish two research projects during that time—one on the history of Egyptian feminism and one reviewing ethnographic writing about Middle Eastern women. The irony that I, an American woman, was writing about Egyptian feminism while relying on Egyptian women to cook my meals and watch my child was not lost on me, and I felt it was time for us to start taking care of ourselves. I was particularly worried about the health of Auntie Abla, for she was diabetic and nearly blind. Convinced that Rakaya's loud and bouncy presence must be an aggravation to her, I began searching for an apartment so the three of us could get out of their hair and Auntie Zuzu could reclaim her bedroom. Bassel was ambivalent about moving out, but I dismissed his ambivalence because I knew Auntie Zuzu's cooking would outweigh any objective considerations. When faced with a table laden with *koushari* and *mulukhiyya* there was no point in expecting him to behave rationally.

Of all the mistakes I made while I was in Cairo—which were countless—the insistence on finding a place of our own was probably the worst. They all assured me that they wanted us to stay, but I assumed they were just being polite. I'd read enough about the glorious treatment of guests throughout Islamic and Middle Eastern history, including the adventures of Hatim, a figure from medieval Arabia who proudly let his own family go hungry before turning away a needy traveler, to know that we'd never be outright *asked* to leave. Determined not to overstay our welcome, I felt we would have to take the initiative ourselves.

What I'd failed to consider was that my husband and daughter could hardly be considered guests in that household. As in most countries, the word "family" in Egypt implied a larger unit than the nuclear one. Auntie Abla and Auntie Zuzu had never married or had children of their own, but their attachment to their nieces and nephew was as strong as any parent's. When we first arrived, I pointed to each family member in turn and carefully introduced them, hoping Rakaya would quickly learn to match names with faces. When I got to Auntie Abla, however, the woman rose majestically in her chair and rejected the name she'd been using since my husband was a child. "I am *Teta*," she said, in English, drumming her knuckles against her chest. This was obviously something she'd thought about. "Teta" is the Turkish word for "grandmother," an old, aristocratic term that commands immediate respect. Rakaya's birth had bumped Auntie Abla up a generation and she wanted recognition of her status as the family's matriarch, a status she had earned despite having had no children of her own.

Still, the strength of their opposition toward our moving out didn't hit me until Bassel's thirteen-year-old sister took me aside and asked why I wanted to escape them so badly. Escape them! I told her my rationale, but she couldn't understand. Children keep you company. They're not a burden. All of my husband's female relatives were professionals, but work was secondary to their duties as daughter, mother, sister, wife. The same was true for men, who were first and foremost someone's son, someone's father. Bassel told me that when his grandmother was dying, his father would always greet her, sometimes in tears, by kneeling over her bed to kiss her hands and forehead.

Auntie Abla had accepted the fact that she'd had no children of her own and that the children she did lay claim to spent long periods of time living away from her in France and Kuwait and America. But when they *were* present she couldn't accept that they'd desire to be anywhere but next to her. We abandoned any plans to move, and stayed with them until it was time to return to America.

❂ ❂ ❂

As I adjusted to my new role as a mother in this country, I recalled how I'd been perceived as a childless newlywed. Early in my marriage, my husband and I lived in a converted slaughterhouse on the edge of a Cairo slum. When the electricity blew out one evening, I ventured upstairs in search of candles. The family I knew on the second floor was not home, so I went to the third floor to ask the family I'd not yet met. I was greeted by a girl in her teens, her infant daughter, and her mother. They invited me into the bedroom, a gesture that touched me because even though I was a stranger and a foreigner I was first and foremost female, and thus didn't need to be entertained in the more formal sitting room as my husband would have been. I climbed up on her giant double bed and held her sleeping daughter as she lit the kerosene stove. They asked me about my husband (at work) and my mother (a teacher in America) and then wanted to know if I was pregnant. "*Lissa*," the girl said with a nod, softening my "no" into "not yet." Her mother assured me that my marriage was new and that there was still time.

At nineteen I was already older than this girl, but in good American fashion I had married before I was ready to buy furniture, much less reproduce. In Egypt, the average woman doesn't leave her parental home at all until she has finished her education, purchased an apartment, gotten married, and is prepared, in effect, to start life as an adult—a life that will, God willing, include parenthood as soon as possible. Transition happened all at once, not in stages as it so often does in the United States. In Egypt children were the heart of the family and the family was the heart of society. Particularly here, in this lower-income district, the possibility that we'd deliberately wait to have children, much less not want them at all, wasn't even entertained. Her gentle "not yet" was meant to steer attention away from any fear that I might be infertile, and, perhaps, to save her sleeping infant from the Evil Eye, lest I be jealous of her good fortune since she had a baby and I did not.

Her response amused me, but it also comforted me. I wanted children, but it was a desire I usually kept to myself back in America, where most of my friends responsibly wanted one, maybe two, once they were in their thirties and had two shiny cars and a house with a nursery. I wanted half a dozen and I wanted them immediately. I knew this was impossible. We barely had money for rent, let alone diapers and daycare, and the American media makes it seem almost abusive to have kids without buying them snugglies, swingsets, and developmentally appropriate mobiles to hang above their cribs. Certainly we'd at least need the crib itself, with slats no more than 2 3/8 inches apart, since American babies sleep separately from their parents and can suffocate if no one is watching. All of this was out of reach financially, and thus, so it seemed, was parenthood. But sitting there, where a baby slept in a darkened two-room apartment and shadows from the kerosene stove flickered against the wall, child rearing seemed remarkably uncomplicated.

Of course, the nostalgia I have for that evening involves a

romanticism that glosses over the Egyptian realities of a high birth rate, high infant mortality relative to industrialized countries, and the hardship of raising many children in poverty. As a response to demographic pressures, Egypt has enacted a population-control program that sings the praises of small families, and couples have responded favorably. The birth rate has dropped, in part because of this campaign, in part because of overall economic development, and in part because the housing shortage in urban areas means that marriages are delayed. Girls as well as boys are entering school in greater numbers and staying there longer; this, too, mitigates the desire to have lots of children.

Auntie Abla and Auntie Zuzu often commented on Rakaya's personality—"she's very verbal" or "she really likes eggs"—but they rarely offered any opinions or judgments on her upbringing. Auntie Zuzu did remark favorably on my habit of going for a morning walk with her, though they all agreed that this idea of walking around without a destination was a western proclivity, much like "jogging," an activity in which American women donned inelegant clothing and ran through the streets even when no one was chasing them. For the most part, though, their relationship with Rakaya, and with me as her mother, was one of casual cohabitation. They hoped, of course, that she would grow up to be intelligent and hard-working, but that was a matter of temperament, not something that parents could control.

Such flexibility is perhaps most evident in the words Egyptians use to describe parenthood. One afternoon we were sitting in the garden with our friend Sam as Rakaya was wandering about, rubbing the rough leaves with her tiny fingers, and pointing at the stray cats on the rooftops.

"I can see it," Sam said, all smiles and satisfaction. There was the sound of cars somewhere in the distance, old men talking behind the gate, a breeze through the backyard. "I can see sitting here like this and watching her grow up."

That word—"watch"—clicked with me. I'd heard Egyptians use it several times in reference to child rearing. It was always "watch," never "raise." After so much time in Egypt I'd come to associate "raising" with soccer practice, PTA meetings, baby Tylenol with childproof caps, antibacterial soap, air bags, naptime at 3:00 P.M. and toilet training on a schedule. "Watching," on the other hand, implied acceptance, humor, and trust.

"Children are from God," I was reminded repeatedly. The statement wasn't meant to conjure images of little blessed angels. It was just an acknowledgment that melodramatic attempts to control the destiny of one's offspring will probably be met with frustration. It didn't justify inaction, but it did alleviate guilt when things went awry, and it helped explain away both the joys and disappointments of a life lived in constant flux. A mother's time is best spent enjoying the family she has, whatever its faults, whatever her circumstances. Life is short.

Wasabi Was the Bitter Herb

Karen Rosenberg

The phone rang in my tatami-mat apartment on a chilly January afternoon. Even after seven months in Japan, that ring still sounded so damned foreign to me. A sustained, unbroken tone, instead of the familiar staccato imitation of a trilling bell. I'd come to fear these rare afternoon phone calls, when it was night in the U.S., and the caller was most likely Japanese. And would most likely chatter to me in Japanese. I'd mumble "I don't understand," "Oh really," and "Yes." Then ten minutes later someone would appear at my door, all ready to take me bowling or to a flower-arranging class.

So it was with more than a little trepidation that I lifted the receiver and began with my timid "*Moshi-moshi.*"

"Moshi-moshi." A male voice, who then asked in Japanese, "Are you Karen Rosenberg?" His Japanese was flawless, but so was his pronunciation of my name, no pinching of vowels or blurring of consonants.

"*Hai,*" I assented.

Then, in perfect English, "Are you a Jew?"

I shifted uncomfortably on the tatami mat. I must not have

replied, because he soon repeated, "Jewish. A Jew. Are you?" It sounded like a slightly sinister nursery rhyme.

"Uh, yeah."

"Well, that's great," the speaker announced. "I thought—"

"What the—" I began, then caught myself. "I mean . . . if I may ask . . . who are you? And how did you get my phone number?"

The story came out quickly enough. Paul originally hailed from Pittsburgh and had spent the last decade in Japan, as a Buddhist monk. But he was a Jew, too. "Buddhism isn't a jealous religion," he explained, "it doesn't demand that you give it all up for Buddha." The more he practiced Buddhism, the more he explored his own Judaism. He currently served as the sole caretaker of a Buddhist temple and got my name from the organization that hosted foreign English teachers. And, he concluded, "I'm calling to invite you to a Passover Seder I'm planning. It'll be in Beppu, three months from now. You in?"

"You're really hosting a—" It was hard to imagine. A Seder—a ritualized meal celebrating the exodus of the Jews from Egypt—just a couple of hours from Amagi, the small farming town where I lived.

"That's right. A Seder. Isn't it great? There are synagogues in Tokyo and Kobe, but nothing on the whole island of Kyushu. I've done some research and I have reason to believe that there hasn't been a Seder held in southern Japan for over 200 years. You in?" he repeated.

I wanted very much to be in. I also wondered if he was some freak-psychopath devising an elaborate plan to lure me to his so-called temple, which even he described as "terribly remote." But that seemed, well, paranoid. Besides, I had almost three months to mull it over.

I come from a family of reluctant Jews—I had no Hebrew-school Sundays or bat mitzvah, no mezuzah on the door, no Shabbat dinners. My folks ate cheeseburgers, shrimp, and ham without a second thought (though not generally at the same time). When my grandmother was a kid, she played tambourine for the evangelical Christians that proselytized on the Lower East Side. My father wanted his pastor friend to officiate when I got married ("but I thought you'd like her," he said, genuinely surprised. "I mean, she's a feminist, she works with the homeless and she's a painter. . . ."). In New York, we didn't need to actively observe to be Jews, Jewishness was everywhere. It was a fact, one that we didn't hide from, but never embraced either. Moving to Amagi, where I could count the entire Jewish community on one finger, my Jewishness took on a new significance. I felt a pull toward Judaism, and so it was that my year in Japan marked the beginning of an awkward religious exploration.

But I didn't embark on this now-nostalgia-tinged journey without suffering through a lot of good ol' culture shock first. I felt incapable of describing how *weird* everything was in Amagi, and felt like I'd die if I couldn't convey this *weirdness* to my friends at home (who, meanwhile, had the nerve to continue their own lives, and didn't fill my mailbox with long, heartfelt letters about how *amazing* I was for dealing so *amazingly* with all this weirdness). My letters and journal entries from this time are filled with lots of capitalization and exclamation points. Like, "you wouldn't believe what I ate last night—A SQUID LOLLIPOP! It was so TOUGH AND BOUNCY I thought I wouldn't be able to get it down!"

Or, "You'd never guess what the regional specialty is here. . . . OK, I'll tell you. It's called *basashi*. It's RAW HORSE! People eat it with SOY SAUCE, just like sashimi!"

Or, "I got sick and Mr. Yokota took me to the clinic. They tried to give me a shot and when I asked what it was he just told me it was the FEEL-GOOD SHOT and I made him ask the doctor exactly what was in it. So Mr. Yokota and the doctor jabber away for like two minutes and then Mr. Yokota turns to me, and in this complete monotone says 'THIS TYPE OF TECH-NOLOGY CANNOT BE EXPLAINED!' So I refused it and I hope that Mr. Yokota isn't mad at me. . . ."

In some ways, this first wave of culture shock was the easiest one to deal with—adjusting was my full-time job. All my energy went into learning how to send a letter at the post office and to read the bus schedule. If the Japanese folks who spotted me in Amagi thought I was an alien, I was equally convinced that I had landed on Mars.

However, while I moved beyond this phase, many of the fair residents of Amagi never did. One evening, I headed home from the large grocery store in town. I'd figured out a couple of months before that the day's sashimi went on drastic discount a half-hour before closing, so I'd made a habit of turning on the rice cooker and cutting the large sheets of nori in half before running to the store for a few slices of tuna. I'd then roll my own sloppy sushi and drink hot, canned tea or cold beer from the vending machines by my house. This simple ritual helped make Amagi feel like home.

On this particular evening, I supplemented the meal with a few persimmons and a junky chocolate cupcake whose packaging boasted, "Confidence of creating deliciousness. This type of tastiness cannot be carried even by both the hands." I chitchatted about typhoon season with the cashier.

I took a winding route back, down the narrow alleyways in the center of town.

A maudlin rendition of an old Japanese folk song drifted out of a karaoke bar. I passed a tofu store, a hostess bar, and a vegetable stand selling long, bright eggplant and *nashi* (Asian pears). The street smelled like sake and fish. The town of Amagi, whose written characters mean Sweet Tree, is nestled in a valley. A wide swath of rice paddies surrounded the knotted cluster of stores. Rows of tile-roofed houses line the edge of the fields, and high, cedar-covered hills ringed the valley. Evenings like this, I felt like I could stay for years.

Then I saw the Japanese man on the bicycle, headed towards me. He was young and wore a white polo shirt and thin gray slacks. I groaned inwardly as I saw that all-too-familiar look: a slight squint (the cartoon bubble reads, "Do I—do I really see—?"), then eyes and mouth stretched open ("Holy shit, a *gaijin!* Right here in Amagi."). I averted my gaze, bowed almost imperceptibly and flattened my lips into a slight smile. It was my best "I come in peace" look. He continued staring even after we passed each other.

I was in front of the rice store when I heard a clattering crash and a muffled yelp. *Oh no,* I thought, *he didn't, he couldn't have—*

Oh but yes, he certainly had—so absorbed with the wandering gaijin, the man had crashed his bike into a telephone pole. Bam! He lay in a heap under his bicycle, his slacks torn at the knee.

"Are you okay?" I asked in Japanese.

Grinning sheepishly, he told me not to worry. He'd be fine. And, by the way, where was I from? And isn't it true that in America there is a lot of crime?

Movie star, freak-show escapee, zoo animal, alien . . . as much as I tried, and as earnest as my intentions were, I never blended in, never ceased to draw attention to myself in Amagi. Families I had eaten with for months still conveyed their shock at my facility with chopsticks. Nursery schoolers in sailor uniforms giggled and pointed as I passed. "Gaijin, gaijin." Students in the high school where I taught English whispered it behind me in the hallways. "Gaijin" is the Japanese "gringo"—the slightly derogatory, but guilty-as-charged term used for foreigners. Literally meaning outside person, gaijin is a terminal diagnosis, and no amount of time or good, assimilationist tendencies smoothes its edges.

The Japanese assumed I was cut from the same (hilarious, odd) cloth as all the other gaijin they had encountered, and I met many gaijin who took solace in their similarities with other westerners. Although I had my share of easy, feckless friendships with other foreigners, and tried my best to dim the sense of alienation by making fun of our Japanese hosts, something else was at play. I wasn't only seeing things as a westerner or an English teacher or a tourist, I was also seeing things as a Jew.

I first experienced this realization on Sports Day, the yearly homecoming-type event at the high school where I taught English. I sat with the Japanese teachers on the sidelines and watched the students do fencing and judo demonstrations, play taiko drums and form human pyramids and an impressive array of other geometric shapes. Under the strong September sun, with only a single can of iced barley tea, I was quickly lulled into a spectator stupor. Hours passed. I found myself staring at my nails and forced myself to look up and feign interest.

Rows of boys in matching gymsuits marched in a lazy goose step, right arms extended. The boys looked bored as they circled the dusty playing field. My breath caught. Trying to sound casual, I turned to Mr. Yokota. "This marching," I began, "It looks a little strange to me."

He bit into an *onigiri*, a snack whose name translates inelegantly into English as "rice ball." "Oh, this one?" he threw off with a dismissive wave, "It's a formation left over from World War II. They do it every year. They'll have races afterward, much more exciting."

I fought competing urges to run onto the dusty playing field or off the school grounds. I compromised by excusing myself to the bathroom where I stood in the stall, one foot on each side of the squat toilet. With the sound of flushing all around (women flush as they go to cover the trickly sound of their peeing), I counseled myself to breathe deeply—a mistake in a bathroom, even a clean Japanese one. I was upset, but also relieved. The thought of the old cliché "I might be paranoid, but that doesn't mean they're not out to get me" elicited a grim chuckle. I was sick of people telling me, "no, that's not a swastika, it's an ancient Buddhist symbol," making me feel foolish for remarking on each and every one. I had pegged this marching as Nazi in origin, and I was right.

Soon after I left the bathroom, the moment passed. A group of girls surrounded me, and their giggles and questions helped me feel like a regular ol' gaijin once again. One girl braided my hair as another examined my rings. For once I was glad for their litany of questions—*Do you like the Japanese food? Do you have a boyfriend? Can I show you my (200) pictures of my trip to Australia? In English, can you say 'keep early hours is good for health'? Do they have the same traffic lights in America as they do in New Zealand? Do you think Japan is nice country?*

Sports Day and Yom Kippur, the Jewish Day of Atonement, fell within two weeks of each other. Observant Jews fast on Yom Kippur and spend much of the day in synagogue, reflecting on their wrongdoings and asking forgiveness from God. In New York, public schools shut down, though as a kid I just watched cartoons and ate fish sticks or peanut-butter-and-jelly sandwiches—much the same as I did on Veterans Day or Teacher Training Day. My family had a dinner to end a fast only my grandfather kept. He fasted every year, in honor of his mother who died when he was twelve, and this was seen as a sweet, but kind of odd thing for him to do.

Remarkably, Yom Kippur fell on Respect for the Aged Day, a Japanese national holiday. No school! I decided to fast that year— being so far away from home made me want to connect with "my culture." Though it involved more than a bit of fantasy on my part (I'd have to skip back a generation or two to find "my people" doing "my culture" sorts of things), fasting on that bright and warm September day I did feel part of a larger community. I wandered through the rice fields and out to an old shrine. I passed groups of old women singing and dancing, schoolkids chasing each other; I heard the dull echoes of housewives beating the dust out of their futons. The shrine smelled like incense and oranges. I met an old monk who explained to me in broken English that this was the Long Life Shrine. The original caretaker of the shrine outlived his entire family. When he was 124, he built his own tomb, lay inside and began to chant. He figured that when he stopped hearing his own voice, he'd be dead. He chanted for a week.

"That's amazing," I said.

"Yes, but you know that in Japan, there are many—more than 5,500—who are over 100 years old. It is difficult to live without your people."

"Yes, it is," I agreed. I said something to the monk about Yom Kippur. Though it was quite clear he didn't understand a word of it, his calm face and reassuring smile comforted me nonetheless. I bid my farewells and continued on.

I spent most of the afternoon writing truly awful poems about trembling rice grasses, dragonflies, farming, God, and New York. I read poems by Mary Oliver and Yehuda Amichai out loud. I marveled that Jews around the globe were fasting, just like me (though I tried not to dwell on the fact that I was thirteen hours out of sync with many of them in the US). When it came time to break my fast, I called up two other foreigners who lived nearby and we met at a restaurant. They made gentle fun of me for fasting all day and I chafed at the criticism.

Time passed. I didn't light candles every Friday or read the weekly Torah portion, but something was shifting nonetheless. Against this backdrop, Paul's call felt even more bizarre (perhaps even a *sign?* I asked cautiously in the privacy of my journal).

Passover was the one Jewish holiday I'd celebrated more or less traditionally as a kid. My mom and I used to take the Long Island Rail Road from Manhattan to Great Neck or Oakdale, where different branches of the extended family held Seders. I always looked forward to these events—with the endless reading of the Haggadah, choruses of Hebrew songs, homemade gefilte fish, sweet *tzimmes*, hiding of the *Afikomen*, four cups of grape juice. These Long Island worlds bustled with life and activity, but they felt so foreign. Still, Passover was the only Jewish holiday I could honestly say that I had celebrated almost all my life.

Though I would never have admitted it at the time, I think I anticipated Paul's Seder as a homecoming of sorts; I wanted to slide open a rice paper door and step into a room that smelled like sweet potatoes and pot roast, with a bunch of New Yorkers arguing politics and a gaggle of grandmothers pressed into a hot kitchen. My presence would be both essential and completely taken for granted—the guests would give me a strong hug or a kiss on each cheek, then continue arguing as if they had always expected me to show up. "What took you so long?" they would chide me later, and then, with a wink, "It's good to have you back."

What I found was a mix between a chaotic dinner party and a UN conference. Five tables were arranged in a giant U and tourists from around the globe sat in molded plastic chairs. It took twenty minutes to do introductions. The lingua franca was English, which the Eastern Europeans spoke with intense difficulty, the Brits with snooty precision, the Israelis with bellowing confidence, and the Americans with a jokey sloppiness. It was a sobering moment, looking around this room of strangers.

It only made it worse when I discovered that the guy sitting next to me had gone to high school with a friend of mine from college. "Isn't this great?" Doug kept insisting, and—putting my fragile hopes into words—"We're really like one family here, aren't we?" Hearing it out loud, having it feel so untrue, made me cringe and hate him. How could he have a sense of irony about his state of origin ("C'mon," he prodded, "New Jersey. Aren't you going to ask me what exit?"), but not about this Japanese Jewfest? He really seemed to find a spirit of kinship amidst this mélange of imported foods and guests.

The Seder dragged on, in several languages, with whispering adults and crying kids. Paul—bald, draped in monk's robes, and looking a bit like my cousin David—supplemented the Haggadah with musings of his own. Like I had during the Seders of my youth, I worried that perhaps it would never, ever end. They had all the ritual foods, and made a big fuss about each one. Wasabi was the bitter herb, and I took too much, appreciating the pain and the excuse to cry a little.

But then, by the third cup of wine, I looked out at this group of strangers with more humor and something akin to affection. Doug was telling me about his synagogue, and asked about mine. "Nope," I said, "no synagogue."

"I mean, growing up," he clarified, "when you were a kid."

"Yeah," I repeated. "No synagogue." I told him a bit about my family, how my grandmother resented Shabbos, the day of rest, because she couldn't iron her clothes or do her hair in time for her dates on Saturday nights, how she had only kept a kosher home out of respect for her mother, and her mother had passed away long ago. I told him about how my mother refused to let me go to Hebrew school, because her post-Holocaust education had been racist and mean-spirited. Doug looked confused.

Paul began another speech. I only heard the words "Jew," "Jewish," "Judaism" strung together again and again. How funny the whole thing seemed to me then—this chasing down of Judaism to find a sense of family, when my family seemed to be running the other way. The group then broke into an energetic, if off-key, round of *Dayenu,* the familiar Hebrew song whose chorus translates roughly as "it is enough." This would have to be enough for now—this clumsy yearning, the object of which seemed to shift and flicker and change as I tried to move closer. I looked around at Doug and the others, singing and rapping their fists on the table. With the keen sense that my family was nearby—snickering, shaking their heads, or smiling, I wasn't sure which—I joined in.

Making a Stir-Fry in Eastern Europe

Stephanie Loleng

When I remember living in Prague I think of cold weather and heavy food. From October to May, Czech people pile on layers of wool, polyester, and cotton to trudge to work, weary from the weight of their clothes. The tram and metro are filled with forlorn souls in what look like Soviet-issued identical fluffy hats and wool coats. I was the odd one out with my cotton-poly-blend coat revealing flashes of flannel shirt from underneath the lapel. My suede SKECHERS sneakers and black wool beret made it even more obvious that I wasn't accustomed to this harsh winter weather.

To escape the cold, I ducked into restaurants, cafés, and bars, only to find myself eating and drinking far more than my 5'2" frame could accommodate. Beef, bread, and beer—the three Bs that signified the beginning of the end of my healthy California-cuisine-trimmed figure—quenched my palate. Big salads toppling over with leafy greens and skinless chicken were replaced by plates of breaded fried pork, French fries, and pints of pilsner. A vegetarian friend of mine who complained about having a hard time finding fresh vegetables at restaurants ate only pickled cabbage, breaded fried cheese, and stale rolls.

A popular meal among Americans living in Prague was a hearty serving of beef goulash with bread dumplings. I could practically *feel* my arteries clogging as I sat on the metro afraid of the cold weather outside. A jogger at heart, I can't remember a day in Prague when I actually ran for reasons other than meeting friends at a local pub. I conveniently forgot my running shoes back in California and didn't have the motivation to search for a pair at one of the shoe stores in Prague, let alone the will to start up running after months of beer drinking.

Some restaurants served non-Czech food, including one that specialized in Tex-Mex, another that offered vegetarian pastas, and a few that made tasty pizzas—all appealing to the expat community. But I quickly tired of these options and found myself craving flavors from my mom's kitchen such as fish sauce, shrimp paste, and soy sauce, things I'd only eat in Prague if I made them on my own.

Through word of mouth, I found a one-bedroom apartment. After living in Czech dormitories during a semester-long study abroad program, followed by a short stint rooming with a Czech woman who liked to cut hair in the middle of our kitchen, I was relieved to have my own place. The apartment was in a huge gray block of a building with rows of windows on each floor. It looked more like an office building than a home, but had a certain appeal as a reminder of Prague's communist past.

As soon as I moved in, I bought a few good pots and pans. (Although the kitchen was well-equipped with plates and utensils, there was little else.) Cooking didn't come naturally to me, but I had lots of time on my hands, and craved home cooking: Filipino dishes of seasoned vegetables and meat or fish, accompanied by the sweet smell of jasmine rice. I missed the satisfaction of eating a mound of rice with every meal, so I decided to take matters into my own hands.

My first attempt was a chicken stir-fry—a dish my mom often made while I was living at home. I headed to Wenceslas Square, one of the main city centers, and walked down a side street to Kmart. (Yes, the American conglomerate planted one of its own in the post-communist, newly capitalist Prague.) In the basement was one of the largest, best-organized grocery stores in the city. Weaving through the Kmart basement was an adventure in itself. It was usually crowded with Czechs and expats, occasionally bumping grocery carts in the narrow aisles. The produce section wasn't too hectic but I always had to remember to weigh and sticker the fruits and vegetables myself, before heading to the cash register—otherwise I had to race back to do it while my groceries were being rung up, annoying everyone in line behind me.

It was a challenge to find vegetables in the middle of winter, but I was lucky to come upon some broccoli. Garlic and onions were easier to find so I snatched up the few that weren't spoiled and placed them carefully in my cart. I also located a packet of chicken breasts. Scanning the aisles, I searched for condiments such as oyster sauce (and yes, I found some imported from Vietnam), soy sauce, and garlic powder. At last, my search completed, I pushed my cart over to the register, paid, and left for the tram.

Juggling two plastic grocery bags on public transportation is a challenge. Even more so in Prague because you have to be careful that no one tries to grope for your wallet or tug at your bag for a loose zipper. You also have to be careful of the more personal grope, which consists of a brush of the breast or a quick grab of a butt cheek (more advanced gropers are bold enough to go for both cheeks). That night, I managed to make it to my apartment grope-free and began to assemble my stir-fry.

I cleaned, trimmed, and chopped the chicken into bite-sized cubes, washed and cut the broccoli, then fried it all together with the garlic and onions. I topped it all off with the garlic powder, oyster sauce, and soy sauce, and the familiar smells immediately brought me to another place. For a moment, my senses tricked me into thinking I was back in California, in my mother's kitchen. This was one of my most distinct moments of homesickness: Suddenly I was back at the family dinner table savoring the salty vinegar flavor of chicken *adobo* and the tangy-tamarind taste of fishy *sinigang* soup. It surprised me that living on my own in Eastern Europe had brought me closer to my Filipino heritage. Here I was, living in Prague, learning about Kafka, the Czech language, and how to drink four pints of Pilsner Urquell in one sitting, yet I felt a need to connect to the culture I had left behind.

In particular, I craved the familiar scent of steamed rice. Intent on making the stir-fry as authentic as I could, I poured two cups of uncooked rice into a pot, then filled it with water, and began to clean the rice by stirring it in circles with my fingers. I drained the pot, refilled it with more water, then drained and refilled it again. I carefully measured out the water by touching the tip of my index finger to the top layer of rice and seeing if the water was reached the first joint of my finger. After making sure there was exactly the amount of water needed to make a good pot of rice, I placed it on the stove and set it to boil, then to simmer. I wasn't used to the stovetop method of cooking rice, having grown up with two— maybe even three—rice cookers in the kitchen. Back in California, my Asian-American friends and I talked about how we didn't know how to cook rice in a pot, while our white-American friends found rice cookers too foreign.

I sat next to the stove and waited for the rice to cook. Stirring it a bit, I let it simmer until the liquid began to dissolve, cooking the rice. Grabbing a plate, a fork and a glass of juice, I served myself, sat down with my feast and started to gorge. The familiar tastes tingled on my tongue and I was nostalgic for home again. It was pure joy. Looking back now, that was probably one of the worst chicken-broccoli stir-fries I've ever made, but sitting in that kitchen after seven months of bread, beer, and beef, I felt a sense of accomplishment and a sense of home. I had brought a piece of home with me to Prague, and was able to bring the flavors from my family's dinner table to my own.

My cooking skills improved as the days passed, but when cooking seemed daunting, I walked across the street to a Chinese restaurant on the corner. Using what little Czech I knew, I ordered chicken with bamboo shoots, broccoli beef, or just hot-and-sour soup with a side of fried wontons. In the States, I'd have considered this restaurant's food to be one step above the Chinese-buffet-style food that is usually found sitting under radiating red heat lamps, but in Prague, where it is almost impossible to find good Asian food, it was comforting. I could sit in the warm restaurant with a book for a couple of hours, and the wait staff would still smile and pour more tea.

One time, after I paid the bill, the waitress handed me a green circular pin with a painting of a panda bear. I took it as a sign of friendship and thanks for coming regularly to her restaurant. I still have that pin in my box of travel memorabilia. I felt that same unspoken bond with other Asians while walking around the streets of Prague. It wasn't something overt, but rather a subtle smile with a nod or a look of curiosity that asked, "How did you arrive in Eastern Europe?" I also began to notice local Asians and discovered an open-air market dominated by Vietnamese immigrants. I was curious about how these Vietnamese immigrants had come to be here, but didn't find out until much later that most had come to Prague as students and workers between 1975 and 1989, to repay a debt owed by the Vietnamese government after Czechoslovakia supplied North Vietnam with weapons during the Vietnam War. In college, I hadn't been involved with student organizations whose main purpose was to analyze and create dialogue about cultural identity. But in Prague, I found myself noticing other Asians, seeking comfort in Asian food and recognizing a connection between myself and Asian culture.

My original motive for moving to Prague had been to live thousands of miles away from home, in a place completely different from California. I hadn't realized that I'd yearn for the tastes of home and seek out the very ingredients of the culture I hadn't fully embraced. The dishes I made not only nourished my body, but reminded me that home isn't just a physical place but something that's stashed away inside us.

After the chicken-broccoli success, I began to crave other dishes, so I decided to call my mom for more Filipino recipes. From the local pay phone (my phone only accepted incoming international calls) in the sharp winter air, I asked her which specific ingredients went into her chicken adobo, sinigang, and tasty beef stew doused with fish sauce. Grabbing a pen and pencil, I quickly jotted down what she dictated to me. (Luckily, a lot of the ingredients, such as *patis* (fish sauce), rice, and oyster sauce, could be found in most Prague grocery stores, thanks to the large Vietnamese immigrant population.)

As we spoke, I sensed a smile on her face and a feeling of "I told you so" in her voice. She had often said that one day I'd appreciate the Filipino flavors that she brought to our family table, but I would never have guessed that that day would arrive in the middle of an Eastern European winter.

Muddy Waters in Borneo

Meg Wirth

The village was abuzz. Following the eyes of the crowd, I saw him coming, shirtless and gyrating across the rice field, heavy rain clouds blanketing the horizon. The crowd's attention shifted as the music intensified and Pak Ali whispered that a man in another village was being "called" by the music. The gamelan orchestra and drums worked to a persistent, eerie rhythm as the figure approached. He arrived to a furious drumbeat and began dancing as the children ran away screeching and the crowd fell back, widening the circle around him.

Neither my books on Javanese customs nor my six months' stay in Indonesia had prepared me for this demon.

The "called one" donned a grim red wooden mask and began a frenzied dance, grabbing a sword that he waved as he grunted, dipped, turned, and swayed. My heart pounded. He rushed toward me and away, sputtering as he chewed and spat bunches of grass. He moved in a strange, jerking dance, sometimes falling to the ground or standing on his head. But what was most unnerving was the possessed expression on his face, a fixed grimace and blank eyes.

And to think of the catalogue of fears I'd amassed in the months leading up to my move to Indonesia. Such a different set of terrors. Tsunamis. Leeches. Volcanos. Earthquakes. Snakes. Headhunters employing poison arrows to hunt down human prey. Monsoons. Malaria. Wasps with a sting that blinds for an hour. Forest fires. Dengue fever. Komodo dragons, Dayaks, wild orang-utans, pythons—all in the Ring of Fire, the infamous volcanic perimeter that encircles the Pacific Ocean and includes east Indonesia.

I was sojourning to work in Borneo, indisputably an adventurous, daredevil spot, and that was certainly part of the appeal. Extreme and terrifying—imagined risks or real ones. "Isn't that where that Rockefeller boy disappeared?" said the naysayers. When I spun the giant globe and stopped it with my finger on Borneo it was clear even without measuring that this tropical locale was the farthest I could possibly go from the Eastern Seaboard. The "going" part of it was all thrill and adventure. It's the "staying there" part of it for which I couldn't have begun to prepare.

I came to this corner of the earth to work on an "invisible" epidemic: the all too frequent deaths of women in childbirth. Intrigued by international health issues, in need of field experience and obsessed with Asia, I simply had to go when the opportunity arose. I met with the experts, spent weeks being briefed in Washington and London and took a month-long intensive Indonesian-language course in Java. I then joined the local team to tackle maternal mortality. Run out of an office with links to far-flung clinics and communities, the project's mission was to counsel, teach, and train health workers, hand out books and pamphlets, blast messages over the radio and over the loudspeakers of village mosques—whatever might stem the hemorrhage of unnecessary deaths. My expectations were high.

When I stepped off the plane onto the tarmac of the Banjarmasin airport, I was greeted by 1950s-Soviet-style painted figures who grinned from a giant billboard. "Welcome to Banjarmasin, The Venice of Southeast Asia." I had seen this enticing slogan on a website and it had me all aflutter. How beautiful—just imagine, a tropical Venice! Equipped with my new language skills, I sang out to everyone I saw, "*Selamat siang.*" "Hallo mister!" they replied.

Dusty and dirty, punctuated by an occasional Mobil station, the road to this Venetian paradise was not promising. A few people in impossibly grimy clothing begged in the exhaust at the side of the highway. Nearer the center of the city, the roadside buildings became more densely packed. Wild jungle foliage encroached on any patch of land that wasn't packed mud or built upon.

Home to some half a million people, located three degrees south of the equator, Banjarmasin is something of a frontier town. It hangs on to the fringes of the jungle and the shore of the giant Barito River, catching the plunder ripped from the rainforest that stretches across Kalimantan. It seemed as though either the river or the jungle could swallow it in a blink, so flimsy and temporary was its construction.

⊕ ⊕ ⊕

The man in the trance was bare-chested; his sinews glistened with sweat, his chest heaved from the effort of contorting and writhing on the grass. The buzzing chimes of the gamelan heralded a second participant wearing a black-and-white polka-dot frock and a distorted white mask set in a permanent grimace. The two danced around each other in careful, calmer steps. I exhaled slowly as the performance took a slower pace.

When I ventured into Banjarmasin's canals for the first time I was punted along the waterway in a long wooden boat. From this vantage point, I could see the canals for what they are: sewers and streams, the arteries of life for most of the city's inhabitants. Large tracts of Banjarmasin consist of simple huts on stilts alongside these canals; every inch of space along the water is packed with human activity. The stench of the water made clear its primary use as the communal toilet. But there, just in front of me, was a woman washing pots in the water. And just above on a platform attached to her house, a beautiful girl was wrapping her head in a towel from an evening's hair wash in the canal. Further above, a group of boys jumped from a bridge into the water as "cannonballs," quickly surfacing to watch the reaction of the "funny white lady in the boat." Around the bend and on every side, "street" life abounded—old men brushed their teeth, leaning over to rinse the brushes in the water; a baby with bulbous welts on his forehead rested in the arms of his beautiful mother; some boys flirted with the girls walking home from the market; a lavatory door slammed shut; the street vendors called from over the houses. As I peeked into houses, I could see women cooking. With their straight backs, jet-black hair, long-sleeved lace tops and elegant sarongs wrapped perfectly around their waists and legs, they looked impossibly graceful in these environs. I felt like a voyeur, glimpsing intimate portraits of human life. Exquisite beauty and joy was everywhere along this sewer.

Yet I couldn't imagine how this place could become my home. My heart sank. I felt a heart string slowly stretch and then break apart. This was no Venice of the east, but a vast urban sewer populated by people with whom I had nothing in common.

As the white-masked dancer departed, the 'called one' redoubled his energies, propelled by black magic and the endless ringing of the gamelan. As he swerved from side to side he plunged a long knife at his chest and pulled it away—bloodless. Before I could react, he lunged in my direction, singling me out from the crowd. I became at once part of the performance and isolated from everyone else.

But I had tried so valiantly *not* to stand out. One of my first adventures was on an excursion to purchase an umbrella, to shield me not only from the blaring sun and the monsoon rains, but above all from the staring. I set off in adventurous spirits, shopping instinct in high gear as I discovered the market behind a bus park. The marketplace was roofed with corrugated metal, a maze of tiny stalls linked by corridors, large and small. Everything under the sun was sold here: ladies' underwear, bolts and bolts of fabric, plastic toys, hardware, cigarettes, knives, kitchen implements, roots, herbs, strange potions the color of muddy water, stalls filled with woven wicker baskets, plaid plastic carrying bags that served as suitcases, dried food of all varieties.

I plunged into the bowels of the market, gasping at the sheer variety of wares and the noise, heat, and commotion. I paused for a moment in a shop with rolls and bolts of batik cloth and other enticing fabrics. As I worked my way back through the little stall the owner rattled on in an increasingly persistent tone about what a great deal he had to offer. "Just looking, just looking." In a flash, before I could protest, this tiny, oily man had shoved me into a corner and began to press and grope me, exclaiming "Nice! Very nice!" It was at most a few seconds but it seemed to last forever. I shoved him as hard as I could and ran from the stall into the open corridor, yelling like a banshee in pidgin Indonesian, 'Bad man, very awful man!' No one responded but I escaped from the old man's clutches, heart pounding and badly shaken. I circled swiftly back to the umbrella vendors, selected a deep blue umbrella, and headed home.

Tsunamis and leeches were no longer of concern as caution of a different sort set in. Warnings from colleagues that women in Banjarmasin do not go out alone were suddenly relevant to me. In this Muslim town, young women walked in pairs with effortlessly linked hands, neatly wrapped from head to toe, heads and necks covered by a white *jilbab*. If they weren't with another woman, an older male chaperone accompanied. No wonder I was such an endless spectacle: white as a ghost, a head-and-a-half taller than everyone, and out walking alone.

The trusty umbrella became a protective force field. If I walked slowly, in an effort not to give myself away with my Manhattan stride, and tilted the umbrella, I could block out the entire side of the road where hordes of young men rested on their motorcycle seats or *bejaks*, awaiting passengers. I wore an ankle-length skirt, both to be properly attired in Muslim eyes and to cover the color of my skin. One glimpse of a pasty white ankle and my cover was blown.

It amazed me that I never ceased to amaze them. I had never been a minority before. I felt large, ungainly, and pale. With my damp hair pulled back in a bun, I looked like Olive Oyl. And a little voice in my head kept whispering, "I can never fit in here."

The demon ran at me. He seemed threatened by my difference and wanted me to be afraid. He drove home the point in a ritual witnessed by the entire village and undid all my efforts at blending in.

Who am I without the tapestry of my family, friends, work, and possessions tightly woven around me? In the midst of so much hubbub, I felt entirely alone. Without my music, my food, my language, *my* obligations, I hardly knew who I was.

I felt like a button that had fallen off.

After a week in a seedy, windowless hotel room, I moved to my new quarters—a maternity hospital. It is one thing to work in the health field, but quite another to live in a hospital in the so-called third world. Alone in my space, I carefully draped the rusting, pink baby crib with a colorful batik and moved the IV rack into the hallway.

The threat of wild animals and volcanoes had by now receded entirely. Instead, I battled with revulsion toward the rats that waddled smugly down the corridors and their wilder cousins who ran across the corrugated metal roofs, creating a phenomenal din. The mornings sometimes required a delicate scoop to rid my tiled washing well of a long red worm or two performing graceful pirouettes in the water. Dodging these and other creatures, I would make my way downstairs to the bustling center of the hospital. The only telephone in the facility was in the delivery room; there I received calls from the U.S. on a bench a few feet from women in labor.

Living in a hospital, living with the sick, I was isolated from any semblance of normal communal life. When I had fantasized about life "in the field" I'd pictured a remote hut in a picturesque rural village high in the mountains. I'd imagined myself living a simple life surrounded by natural beauty and passing the time quietly chatting around a fire with neighboring villagers. Urban hospital living could not have been more different.

For the most part, I battled my own mind in the negative

space hollowed out through isolation. With my imagination and mind in overdrive from long stints without communication in my native language, reality became blurred. Many a time I had to talk myself out of the illusion that I was deathly ill and remind myself that I just happened to be residing in a hospital. Too much time spent alone and one begins to cling to whatever is familiar—even if it means watching *Alf* reruns and rushing home from the supermarket to catch a little of *Baywatch*.

I turned within. I reviewed my memories—I played them forwards and backwards. As a game, I searched for lost or forgotten memories, enjoyed the challenge of recalling moments that had gone unconsidered since they'd occurred. There in my room I distilled my life. I was neither making decisions nor reevaluating, just pressing rewind, again and again. It's possible that I retreated to what I held in my own mind simply because it was familiar. Mulling it over was like praying with rosary beads, repeating a familiar pattern again and again in the hopes of finding something greater. Perhaps I was here in Borneo not solely to work on public health, but to extract my self from my life and home, to view that life and that self separately, to hold my self out at arms' length and get a good view. But to simply recall one's life without injecting fresh or alternative viewpoints can be a form of torture.

Each time the dancer spiraled out of control, his handlers would draw him over toward the gamelan orchestra and calm him, giving him small amounts of food and letting him breathe the smoke from the fire. They would whisper in his ear and stroke him as if he were an animal, touching him gingerly as if to ward off the evil spirits. The crowd looked on calmly, children now seated in an inner ring, adults standing or squatting casually behind them.

My respite came in the cool of the evenings when I rode the *bejaks*—three-wheeled rickshaws pedaled by thin and wiry elderly men or young boys. As dusk settled over my equator town, people returned home and the streets were subdued. With the sun's reluctant demise, the relentless, excruciating glare ceased and the thick dust and exhaust hovering over the roads was obscured. As the light slipped away and gas lanterns were lit in the roadside stalls, the place took on a singular charm. Rivulets of sweat coursing down my body became a lighter coat of moisture that blanketed me for the evening. At a leisurely pace, we passed all the little food and dessert stands and stalls, crossing over bridges that span narrow canals lined with houses and constant activity.

I could relax under the cover of night; I was no longer the main attraction.

At this hour, all the doors to the houses were open wide and I glimpsed families sitting down to dinner on the floor, bathed in an orange lantern glow. I saw a woman kneeling, laying aluminum pots filled with fragrant curries on the floor. A few pieces of furniture stood against the wall, metal-framed family portraits were hung at the high juncture of ceiling and wall, sheets of adhesive

flooring mimicked real tiles. Relaxed and content, husband and
sons sat cross-legged on the floor, spooning out sticky piles of rice
and, with their hands, combining rice and vegetables in a mouth-
watering lump.

Gulp, and it was gone. Peeking into all these intimate scenes
was a magical pastime. And here, just as we turned past the arched
footbridge, my favorite fruit market, where every variety of fruit
imaginable hung in the incandescent light—rambutan, mango,
sawo, jackfruit, pineapple, several varieties of banana, papaya, and
the famous durian. I could smell the durian from the bridge—a
heavy, sticky stench so thick it lodges in the back of your throat.
It's a fruit that people go crazy for, a fruit that makes elephants
drunk and prone to rampaging through villages. Its strange
odor—repulsive, sickly sweet and yet alluring—was unforgettable.
It filled up all the corners of the night.

It was in these moments that I felt I lived somewhere magical.

*Refreshed, the possessed figure commenced galloping and leaping
about the inner circle of the crowd. Someone shimmied up a coconut
tree, plucked a ripe coconut and tossed it to the handlers below. The
performer ferociously tore the shell open with his teeth, bit into the
meat and spat it out. He whipped and beat himself with a rope—
leaving no mark. He lunged into the crowd and rolled his eyes back
in his head, groaning and grunting. I gasped as he ingested a lightbulb, crunching shards of glass.*

This masked man leapt about on a sinisterly painted wooden horse—the sort of scene that circus nightmares are made of. My mind and heart raced as the djaranan *unfolded. With each lash on his back, my own body reverberated.*

When magic gave way, I tried to focus on what had brought me here to this remote land. Work excursions to rural areas formed the high points of my days and weeks. Whether by car, bumping over dirt roads and being ferried across the wider rivers, or by boat, speeding up the immense muddy river choked with brilliant green weeds, I was in my element. I felt a rush of adventure and the thrill of discovering something new each foray upriver. The area surrounding Banjarmasin is either flat and swampy with Seussian trees rising up from the swamp or covered with rice fields that spread out below distant hills and mountains. A single road cuts through the landscape parallel to a small river along which all the village houses cluster. Punctuating the low skyline of every town is a local mosque, or *masjid,* the domed cupolas often made of hammered tin and painted a beautiful faded turquoise or brick red.

On one particular visit, we traveled for hours upriver to study a remote village's emergency-transport plan. A welcoming party met us at the dock and escorted us in the village ambulance to the house of the "village head."

After an elaborate exchange of pleasantries and speeches we sat down for a meal on the wallpapered floor. When no one was looking I scooped my fish onto Pak Ali's plate, for it had apparently come from the river underneath the house—part sewer, part food source.

After a few hours, we finally got to work and interviewed health officials and clinic staff, village elders, village midwives, and other people in the community. Wearing an official cloak and being out and about on business was much more legitimate than prowling around Banjarmasin on the weekend. There in the outlying villages I felt that I was part of a mission, not just biding my time.

On tours of the clinics we generally saw very few patients making use of their services. No one was there—was no one sick? Although rooms were littered with used syringes, equipment looked dusty and old and faded posters on the merits of breast-feeding or some other topic curled on the walls, the decrepitude of the clinics and the barriers to proper health care were not unduly depressing—everyone was working to improve the situation. In one clinic, the doctor had stored rows of little ceramic pots families could use to take home the placenta after birth, something that is extremely important in the local culture.

Most interesting were the meetings with the *dukun bayi*, the traditional birth attendants or healers. These very old women are the medical personnel of choice for most women in Indonesia. "Dukun" means "healer," a position that includes mystical powers as well as other professional skills. Although they lack official training, these women carry the knowledge of generations and hold the respect of the community. A dukun assists with births, cares for newborns, and even aborts babies in some cases. These women tapped into the same elements of mysticism as did the dancer I was witnessing.

Our project sought to encourage visits to doctors and midwives in the local clinic—often hours from a woman's home and bereft of religious services. It was increasingly clear that the practices and traditions we were trying to change were deeply rooted. If I were a woman in a remote village, I'm not sure I would act any differently. Would I read the pamphlets given to me or would I do just what my mother had done when she delivered me? Wouldn't I go to a dukun with years of experience, prestige in the community, and the ability to offer medical and spiritual services in the same visit? To grapple with culture, religion, and tradition all at once is already quite an undertaking, but to change behavior that works for the majority in order to save the lives of a minority is a formidable challenge. Given the powerful underlying current of the mystical and supernatural, our western medical advice was met with considerable skepticism.

Doubt about our endeavor unraveled another cord inside me.

Men in elaborate costumes sparred on hobbyhorses. I fixed my gaze on a scrawny chicken, who stood placidly in the rain, his little leg chained to a door, awaiting his fate. I'd been told in advance that the chicken would be eaten live as part of the performance. I heard the scuffle but couldn't bear to watch as the bird played his part in the drama.

I couldn't tell whether the crowd was simply amused by or half believed in the performance. The children's shrieks could have been part of the act. Adults smiled, but gazed fixatedly at the spectacle. When I turned to Pak Ali—my bedrock—he assured me it was all a genuine trance. I was crestfallen—I had wanted him to say it was all in good fun, just a game.

This sort of public theater laced with the supernatural was the very thing that made Indonesia fascinating and that drew the closet anthropologist in me to this faraway land. And yet something made me unable to enjoy it.

I don't know what happened after witnessing the trance and subsequent events. There was nothing truly threatening about it, but despite the ceremony's relative harmlessness, it altered my ability to stay on in Banjarmasin. Perhaps it was its divergence from anything I'd seen or imagined, the event itself or the fact that it coincided with Christmas.

I had voraciously read anything I could find about Indonesia— on the supernatural, popular culture, art forms, street theater—but Javanese mysticism in action had affected me differently than written accounts. Had I been able to turn to someone and comment on the scene before me, or report it to someone when I came home, I think I could have experienced all of these events as a purely an amazing spectacle. But I had overestimated my ability to nourish myself on the culture and spectacles of another land, to live in a pure intellectual appreciation of this foreign space. I craved a reference point, another warm body off which to reflect. To simply *observe* and not to *live* was unsustainable. I had viewed my ability to stay and endure the isolation as a survivalist challenge, and tried to wear it as a badge of courage. Like a bowstring, I had stretched my psychological capacity to endure, viewing each incremental stretch as a success, until it snapped.

Shortly thereafter, I became seriously ill and lay in my hospital bed for a week with a persistent fever. My bones hurt and I had the constant sensation that the inside of my skin ached. I was too weak to get out of bed and had no phone in my room so I could not call for help. Afraid I was dying of malaria or dengue fever, I read my book on tropical diseases to try to figure out what I had, but only succeeded in further frightening myself. I wondered if the dancing fiend had exorcised something from me, leaving me weak and susceptible to disease.

Finally someone from work came by to check on me. I bought a ticket home and recuperated for two months before returning to work for six months in Jakarta under very different circumstances.

Looking back I realize that the very event that was my undoing was also perhaps the most fascinating thing I witnessed. Was this a phenomenal experience? Certainly it was acute. Banjarmasin is crazy and crowded and polluted, yet strangely beautiful. It must be something about the proximity to the equator, but the sunlight is different there, making things appear golden. I can read in letters I wrote during my time there that I delighted in wandering around, soaking in all the sights and sounds while saturated in my own sweat. It sounds like a tropical Venetian paradise. I can also recall the period as one of echoing loneliness and terrifying estrangement. It all depends on my frame of mind.

⊕ ⊕ ⊕

The djaranan slowly wound down. The dancer gradually shook off his trance and slumped against a coconut tree, spent from his efforts. Wooden horses, painted eyes rolled back, were left propped against the new town hall and the crowd moved inside to devour chicken satay and banana cakes. I walked away slowly, turning back to take in the smoke still rising from the fire, the aroma of burning coconut and the last jarring notes of the gamelan orchestra.

Never-Never

Juleigh Howard-Hobson

They ended everything with the word "YANK." For instance: "G'day, YANK." or "Why'd ya come here, YANK?" And it wasn't a good YANK like the way it was when our grandparents' generation sang "The Yanks are coming" or even the way the British said it thirty years later: "The Yanks think they won the bloody war." No, make no mistake, this was a sneer, an inflection, dripping with deep nationalism—this was "YANK," like some people say "BITCH."

Let's backtrack now. I grew up in Greenpoint, Brooklyn, on streets and stoops that I knew prenatally, that my great-great-grandmother knew, that *her* daughter knew, and *her* children and *their* children. Five generations in all: cousins, aunts, uncles, and neighbors whose great-grandparents were neighbors of my great-grandparents. I belonged to a huge living mass of interconnections, mutual histories, and familiar lives. We all ate orange-cream popsicles in the summer, wore Catholic-school uniforms that displayed our particular school's initials in little diamond patches on the right breast, played Barbie, read *Mad Magazine* and *Cracked*.

We all ate bagels, corned beef, knishes, and hot dogs off the cart and jelly-filled doughnuts from the local bakery.

We lived in apartments in solid, three-story brownstones fronted by slate sidewalks and pointed iron fences. We had steel milk boxes in the vestibules and big bay windows that our mothers leaned out of to yell, "Hey, youse, time to come in" or "It's getting dark, c'mon already." We'd ring the buzzers and they'd press the button; the door opened and the kids went in.

Birthdays were marked by candy corsages—Tootsie Rolls for your ninth, SweeTARTS for your tenth. Summers were muggy, winters snowy. If you had a cat it would most likely get hit by a car, and if you played in the gutter *you'd* get hit by a car. We played in the airy ways, on stoops or, like on my grandmother's block, round the alley—we played freeze tag, we played dolls, we played jump rope. Summers we put on bathing suits and splashed under the spray of an opened fire hydrant. Then, driven inside by the warm sun, we'd ask each other, "Hey, how about a nice Hawaiian Punch?," smug in our certain knowledge that this was really funny—really witty—given that our mothers always served up Bosco instead, claiming the milk would help us grow.

It never occurred to me that any of this could change, that any of this wasn't completely and infinitely universal. It never occurred to any of us—why would it? It just *was* . . . as it had been for generations before us. All of it, the milk boxes, the slate sidewalks, even the Bosco.

It was New York, the gold standard of cities, the home of

Barney Miller, Mad Magazine, Lenny Bruce, *Midnight Cowboy,* Greenwich Village, the Statue of Liberty, *HAIR,* FAO Schwarz, the Empire State Building, Ellis Island. Andy Warhol painted here, Edna St. Vincent Millay wrote here, Woody Allen filmed here. If it wasn't here, it just didn't count.

I was eleven when I went to sleep in New York for the last time on May 27, 1974 in my aunt's old railroad apartment, surrounded by faded horsehair couches, family photos, and the smells of kielbasa and cabbage. And suddenly, the next day, it was all gone.

My parents, tired of all the crime, tired of pollution, crowds, apartments, and noise, had decided enough was enough, and moved us as far away from all that as they could possibly get: an Australian suburb. Not Sydney itself—they'd had more than enough of urban living—a suburb. A world of council houses, gum trees, poisonous spiders, backyard barbecues, schools that looked like POW huts squatting in the sun . . . and Australians. It was like nothing I had ever known.

Everything was suddenly insane. Even the English language was just so much garble in my ears. "G'day owzzat gown, mite?" (That's "strine" for: Good day, how is it going, mate?) It was a nightmare: the hiss-hiss-drip-drip of the Australian accent whined in my head, replacing the comfortable Polish/Irish slur I had grown up speaking.

No more "oh yeah," no more "youse guys," no more "wisenheimer."

No more stoops, no more ancient creaking banisters in hallways. These houses were flat white squares with red-tiled roofs. Screens and plastic multicolored flystrips obscured door and window, and everywhere, everywhere, there was blue, blue cloudless sky.

Sunlight beat down on the red dirt of the yards, cicadas droned from yellow fuzzy wattle bushes and no children played on the sidewalks, it was too hot.

And I was stuck. Thousands of miles away from every single thing I had ever been about, ever considered part of me—all gone in a single flight. Perhaps if we'd gone by ship, if we could have watched one shoreline recede and a new one emerge and grow in our vision, perhaps it wouldn't have been so devastating. But we didn't. We flew twenty-seven hours on a 747 and my life fell away like the gallows floor under a hanging person. Bang. You're gone from here.

As potential immigrants, we were warned about culture shock, but the government pamphlets we'd gotten from the Australian embassy, with their dry titles and emotionless texts ("Facts About Emigration" stated one; "Immigration?" posed another; a third, sporting a full-color picture of three happy immigrant children skipping merrily through a patch of clover, informed us: "Australia is an island continent of 16 million people situated in the southern Pacific Ocean.") made culture shock seem like a case of sunburn, something annoying but not serious, something so common and mild there was no need to worry.

It's no sunburn.

Not to put too blunt a word on it, it's death. Part of me died then. Everything that I had thought counted—the names of the presidents, black cherry Kool-Aid sipped in aluminum folding chairs, rulers marked with inches and feet, Thanksgiving dinners of sweet potatoes and Butterball turkeys, color TVs that blared commercials for Band-Aid brand bandages—was no longer any good to me.

Embroiled in a sudden breakup (50 percent of all immigrant marriages end in divorce, a statistic those government pamphlets had given us, but one that we never thought might apply to us until it actually happened), my parents had troubles of their own, so I had nothing, not even family, to help me get on in Australia.

My mother, waking up to the shocking reality of the situation, just wanted to get the hell out, but, as my parents had signed a contract to stay in Australia for two years in exchange for assisted passage down there, we weren't able to simply turn around and go home.

Instead, my mother retreated to a sort of voluntary nonparticipation in the customs of the land.

We were not allowed to celebrate Australia Day, she refused to cook Aussie-style food (we'd never seen a barbecue, in Brooklyn, anyway). We weren't allowed to speak "strine." We weren't allowed to look like the Australians did in their Aussie-casual micro-miniskirts, surf-inspired stringy bleached hair, "stubby" shorts, British-throwback hand-knitted cardigans, or dazzling summer whites. In our shorts from JCPenney, machine-knit sweaters from Sears, and our dress hems firmly situated midway between knee and thigh, there was no way we would pass for native.

All these things were sent in boxes from relatives. My mother called them "care packages" (at the time I didn't get the allusion). In addition to basic North American clothing, my relations sent us anything they could get into a cardboard mailing container: Girl Scout cookies (peanut butter and chocolate mint), Hi-C, Ultra Fresh toothpaste, 3-packs of Dove Beauty Bars, Fruit Stripe gum, and Pixie Stix—all things we took for granted back in Brooklyn, but they were impossible to come by in Australia.

Meanwhile, my grandparents died, my great uncles and aunts dispersed to Florida and California and my cousins left for upstate New York. So, even if we *had* gone back, the family wasn't there. It was as if our leaving had pulled a thread out of the fabric that was all of us and, once loosened, it quickly unraveled. Gone. All I had ever known and loved. When I had thought that we'd return, when "home" was still there, I could hang on to who I had been, even if only deeply within myself, but when it all fell apart back there, the last part of my childhood self fell apart too.

That was when I began to change and I began to hate: hate my old self, hate my relatives who had moved away on me and, although I never hated my old home, I began to hate *my* American-ness.

It was hard to not be an Australian there, you understand. Since I was not a wog (*anybody* foreign/dark/non-Anglo), locals figured me "fair dinkum" until I opened my mouth. So, when I *did* open my mouth and my American-ness revealed itself, it was as if I had somehow betrayed something—some assumption, some down-under club. It was amazing to see the change in people's expressions once I'd spoken.

"G'day," one of them would say.

"Hi," I'd answer.

Silence.

Then: "Are you a YANK?"

Silence.

I refused to identify myself as a YANK, but I couldn't deny it either.

"You're a YANK. Hey, she's a YANK"—then, inevitably: "*I hate* YANKS."

I was never told that anybody loved YANKS, or even liked them very much—but I was always told that we were despised.

I was ill-equipped, the playing field was not even. They knew all about YANKS, could sing my national anthem at me, mimic national icons, tell me to go back to Disneyland, Hollywood, the Grand Canyon, or Jellystone National Park (I was too young to smirk at that one). They could mock peanut butter and jelly, tuna fish, and fast-food franchises; every lunchtime would bring its refrain: "Yankee Doodle went to Sydney, riding on a chicken, stuck her finger up its bum and called it FINGER LICKIN'." They mocked; they taunted with a quick familiarity gleaned from American TV, American goods, and American tourists.

I had none of their weapons. When I first got there, I didn't know that Australia even *had* a TV show of its own (it did—quite a few, as a matter of fact—*Skippy The Bush Kangaroo* being the most beloved). I had no idea what they were talking about when my classmates would say things such as "*This arvo we're going to have a perve at the lollies down the milk bar, coz there's only Matchsticks at the tuckshop*" (roughly translated, this means that they were going to go and have a look at the candy for sale at the local shop that afternoon as there was only a certain type of pastry available at the school's cafeteria).

It was up to me to find out that milk bars were sort of like old-fashioned American soda-fountain drug stores that sold milk shakes, ice cream, ice blocks (known as Paddle Pops and advertised on the "telly" by a man dressed in a giant lion suit; he was called the Paddle Pop Lion and he rode a bicycle into the hearts and freezers of Australians everywhere) and candy—or, rather, lollies.

Perving was "looking", and *tuckshops,* well . . . to say they were akin to American high-school cafeterias is . . . well . . . wrong . . . but how else do you describe one? They are like little roadside stands built into the sides of school buildings, where students line up before morning assemblies and order strange foods—like beetroot sandwiches, pies, and sauce or salad rolls—to be picked up at lunchtime in a little white paper bag with the student's last name written in pencil across the top of it. If you were hungry while you were making arrangements for lunch, you could purchase a pastry—they were well stocked with buns, currant scones, Vegemite toast, lemon slices (somewhat like a square slice of key lime pie, minus the meringue but with the addition of a tangy icing) and Matchsticks.

There is no equivalent for Matchsticks and I never knew how one went about eating one politely. These rectangular flaky pastries, filled with a thick yellow custard pudding that oozed out all sides at the first bite and topped with a vanilla-and-chocolate icing, were always sold in as tough and stale a state as possible. Why they were called Matchsticks was beyond me. To me, coming straight from European-bakery-filled New York City, these seemed to be negligently baked chocolate éclairs trying hard to be taken for bad napoleons. Aussie schoolchildren ate them like Pop-Tarts.

But, of course, there were no Pop-Tarts. Nothing even close.

They ate things I never even knew existed—*bangers* and *snags* (big sausages, eaten almost daily), Spaghetti Bolognese, Chico Rolls (sort of a mass-market spring roll), chokos (a funky fuzz-filled squash—very popular, and unheard of outside of Australia, I think), sausage rolls, pies and sauce and blue pumpkins (orange-fleshed, dark-skinned cooking pumpkins eaten at every meal, an unofficial national veggie). They put paper cuffs around cakes instead of icing them. At bake sales, they sold hard little toffees in cupcake papers instead of cupcakes—they had never even heard of cupcakes.

Some things were familiar, but they had different names. Potato chips were Crisps, Jell-O was jelly, cookies were biscuits, ketchup was sauce . . . even the Burger King in downtown Sydney was named Hungry Jacks, the letters still shaped like hamburger meat stuck in the logo bun.

And it wasn't only food. During one of my first school weeks, we were told to bring our art supplies to class the next day—and not to forget our Perkins and Textas. Assuming it was a book of instructions, I searched at the newsagent's (a newsstand that sold books, magazines, art supplies, and even shoe polish) and then at a local bookshop—but to no avail. I couldn't find any art book by Perkin and Texter.

It turned out Perkins paste is the Aussie answer to Elmer's glue and comes in little pink plastic jars with paste-paddles built into the white snap-on lid. Every schoolchild owns a jar. Textas are felt-tip pens that come in every color and every thickness—otherwise known as Magic Markers.

There was so much to learn. It was hard to remember it all, hard to keep it straight in my head—which word was "ours" which was "theirs"? A year after I'd arrived, I asked someone at the school tuckshop to please pass the ketchup.

"Ya mean sauce, doncha, YANK?" I was answered.

"No, I meant ketchup, that's what it is," I spat back, sick of making stupid mistakes and being called for each and every one of them, each and every time.

"God, you are aggressive, don't you reckon?" (*"Gawd, yer ergressif doncha rekkun?"*)

And, right then, something clunked deep inside. I *was* being aggressive—not out of any of my own character traits, but out of some deeply held sense of honor. By clinging to my old self, I was defending my honor, or America's honor, or some other misbegotten theory of honor that had nothing, absolutely nothing, to do with what I really felt or thought or cared about. I had nothing to gain from it.

So I just stopped. Like the old Brits used to say back when they roamed "Inja's sunny clime," I went native. Only took me one year.

And suddenly, although my mother couldn't say what ANZAC stood for, I knew. (Australia and New Zealand Army Corps, ANZAC Day is observed April 25 in commemoration of the huge losses but overwhelming bravery of the ANZAC soldiers in World War I—mostly in the Gallipoli campaign.) Although my family refused to eat Smiths Crisps (potato chips) and Cadbury Caramello bars, put butter on steak, or take Bex (aspirin powder), I did. They didn't acknowledge that erasers were now rubbers, sofas were lounges, parlors were loungerooms; that Father's Day is held on a different day down under; that college is a private grade school and *uni* is where you go after high school—I did. I took it all in, made new friends who had never heard I was from America and, by the second anniversary of our arrival, I'd even forgotten it myself.

I thrilled to the stories of my new nation's convict past, entranced to hear that that there had been two Howards aboard the first fleet of ships that brought the prisoners from England's jails to the Australian shores. I cheered our teams in the

Olympics—not even noticing how the American teams fared. I protested the damming of the wild and beautiful Franklin River (how dare they do that to my country?). I decided to become a great Australian writer.

It never occurred to me, fair dinkum, that I wasn't *truly ruly dinky di Aussie*. When the radio commercial sang "We've got football, meatpies, kangaroos, and Holden cars," I knew it was me and my world they were singing about. When the TV played "Advance Australia Fair" or "My City of Sydney" at the end of its broadcasting day, I was moved to a self-satisfied smile—these things were Australian, these things were great, these things were mine.

I came to fall in love with that country: its red soil, its flies, its ornery language, and its history. I loved walking down footpaths that curved around huge gum trees with peeling bark hanging in the hot sun, loved the spicy chemical smell of Aerogard (insect repellent), which hung in the air on summer evenings when everyone did their traditional Thursday late-night shopping. I loved it all: the cold rains in the middle of July, the crispy fried-butter smell of fish and chips in the train station (even in the early morning those chip shops were working hard), the almost-deafening call of the cicadas on blazing afternoons in December. When I looked at a map, I automatically turned to Australia, mesmerized and enraptured by its shape, its coasts, its place on the underside of the globe. I thought its flag, with its Southern Cross of seven-pointed stars spread out on a field of blue, the most beautiful of all. And its old men and old ladies playing *bowls* on the greens in the fading heat of summer days seemed a magical and eternal glimpse of my past and my future on Earth. I loved being part of it—wearing my MacArthur Girls' High School white-and-blue uniform with my black shoes, my school-crested jacket and my prefect's badge. I never thought of leaving, never thought of being anywhere but there, never thought of being with anyone but my mates. I was truly happy, there, then.

Then, all of a sudden, *six years after landing there,* my mother had finally saved enough money for passage home. I was dragged back to the U.S.A., and not even to Brooklyn, but to Sacramento, California—the middle of absolutely nowhere, home of a great uncle and a few assorted cousins I never really knew.

For me it was nothing less than a descent into hell. America! I'd left that place behind. It was something that I no longer *did.* All Barbie dolls, *Gilligan's Island* reruns, and peanut-butter-and-jelly sandwiches—things I didn't want, didn't like, didn't claim as my own. As a matter of fact, Americanness repulsed me: the sound of those broad flat accents assaulted my ears, the clothes were ugly and out of date (Australia was in the throes of a second English invasion—punk rock had hit and hit hard—jeans were pegged and zippered, shoes were pointed and black, hair was spiked and everything, *everything,* was black, safety-pinned, and edgy). California manners were brusque and crude compared to the easy graces of the Empire-hatched Australian mentality. There was no "if you please," no "thanks, love," no "ta, mate," no "mates" at all, at least not for me.

The things I loved and celebrated—the Arnott's Iced Vo Vo biscuits, with their ribbons of raspberry jam and their coating of coconut flakes; the passionfruit shakes, with their sundrenched tang and creamy coldness; the Crystal Cylinder brand T-shirts that we begged and begged to be allowed to wear; and Sydney's brilliant *Billy Blue Magazine,* which had just promised to consider a short story of mine—were taken as so many incidental trifles by my "new," California-based family. Even my small koala made of kangaroo fur—only the greatest icon of Australian pop culture (every good Aussie kid has one)—was considered by my new countrymates to look "like a dead sewer rat."

I remember the burning desire to go back down under, to go back home. I remember the day I realized it was all over for me, when I sent my letter to the Australian embassy asking, now that I'd turned eighteen, for a visa to go home, and they replied that I needed to apply for emigration. Emigration? That's for immigrants, mate, I was Australian. I applied again—I sent photos of me and my friends in Sydney, in my white-and-blue micro-mini school uniform, on Bondi Beach, in the bush; copies of my ANZAC Day writing award, my Fellowship of Australian Writers papers; my publications in Aussie magazines; my Higher School Certificate results and my acceptance letter from the University of Sydney. Surely they would just let me come home?

And, to be sure, they were considerate. They told me they had considered my letter, but, still and all, *to be sure*—seeing as I was never made a citizen of Australia—well, if I wanted to go back as anything more than a bloody YANK tourist, then I had to apply for emigration.

As a *YANK*.

Which was something I could not do. Insane as it was, all I had to do was apply. Who the heck cared how I got back, right, *so long as I was back?* I couldn't do it. I couldn't go back to being an immigrant. Not even if it was only on paper.

If I had to apply to migrate, then I never really was an Australian, was I? Australia wasn't my home. I was home—in America.

Gradually it came home to me, and gradually I really came home. I realized that I was not an expat anymore. I was an ex-expat. An *American*. Never, never just a YANK again.

First, the Blanket

Kate Baldus

The first week I lived in Dhaka, Bangladesh I was not sure I could ever find life there normal. I moved to Bangladesh to teach in a private English-language university and, although comfortable in my office and apartment, I felt disoriented when I walked in the crowded streets. Before I left home I did not think of any of the difficulties of living in Dhaka because all of my friends and family did that for me. No one wanted me to go because they were all worried that I would die of something—diarrhea, floods, arsenic poisoning. In order to convince them that I would be all right I focused entirely on the positives—my job, learning Bengali, the people I would meet, and places I would visit. In my attempt to make Bangladesh seem desirable to those who did not want me to go, I had lost sight of the potential difficulties of life there.

At first, everything intimidated me: I was afraid of riding in a rickshaw. I was stared at whenever I left my house. I didn't know if I could tolerate eating curry once or twice a day, let alone eating it with my hands. I was assaulted by beggars. I had an allergic reaction to the dust. And, foremost in my mind, I was cold.

I arrived in January and had not expected the weather to be

so chilly—50 degrees. I lived in a modern high-rise in an apartment large enough to house a three-generation Bangladeshi family but furnished with only a bed, a dining-room table, a couch, and a TV. With no rugs on the floors or paintings on the walls, it felt like a cold and drafty train station. Each night I crawled into bed bundled in jeans, layers of T-shirts, and a fleece. Despite the layers, I woke with a frozen red nose and a chill down my spine. Perpetually tired and cranky, I knew I needed more insulation. The stress of a new job, a new home, and life in a new country made me forget all my reasons for coming to Bangladesh in the first place. For a moment I wanted to run back to California, but I convinced myself that I would be okay if only I could get a blanket.

Getting the blanket, however, did not prove so easy. I did not know anyone well enough to borrow one and, as the university was officially closed for Ramadan, requesting a blanket through administrative channels was not an option. I spent my first weekend looking into the windows of the many shops that lined my street. I could buy CDs, shoes, computer equipment, dishes, packaged import foods, and even a cow—but no blankets. One shop looked promising—it had imported sheets and towels in the window. I entered the store to find a small space in which two men stood talking behind a counter. There was no way to browse, as all of the merchandise was stacked behind the men; I had to speak. I knew about ten words of Bengali, so I said, "Excuse me," softly in English, as a way to disguise that I was not speaking Bengali, but loudly enough to get their attention.

"*Ji* Madam (Yes Madam)," a small man dressed in a fake Polo shirt said quickly.

"Blanket?" I said, hoping he would understand that this question was a request.

"Blanket," he repeated back to me and I nodded and smiled. The men looked at each other and then turned to their shelves. First one pulled out a towel, and I shook my head. Then a sheet, I shook my head again. And another towel. After a few minutes of shaking my head I waved my hand at them and went back out into the dusty streets.

As I walked along Kemal Ataturk Avenue, my head hung low. I looked at the ground in an attempt to feel less visible and to make sure I did not fall into any holes. The air smelled of dust, leaded gas, and spoiling trash. Suddenly I wanted the convenience of Safeway and a telephone in my apartment. I wanted to feel comfortable and I wanted to know where to buy that blanket.

"Blanket" floated in my head all weekend long. A friendly American woman I had met on arrival took me to a handicraft shop that sold bedspreads and wool scarves. I bought a scarf and wrapped myself in it like a mummy before bed—but this was still not enough. On Sunday morning, the first day of the Bangladeshi workweek, cranky from too many nights of cold sleep, I went to work. Because it was Ramadan few people were there. The only other regular in the office was the chairman of the department, who sat all day at his desk reading books and surreptitiously eating crackers from a package hidden away in a drawer. But on this Sunday a friendly colleague, Nasreen, came in to chat.

"How are you adjusting to our country?" she asked.

"Oh, I'm fine," I said, "but cold." It slipped out unintentionally. As soon as I said the words I was sorry. I tried to recover. "I mean, I'm fine. . . ." How could I complain about my discomfort when Nasreen had been fasting for three weeks?

"Cold? Well, it will get hot soon enough. And you have a scarf," she said, pointing to my body. I was wrapped in my rose-colored hand-embroidered scarf.

I smiled, "Yes, I got it this weekend. Now all I need is a blanket."

"The university didn't give you a blanket?" Outrage rang in her voice.

I shook my head meekly. I was half surprised by her emotion and half elated.

"You need a blanket," Nasreen said firmly and then volunteered to take me shopping. I was ecstatic. Her directness, her passion, and her desire to help gave me hope: with help maybe I could build a life for myself here.

We were to go to a shopping area called DIT 1. One of two traffic circles in a nearby neighborhood, it was ringed with a large market, shops, foodstalls, newsstands, shoeshine stands, offices, parked cars, empty rickshaws, begging kids and begging adults, buses, crowds and cows weaving in and out. I had passed DIT 1 once in a car, but had no idea how to get there. Nasreen said we could take a rickshaw. Although they are the most common form of transportation in Bangladesh, this was to be only my second experience in one. So far I had chosen to walk everywhere I went, even if it meant a long trek through a cloud of dust and beggar children.

We climbed into the rickshaw, a three-wheeled bicycle with a covered seat for passengers. Rickshaw seats are small and Nasreen took up two-thirds of ours. As I squeezed into the edge of the small box I had a flash of fear that I might fall out, but soon that was the least of my worries. It was about 3 P.M. and traffic was teeming.

"Why is there so much traffic?" I asked Nasreen.

"What do you mean? This is normal," she laughed.

"Last night I went for a walk and there weren't half as many cars."

"You went for a walk?" she said, in a shocked voice.

"I needed some exercise so I went out to see the sun set."

"That's right before we break our fasts and everyone was praying. Now people are trying to get home to pray."

If this was normal I was not sure how I was ever going to get used to the dust and noise and abundance of vehicles. We were one of hundreds of cars, cows, buses, rickshaws, baby taxis, people, bikes, and pushcarts pushing their way through the streets. The air was thick with the smell of leaded gas and dust. I copied Nasreen and covered my mouth and nose with my scarf. As the rickshaw began to roll down our bumpy street and out to the main road I was reminded how far I was from home. A skinny old man held out his hand and called to me, "Madam, baksheesh." Car horns honked constantly and our rickshaw came to a sudden halt, knocking into the rickshaw in front of us. Tension began to rise through my belly and make my face red, until I stopped it with the word "blanket." One challenge at a time.

"And so my father went to south India to get surgery." Nasreen was chatting calmly about her family, as if we were in the quiet sanctum of a kitchen nook or coffee-shop booth.

"Was that difficult?" I responded with words that I knew would be appropriate but I really did not know what I was saying—all of my attention was focused on the traffic and the maneuvers of the rickshaw *wallah,* who was trying to turn into a busy street. It did not look like there would be a break in the traffic for at least two hours, if not two days. He was standing up and rocking back and forth on his bike chain as he looked both ways. Rock-look, look-rock, rock-look. Rock-look, look-rock, rock-look. It looked hopeless, but suddenly he rocked, cranked his bicycle chain, and plunged us into the stream of vehicles. We were heading into moving traffic that was going with us and against us and away from us all at once. I wanted to scream or pull out my hair, but made myself think about waking up warm the next day, beneath my new blanket: I tried to listen to Nasreen.

"We decided to send him there because the care is much better than what we can get here in Dhaka."

"That makes sense."

We were safely on the other side of the road, heading in the right direction. "But the procedure was more complicated than we thought it was going to be and we actually had to . . . *da-ney, da-ney* (right, right)," she interrupted the flow of her story to scream at the rickshaw wallah and tap him on the back. Just when my heartbeat had returned to normal, we made another turn and had to cross another torrent of traffic heading every which way. Nasreen's voice became background music and my eyes returned to the wallah.

Again he looked right, then left, and I furtively looked with him. If I had been biking I would have gotten off my seat, put my hand out, made all the traffic stop and walked my bike safely across the street. He, however, only paused for a second to look both ways before diving into the flow of moving cars and buses and baby taxis. This time I tried to watch what happened as we crossed the traffic stream. Although no one stopped moving, everyone was quite aware of other vehicles. There was a natural rhythm between all the parts of the traffic that slowed and weaved and avoided each other. At home all these different types of vehicles negotiating the street together would have resulted in a hideous pileup, but here they all fell into their respective places, and we safely crossed the street.

"And I really liked visiting him, because south India is a very nice place."

Nasreen was still talking about her father and his latest surgery as we traveled down a quiet street. I felt momentarily comfortable because the traffic flowed only in two directions and everyone stuck to their side of the road in an orderly fashion. The smell of gas was not so strong here and as I pulled my scarf from my face I relaxed and took a moment to observe the situation—we were being dragged in a cart by a man who was one-third our combined weight and dressed in a men's button-down shirt and a lungi (a piece of fabric wrapped around his lower half). He was barefoot and had a checked towel tied around his head. Two weeks ago I would not have been able to imagine any of this, but now I was riding with a woman for whom this was entirely normal. She did this yesterday, she would do this tomorrow, and for the rest of her life—soon, so would I.

"And so we were all worried about him. He was only fifty-three but not in very good health and who knows what could happen."

"That must have been hard."

We hit a bumpy patch on the road and our heads rocked, voices rattled, and bodies jerked as we bumped through potholes that had not been repaved since the last floods. Of course this was normal to Nasreen, just like riding the bus or driving alone was normal to me in America. But could this ever feel normal? Would the traffic, crowds, potholes, pollution, and constant noise ever fade into the background of day-to-day life the way Nasreen's voice did? I was not sure. Overwhelmed by such an epic question, I knotted my hands in my lap and I repeated that word again, "blanket." First, the blanket.

"But now he is back in Sylhet. Do you know where that is?"

"The ah—" But Nasreen began her next thought before I was able to finish my own.

"That's where I'm from, it's in the north and, *ba-mey, ba-mey* (left, left)." She raised her voice to scream at the rickshaw wallah again. We turned left into the market area, a two-story building full of shops, where people scurried up and down the stairs. She screamed again "*Vas, vas, vas* (Enough, enough, stop)."

Our journey was over. My legs were cramped and shaking. My skin was lightly dusted and I only half knew where I was. The people and traffic continued to stream past, even though we had come to a stop. I stepped cautiously out of the rickshaw, happy to have Nasreen as my guide. But underneath the momentary elation over our arrival, I still felt lost and on the verge of tears. If one simple errand took this much effort, how could I ever handle bigger challenges? Maybe the skeptics at home had been right. Nasreen pulled me from my thoughts.

"So, the blanket," she said triumphantly.

"Right, the blanket," I replied, trying to smile.

"We will surely find you something." And we began to climb the broken stairwell to the market.

That night I fell asleep exhausted and warm. I slept in a T-shirt, protected by the thick handwoven cotton blanket that I now called my own. The rickshaw ride home from the market was not as scary as the ride there had been; I now had a blanket.

When I woke up the next morning my nose was not red and

I felt rested. I got out of bed and looked out the window. On the unpaved road below, a barefoot man carried a pile of fabric on his head. The chicken vendor was arguing with a rickshaw wallah while clutching a group of live chickens in his right hand. The clan of beggar kids that roamed my street had surrounded a neighbor who had just left the building. Looking at the street, doubt began to surface again. Adjusting to this culture might take longer than I had imagined. But then I remembered my blanket. Yesterday I was cold and cranky. Today I was warm and rested. I took a deep breath and told myself, "If you could get the blanket you can get the other things you need." And with time I did.

Beautiful New World

Emmeline Chang

I held onto the pole while the bus bounced along the heat-choked street. *My clothes give me away,* I thought. Riding through Taipei, I was afraid of being discovered at any moment. If you didn't look too closely, I blended in. My hair and features and build were right, but my clothes were too casually American: rubber-and-Velcro Teva sandals, a JanSport backpack, a white men's under-shirt and a rough wraparound skirt. Fortunately, the people on this bus weren't looking. They dozed or stared out the window, and I stared with them. The concrete buildings and jumble of Chinese signs were familiar, but the streets I remembered—a dusty mix of scooters, compact cars, and bikes—were now gone, replaced by streams of sleek BMWs and shiny scooters.

We bounced over a pothole. The old man standing beside me said something. I turned, smiling nervously. He was talking to me. He had friendly wrinkles around his eyes, and his thin chest was visible beneath his undershirt. He was wearing shorts and flip-flops. In fifteen years, my father might look like him. The old man said something else and laughed. Conversational, friendly—he would expect a response. I tried to relax my smile and made myself laugh as if I understood. I watched him anxiously. Thankfully, the bus lurched to a stop, and he stumbled to the door.

I wanted so much to belong. I had kept those painful summers at bay—those trips from the U.S. where my sister and I sat mute while relatives talked about us as if we weren't there. Despite our parents' explanations, our relatives couldn't comprehend that though we didn't speak Taiwanese, we understood it. One afternoon I retreated from an uncle's living room to cry in the bedroom.

"I can't stand it," I sobbed to my mother. "I can't say anything! I can't talk to anyone, and they all treat me like I'm stupid!"

I'd returned to Taiwan with a strange mix of expectations. A part of me hoped to grapple with childhood impressions of Taiwan as a poor, dusty country filled with roaring traffic and greasy-haired, glasses-wearing people who did nothing but work and study. I remember how startled I was, at eight years old, by Taiwanese city streets: at traffic lights, motorcycles surged forward, old Japanese hatchbacks and bikes following in their wake. Dust rose. Engines roared and whined as the swarm of vehicles pushed forward. Housewives and old men in flip-flops wove among the traffic on bikes. It was chaos and poverty. It was Taiwanese.

Back in the U.S. our family friends, the Chens, drove an old '70s sedan. The faded beige interior smelled like Mr. Chen's unwashed hair, and the roof's sagging upholstery was held up by strips of electric tape. When we carpooled with the Chens, I looked at the flecks of dandruff lodged among Mr. Chen's oily strings of hair. Up until fourth or fifth grade, I had washed my hair once a week, as my mother had taught me; by the end of the week, I could brush flakes of dandruff past my bangs and smell the oils of my scalp. It was the smell of being an immigrant—of not taking part in the shiny-haired, bouncy lives advertised on TV. The smell of being an outsider. Of not belonging. A smell of shame.

Childhood trips to Taiwan had left me with certain uncomfortable memories. Terrible haircuts: straight bangs and bowl cuts with no angles or layers or sophistication. Embarrassing clothes: flimsy polyester shirts with tacky patterns, cheap pants and shoes. Taiwan was a country of nerds. While there, I catalogued the differences between myself and the others: I had a cotton polo shirt and jeans faded to the right color. Still, I knew that I came from these people—differences were only a matter of degree.

In the U.S., I was a nerd, and this was related to being Taiwanese. I was serious and studious and got good grades—and didn't have the clothes or social skills to make up for those defects. When a classmate whispered, "Chink," as I walked by, I pulled away, flushing with shame at the half-understood insult. I didn't know many Asian Americans—only a few classmates and the families I saw at Taiwanese church gatherings—but a sameness seemed to bind us. I hated the competition over grades, the classmate who wore tacky plaid shirts and Toughskin jeans. There were no Asian American rock stars or political leaders or athletes to shape my idea of who we were, no Asian Americans in the TV shows I saw, or in the magazines or history books I read. There was nothing except ourselves and Asia.

By the end of college, I saw things differently. Our hair styles and clothes and cars had been shaped by political and economic forces. My shame had been a form of internalized racism, a self-hatred I was learning to overcome. While Taiwan had changed (transitioned from making cheap appliances to building semiconductors; gone through an economic boom that brought the joys of Gucci and cell phones; and moved from martial law to raucous, lopsided democracy) I had started to think about identity and diaspora.

On the bus, I stole glances at the Taiwanese women. They fell into two main groups: pale-skinned women with long black hair and careful makeup, dressed in heels, hose, and thin, close-fitting synthetic suits, or shiny-nosed women with tanned faces, hair clipped back in barrettes and Hello Kitty T-shirts. I didn't see the familiar signs that identified kindred social types in the U.S.: hippie-print shirts or political buttons, freedom rings or silver Goddess jewelry. No sign of where I might find what I'd left behind.

This was hardly a surprise. I had expected socially conservative people. When I was growing up, my parents had forbidden me to go out on school nights, and my mother threw a fit when she saw a Thompson Twins poster in my bedroom: rock posters meant drugs and rock concerts and activities that would keep me from ever going to Harvard. "You have to study harder," my parents said. "In Taiwan people work very hard because they have to take entrance examinations to get into college. You have it easy here in America." My parents were against dating in high school and sex before marriage; when I decided to go to Taiwan, they warned me not to stay out late or "your relatives will think you're a bad girl." I had expected to be constrained, and I had accepted it. In return for learning Chinese and learning about Taiwan, I was prepared to focus on the good-student, good-girl side of my personality for a year or so.

In July 1994, a year after I graduated from college, I went to Taiwan. I wanted to connect to the place my family had come from, to speak to my relatives as an independent person, and to experience daily life in the country where my parents had grown up. I wanted to expand my one-dimensional image of the place, to move beyond the distorted view informed by childhood memories, model-minority stereotypes, racist ideas of the third world, and what I saw in other suburban Taiwanese Americans. What parts of me had been shaped by my parents' admonishments? What parts had been shaped by American stereotypes of Asia and Asians? I went as a young woman breaking free from parental career expectations, as a feminist explorer creating an unconventional life, and as a budding writer in search of travel and new experiences.

Once there, though, my ideas were ensnared by ordinary life. My writing had been my first priority, but in Taiwan, it lost its urgency. Writing involved English, and English was a very low priority. What mattered was learning new words—as quickly as possible: "stationery store" and "vegetarian," and then, as life situations continued to press on me, "cough" and "fever," "waterproof hiking boots" and "anti-malarial medication," "answering machine" and "government" and "second aunt on my father's side."

Exploration, too, was problematic. Perhaps if I'd been European American I'd have struck out boldly, befriending inquisitive children with gestures and joking with the women who sold me vegetables. But without skin and hair to mark me as different, I lacked the freedom to flounder adventurously through the society. People would expect me to know the language and conventions. If I made mistakes, they would judge me harshly.

My initial contact with Taiwanese people came through relatives—and even they made me nervous. I didn't worry about the aunt and uncle I lived with: they had lived in the U.S. and spoke English. But when I visited other relatives, I sat nervously, hoping I wouldn't make a wrong move. During my childhood visits to Taiwan, the slightest word or gesture could bring unwanted results. Once, I looked at a canned drink: my relatives immediately bought it for me. It was filled with bits of slippery gelatin that made me gag. My relatives watched me with concern as I forced myself to take sips.

"Is it good? Do you like it?" they said.

"Oh, yes," I lied; it was the only answer good manners permitted.

"We'll buy you another," they exclaimed.

"Oh, no, no—please don't!" I said, watching in horror as they moved toward the vendor.

Relatives walked me to bus stops, served me food when I wasn't hungry, offered kindnesses I didn't know how to refuse politely. Life in a Taiwanese-American home had taught me just enough to guess all that I might be doing wrong—but not enough to navigate this new social world.

I felt freer with expats. Comprehension, communication, common manners—all of it was easier. Nuanced word choices, the subtleties of humor and irony and cultural references were at my command once again. It was a relief to sympathize with people who were also bothered by the choking pollution, the miniature trucks that endlessly circled the streets broadcasting campaign slogans, the vendors and parked scooters and piles of junk crammed onto the sidewalk and the way people pushed onto buses instead of forming lines. Yet I often felt vaguely disloyal when I joined in these conversations. I imagined us sitting over china plates and cups of tea, fanning ourselves and shaking our heads: "These natives just can't get it right."

Occasionally I met expats who were integrated into Taiwanese society. Cheryl, a photographer I met through friends in the U.S., had lived there off and on for ten years. She spoke Chinese, had Taiwanese friends and lovers, and rode a motorcycle like the best of them. Through Cheryl, I learned how to say "It's not necessary" when relatives became too helpful, and discovered that some

Taiwanese people actually have sex before marriage—and even (gasp!) extramarital affairs. For the most part, however, my everyday social world revolved around the Mandarin Training Center, where I took Chinese classes. Many expats there belonged to a different group: the beer-and-*bushiban* crowd, made up of twenty-somethings who taught English in cram schools, hung out in bars with other foreigners and left Taiwan speaking only a handful of phrases in broken Chinese.

I avoided them—and spent time with expats who avoided them as well. Weekend after weekend, we went out with Taiwanese friends who patiently tolerated our horrible Chinese. We sat in tea houses for hours and talked. We had stilted but entertaining conversations, using pantomime and very roundabout definitions to arrive at words like "sweatshirt" and "Patriot missile."

I hadn't expected to express all the sides of myself in Taiwan, but as I became more fluent and met more people, full self-expression seemed increasingly possible. I couldn't celebrate full moons in pagan circles, but Cheryl and I could take moonlit motorcycle rides along the twisting mountain roads outside Taipei. I didn't have my old circle of progressive friends, but found a kindred spirit in one of my language-exchange partners: Ting and I drank milk tea and laughed and talked about everything from parents to travel to social activism to sex. I missed the ready plethora of African, European, and Latin American cuisines available in the U.S., but loved discovering the Taiwanese version of Thai, or

Indonesian, or Korean cuisine. I fell in love with Chinese foods that had felt disturbing and foreign to me as a child, found stores with clothes made of natural fibers and discovered a chain of Japanese drugstores that sold everything from stylish hair clips to acupressure slippers to cruelty-free shampoo.

What I saw in Taiwan was a whole society. How liberating it was! Taiwanese people weren't just aspiring valedictorians, they were taxi drivers arguing for Taiwanese independence, under-shirted men chewing betel nuts, and carefully coifed hostesses in karaoke clubs. They were business families who took weekend gambling trips to Korea, single mothers who wrote radical cultural criticism, a student sleeping with her older married friend. As a concerned Asian American in college, I'd read about the problematic model-minority myth: how it is based on a distorted interpretation of Asian-American incomes and professional standings; how it is used to pit "good" (quiet, hard-working, nontrouble-making) Asian Americans against "bad" (lazy, loud, and always-complaining-about-racism) black people; how it is, to be simplistic, bad and wrong. Still, on some gut level, I couldn't help feeling it was true. I knew this view came from my limited perspective (suburban, middle-class, with professional, educated parents) . . . but, well, I hadn't actually *seen* many *non*model Asians at Princeton. As I lived in Taiwan, my gut feeling shifted. Here was a world filled with every type of Asian. This existed, so all those types of Asian Americans could exist as well.

By the time a friend e-mailed me the phone number of a

Taiwanese lesbian group that winter, I had gained enough vocabulary and confidence to explore this part of Taiwan. Full of anticipation, I dialed the number . . . and got an answering machine. I held the phone for a second, then hung up. Leave a message about lesbianism in my accented, second-grader's Chinese? I couldn't. It was a few weeks before I could try again. I steadied myself and left a stumbling, breathless message. Then I hung up, mortified.

For the next couple days, I picked up the phone expectantly each time it rang. It was Cheryl. Or a student. Or another friend. Never the lesbian group. A few weeks later, I tried the number again, but no one was there. I resigned myself: the lesbian community just would not be part of my Taipei experience. It was sad, but . . . well, perhaps to be expected.

So I was surprised when, two months later, the phone rang and a woman introduced herself. The lesbian group was having a retreat that weekend. Did I want to come? That was how I found myself at a gathering sponsored by Women Zhi Jian, Taiwan's oldest lesbian group. We met in a building on Yang Ming Mountain, just northwest of Taipei. Large and chilly, with high ceilings, fluorescent lights, and folding chairs, it felt like a school cafeteria. I tried to read the program. "Greetings and welcome." "Introduction games." Women drifted in from outside and filled the chairs—there were close to fifty of us in all.

At the front of the room, a woman in a vest tapped the microphone and introduced herself. I leaned forward, trying to catch all her words. She said something and two women stood up. They

were Ah-Fang and Xiao Mei, she said. They had met at a Women
Zhi Jian gathering, and they had been together for two years now.
I watched, perplexed, as Ah-Fang explained how she and Xiao Mei
had met. She went on at length. People clapped after she finished,
and the emcee introduced another couple. I was confused. The
atmosphere was strangely formal; the structured program
reminded me of the Taiwanese cultural programs my family used
to attend for the Chinese New Year and the Mid-Autumn Festival.
But why *did* it feel so strange? What had I expected? Then I realized: groups of women sitting in circles, sharing their coming-out
experiences; a lecture or panel discussion; a potluck; groups of
friends standing around to talk; announcements about upcoming
rallies and political actions. In other words, a Chinese-language
version of queer groups in the U.S.

"Now let's have some activities to find out more about each
other," the emcee said. "*T*s go to one side, *po*s go to the other."
The women around me began to separate. I looked from side to
side. I had never heard these words—*T* and *po*—but I could tell
from the appearance of the women on each side (boyish haircuts,
vests and blazers, dumpy bodies or muscular arms versus long hair,
makeup and tight little skirts) what kind of division was taking
place. I didn't know which way to go, but finally hurried onto the
po side since my fashion and grooming choices more closely
resembled theirs. Later, friends told me that most Taiwanese lesbians chose one identity or the other, and that most lesbians are
suspicious of women who don't choose.

The emcee had moved on. "So remember, I want you to move around the room and meet as many people as you can," she was saying. "The person who has the most responses wins." Around me, women shifted forward in their chairs. "All right," the emcee said. "Find five people who have the same *xie xing* as you." The women around me jumped up and began milling around. *Xie xing?* I thought.

A tall, round-faced woman in a long skirt interrupted my confusion. "I'm A xie xing," she said. "What about you?"

"Uh, well, I'm a Taiwanese American, and my Chinese. . . . Sorry. I don't know what a xie xing is."

"Oh." She began speaking very quickly. "Do you know 'xie'?" I gave her a confused look. She indicated her veins. "You can be A or B or O . . ."

"Ohhhh!" I said. "Uh, I'm type O."

"Oh." She looked disappointed.

"My name is—" I began, but she had already rushed off to find someone with type A blood.

"All right," the emcee called. "Now find a person from every *xin zuo*."

The milling took on a more urgent character. I looked around, wondering if there were some way to absent myself. I'd thought my Chinese was good enough for this retreat. I had learned words like "lesbian," "bisexual," "condom," and "AIDS," but I hadn't imagined needing to discuss my blood type.

I didn't meet anyone until the organized activities came to a close. The women stood in groups along a low stone wall that overlooked the lights of Taipei. I stood alone, wondering how to join a group, when I felt someone beside me.

"Are you lesbian?" The woman was short, with small eyes, puffy boyish hair, and bangs cut straight across her forehead. During my teens, when being an Asian American with good grades put me at high social risk, I would have stayed far away from her.

"Well, actually . . ." I decided to be brave and honest. "I'm bi." When coming out, thick-necked jocks and suited corporate men aside, lesbians were the group I feared most.

"You mean you can be with men?"

"Yes," I said.

"But then why are you here?"

I began a stumbling explanation about confining social assumptions and wanting to be part of a community of women. My Chinese was definitely not up to the task.

"You're not here to find a girlfriend?"

I was surprised. I had never gone to queer groups to find a partner—I had gone for the progressive worldview, or to make friends, or to take part in political actions. Perhaps this attitude was possible because in the U.S., if you spend time in certain circles, you don't need a group to find a girlfriend. In Taiwan, I would find that many people shared this woman's view. That was why many queer groups had trouble sustaining themselves. As another woman said to me, "Most people come here to find a partner, and then as soon as they find one, they leave."

Over time, and bit by bit, I met Taiwanese lesbians who lived with more freedom. I met Eva, an interior designer who had studied in Iowa, and vivacious, flirtatious Jessica, who said she would identify as bisexual if it weren't for lesbian prejudices. I met queer activists Jia Zhen and Bing Bing and Mei Li, who were each active in different lesbian organizations, and dozens of others. Eventually, I met the leaders of the Asian Lesbian Network and learned about their plans for an Asia-wide lesbian conference in August.

By that summer, I rode the buses with my hair clipped up into a wooden barrette. In my long, slim skirts and the tight-fitting tops I had bought in Taipei, I looked Taiwanese. And it was such a luxury to see Taiwanese women everywhere—in commercials, in magazines, on the street, and in the parks. They were beautiful. I was beautiful. To think that all these women had grown up in a society where beauty did not mean being white, or wavy-haired, or large-breasted.

By August I knew enough Chinese to attend talks about transgender or HIV-positive life. I could tighten my mouth for a passable accent and shift between feeling Taiwanese and American by changing what I wore, how I walked, how much I listened. Listen carefully, and I was Taiwanese: competent, comprehending, and able to communicate. Stride aggressively, backpack strapped on my shoulders, and I was American.

The weekend of the Asian Lesbian Network conference, I saw how different my life in Taiwan had become. At a Taipei bus stop, I read the destinations posted on bus windows and got onto the right bus. I watched the city thin out, the roads becoming narrower, the tile buildings and 7-Elevens appearing further and further apart until we were winding through the country. Outside, dusk was falling. I was traveling through Taiwan. Without conscious awareness, I had made a life in the land my parents came from. The Taiwan of their youth was a point of origin: they had emigrated to the U.S. and put our family on one trajectory, while Taiwan continued on its own outward trajectory through the years. Now I, in crossing the seas, had crossed onto Taiwan's path.

I could not experience those last days under Japanese rule, when U.S. planes roared overhead and families huddled in bomb shelters, or the years afterward when neighbors fought over a book of matches. I had not lived under Chinese martial law, sung songs about retaking the mainland, or helped build the factories beginning to make socks, fans, and plastic toys. I could not be with my mother as she worked in her college chemistry lab or camp in the countryside with my father to survey the land for the Cross-Island Highway and bridges. I could not return to my parents' former lives, but by crossing over to see what the other trajectory had yielded—and by living in this place—I could triangulate back towards some vision of the place we all came from. Parts of that origin remained in the shape of a building, the flavor of holiday soups, the tea house discussions, and the incense that drifted across temple offerings. And here I was, an American, helping to build the future of this land that had given my family its start.

The bus slowed to a stop, and I got off at a set of low, Japanese-style bungalows. When I walked in, the organizers waved me over and handed me a microphone. I stood at the front of a room filled with lesbians from all over Asia, and while the emcee led us through introductions, announcements, and a version of charades that had me doubled over laughing, I translated. That night I slept on a tatami floor with women from India, Korea, the Philippines, and Indonesia; the next day I went from seminar to seminar, translating between English and Chinese. I talked with women about lesbian organizing in Korea and India and bought myself a Chinese "Action=Life" button. A group of Taiwanese acquaintances asked me to join them for dinner.

That night, they turned the music up and the lights down: I danced, developed a crush on a Taiwanese woman, and clambered down the steep slope behind the bungalows to wade in a stream with her and her friends. Later, a group of us walked down the road to a hidden hot spring. Dark tree branches moved above us; women's voices surrounded me as I balanced on one leg to get out of my clothes and walked gingerly across the rough stone. I slid in among the women, and breathed the rich, humid air. Half-submerged in the water, looking up at the stars while English and Chinese conversations flowed around me, I knew this was a life neither my parents nor mainstream America had imagined for me. Only by coming to Asia had I found it for myself.

Saudades

Eliza Bonner

Saudades: Unsatisfactorily defined in any dictionary,
it is a unique Portuguese word that describes the
feeling of missing a person, place, or time with a particular profundity, yearning, nostalgia, fondness.

Ana Lúcia and I were on our second trip to Amyr's house in Jurumirim, five hours by car from Rio. It was a cloudy day. We'd given
up any idea of kayaking and the sun had given up on appearing at
all, so we sat side by side on the porch bench, facing the bay where
Amyr's boat, the Paratii, in which he'd made several record-setting
voyages, was anchored.

There were no ringing telephones, no noisy neighbors, or
apartment problems begging to be fixed, just the theatrical setting
of our deserted beach and our beautifully rustic house with no
electricity. The porch was prime front-row seating in that day's
production of life, the beach and ocean the stage. The hills rearing
up on either side of our private cove were the wings from which
an occasional sundry actor (a tourist boat) appeared to do his part

(circle the Paratii and point out the house to gawkers) and then, without too many lines to enact, disappeared again.

"What do you think about opening a coffee shop in Leblon?" I asked Ana. I had to explain the Starbucks concept that had swept the U.S. because to Ana, coffee meant hair-raisingly strong espresso in a tiny cup half filled with sugar. Once she understood my idea she bought into it.

"You could sell your healthy breads and muffins."

"We'd open early in the morning, sell people their coffee and muffins on the way into work, and I could write in the afternoons. You'd be the financial brain."

"The only problem is that Brazilians don't have a habit of leaving the house for breakfast."

"I know. But they will! They'll find out about us and won't be able to resist. Like Celeiro—who would have thought a restaurant serving light healthy food would be successful in Rio where people only eat rice, beans, and meat?"

"Hm, could be. What about your family?"

"I don't know. It's hard being so far away. My baby sister and niece are growing up and I don't get to see that. But I can't imagine leaving Brazil."

Ana smiled. "I don't want you to leave. Don't worry." She dismissed the notion with a quick wave of her hand. "You'll be here a long time."

"Okay, then how about this?" I went on. "If I do go back to the States, I can open a Brazil-themed store, a place that's charming and educational at the same time. The floors and walls could be painted in an abstract representation of the country, and each state would have its own characteristic music and crafts." The more I elaborated, the more she liked it.

"And you can come to Brazil three or four times a year for buying trips. I'll handle the export from this end. Think of all the artisan work we'll get to buy!"

"Imagine having no boss. Responsible to no one but ourselves."

"No boss."

"No Jean-Louis."

"No Marc." She sucked in her breath and smiled radiantly.

"You want some Três Corações?" she asked me. We both loved the instant cappuccino, and often had one after lunch before returning to our too-busy office.

We heated the water on the stove together, talking about non-work things. We'd already talked ourselves out about work on the five-hour drive from Rio. Even though it looked like it would be gray and rainy all weekend, we were so tired we didn't mind the idea of puttering around the house for two days. We'd both been up to the wee hours several times during the previous week because it was earnings season, and time to report the company's financial results.

"Before or after?" she asked me, with a teaspoon full of mix hovering over an empty mug, the water boiling on her left.

I stared at her, baffled, my tired mind unable to decide

whether the mix should go into the cup before or after the water. "I don't know!" I finally blurted. And we burst out laughing at ourselves, at our exhaustion, which made this moment so inane and perplexing. We were soon weeping with laughter, while Ana continued to hold the spoon poised over the mug.

"Okay, okay, after," I gasped.

She poured water into the cups and dropped in the mix. We watched in dismay as it refused to sink, absorb, or blend. Again, simultaneously, absurdly, we were holding our stomachs, laughing as the tears rolled down our faces. "Before! Before!"

Later that evening we set ourselves a beautiful table and took a picture of the omelets and apple-walnut bread I'd made, the wine, cheese, and candles. Although at the time I thought it was silly to photograph the table, I now treasure the memories of that evening when we talked for hours, solving the world's problems as we saw fit. It was one of the best in the six years that I lived in Brazil.

That weekend, after speaking Portuguese the entire time, dreaming in it, and even thinking it to myself, I realized for the first time that I was not exhausted from trying to understand, and I wasn't frustrated at trying to express myself in an intelligent manner. I had finally jumped to the next plane of learning.

I explained it excitedly to Ana. "Learning Portuguese is like a mountain range with lots of mesas. You struggle and sweat to climb the mountain, learn how to conjugate verbs, absorb some vocabulary—then all of a sudden you've climbed the mountain and you're on top. But it's a mesa—flat—so you go cruising along for a while, but it stays flat and you realize you aren't learning much. Then you come to the other edge of the mesa and fall off into the next valley of not knowing. So you work and work, go through the valley, climb the next mountain and finally reach the top of another plane of learning."

Ana couldn't relate directly to my analogy, but she loved it. As time went on, she occasionally asked if I were in a valley or on top of the mountain. I climbed those language mountains ruthlessly, determined to lose my accent and speak Portuguese without the hesitation of a foreigner.

I thought about the mountains I had climbed alone in Brazil before meeting Ana Lúcia. My first months were a spectacular time of discovery of my new home, the food, people, and language. I had always loved the chaos of Latin America—the bustle and excitement, the relentless energy so different from that of the States. The fluttering Brazilian flag was thrilling proof that I was Somewhere Else. At every turn the ocean glittered turquoise or indigo, the long white beaches filled with thousands of *cariocas* (people from Rio) beckoned. Rio's beauty was stunning: the enormous mountains, mysterious green jungle, and massive granite walls, the sudden rocks jutting from the sea. The city itself was a formidable hodgepodge of sleek modern high-rise buildings, communist-style block structures, endless *favelas* (slums), and curlicued nineteenth-century edifices.

But after six months, the newness had worn off, day-to-day

life was a constant struggle and I was tired of working so hard. I found myself in a strange limbo: I had no friends and couldn't speak Portuguese well enough to make any. My supposed future husband had backed right out of his unconditional love for me after his first visit to Brazil. The smells, noise, and bustle had all horrified him. I didn't want to return to the U.S., but I wasn't excited about staying either.

Things began to snowball, and my health began to suffer. I was frequently sick from a combination of loneliness, unhappiness, and lack of antibodies to your basic all-around tropical crud. Disillusioned and lonely, I slept little and was bone weary. It was summer and too hot for my fair skin at the beach. When I went anyway, the beaches were crowded, loud and dirty, and even in the midst of thousands of people having fun, I felt myself to be an insignificant island of anonymity. Sundays dragged, and I longed for the lonely weekends to end so that I could bury myself in the frantic rush of work. Even in the shallow consolation of the office, my composure was a façade and my self-confidence precarious. I explained all this to Ana that cool tropical night in Jurumirim.

"I was so lost and confused that day you walked into my office."

"I remember. I was surprised you worked only two floors below me. What month was that?"

"I'm not sure, but it was just before Easter, the end of summer, because the *quaresmeira* was blooming in Tijuca along our running route," I replied. "I remember seeing you and

Roberto running at 5:30 A.M. on the beach. You started saying good morning to me and I couldn't figure out why!"

"I recognized you from work, and I thought it must be hard for a foreign woman here by herself. I wanted you to have a good experience with Brazilians."

I couldn't easily tell her how her offer of friendship had affected me, because she would have been embarrassed and denied having done anything special. I remember running back to my apartment at the base of Dois Irmãos mountain on dark cloudy mornings, and a tiny woman with Rapunzel-length dark hair and her nondescript running partner waving good morning and startling me out of my isolationist reverie. Some mornings I dreaded seeing them, dreaded having to wave back. It's hard to understand now, but my isolation was so profound that I wanted no intruders. When she appeared in my office tentatively offering the treasure of friendship, my life in Brazil began to turn around.

"You were so careful that I wasn't sure if you were really inviting me to run!"

"And then we started running every weekend. Just us and the animals at 6:30 A.M. in Tijuca on Sunday morning."

"Monkeys, birds, that huge worm, squashed frogs . . . "

"Ick," she shuddered, petrified of frogs and snakes.

". . . and remember that thing we never did identify? It might have been a *gambá*."

"But the best was the puma."

We had seen the puma the weekend before my first Brazilian

Carnaval, when Ana had invited me to a friend's house in Ubatuba, five hours away in the middle of the jungle. Made of river stones, the driveway wound up a steep hill to the house, which was hidden under an overhanging bier of wildly blooming tropical vines. Windows and doors made of dark, rustic wood framed breathtaking views of verdant jungle and mountains. Brazilians have not discovered the convenience of screens, so the nights were stifling with the wooden shutters closed against night creatures. The large patio with its hammock, *churrasqueira* (Brazilian-style barbecue pit) and wooden furniture was the official gathering place. The "waterfall"—actually a pipe set high in a tree—ran continuously into a small pool below, which in turn funneled water to a frog-inhabited pond on the other side of the house. The constant sound of running water and croaking amphibians was loud and soothing. Bats and *pererecas* (jungle frogs) made occasional appearances inside the house, while wall-climbing geckos hunted swiftly and silently in the night, bellies fat from the abundance of mosquitoes and myriad other blood-sucking bugs.

One morning, as we ran along the dirt road, a puma flashed across the road thirty meters ahead of us, more like a shadow than any kind of physical beast. Silence, as our steps faltered slightly.

"Did you see it?" I breathed and looked incredulously at her.

"Did you?" she looked back at me just as wide-eyed. "This is a blessing," she stated, the wild bond affirmed between puma, Ana, and me.

❀ ❀ ❀

I refilled our wine glasses and pulled my sweater tighter against the breeze.

"You taught me a lot of Portuguese during those runs and weekend trips."

"No, you learned fast."

I knew better than to try to convince her of how much I had learned with her. I had adopted many of her speaking habits, and she had even adopted one or two of my mistakes that made sense once I'd explained a certain terminology from my own language. For example, no one says "*Sabe que?*" in Portuguese, which to my mind meant, "You know what?" But she liked it, so claimed it for herself.

For the first time I fully understood what an isolating factor language can be. My own identity and ability to integrate into Brazil were founded in language and my capacity to communicate. I found a surprising side of me, so timid that it hamstrung my ability to interact. No one who knew me from home would ever guess I knew how to be shy, but here I had often frozen in embarrassment, swallowing words I could speak perfectly well moments earlier, creating a lonely cocoon of my own silence. Sometimes the hassle of attempting to communicate was so intimidating that I chose to hibernate in my apartment.

But Ana had listened patiently as I struggled with the nuances of vocabulary and proper verb tenses, offering words until we came to the right one. The daily struggle to communicate about the most basic aspects of life humbled me in its own particular way.

The word-discovery game delighted both of us. "How do you say tacky?" I would ask her, then go through a detailed description of tacky, weaving stories around the unknown word and giving specific examples. "*Pirúa!*" she would crow, and give her own description that would leave us giggling whenever we saw our word in action.

"Buzzard."

"*Urubú.*"

"I like how it sounds in English," she told me. "It has a nice sound. Buzzard. Buzzard," drawing the sound out. "'Urubú' is awful!"

"'Urubú' sounds much nicer than 'buzzard'!" We laughed at the incongruity of sounds and their meanings.

"I want to read you something I wrote in my journal, if you can stand to have me translate it."

Her eyes lit up at my confidence and trust, and she smiled and nodded.

"There is no heart to an onion. No inner seed, no final point to reach before you can say 'it's gone.' No juicy hard pit implying some kind of permanence or regeneration once each successive surface is peeled away. When the layers are gone, there is nothing. The onion smell on your hands is an impermanent stain, a stinking reminder that stays with you for a short time before it too fades away.

"The onion was my isolation and disillusion, one that I kept whole for a long time; a large, healthy onion, replete with not only all its edible layers, but also with that thin, dried-up protective film on the outside. At first I could not even remove that most fragile surface, but preferred to keep the onion intact and closed. Peeling the first layers made me cry, then I became more accustomed to the sting, then the peeling process, and finally I fully embraced healing. The layers fell away more quickly with each dream I had, each poem I wrote, each passing week that I rejoiced in my new life in Brazil."

The next morning the sun came out and gave us a glorious day. We lounged over breakfast, planning a kayaking jaunt before heading back to Rio.

"I don't want to go back. It is too fine here to think about going back to work." My weekends with Ana had driven away the cobwebs of my loneliness and I no longer looked forward to the perverse relief of being buried in papers and meetings.

"Neither do I. But even so, it's always good to be home."

I made a face at her. "Yeah, you're right."

In Search of Zorba

Marci Laughlin

September 1992

"What are you listening to?" asked the slender gray-haired man in the seat next to me. He had immediately identified himself as Robert, a high school teacher from San Diego, when we boarded the Olympic Airways flight to Athens. I was a little embarrassed to admit to him that I was listening to the soundtrack from *Zorba the Greek*. The music had been a mantra for me since my decision to return to Greece. What exuberance and passion I felt when I heard Greek music!

"I love *Zorba the Greek*!" Robert exclaimed when I confessed my obsession. "I have seen the movie so many times, I can recite every line." Encouraged by my fellow Zorba enthusiast, I told him my favorite line in the movie was when Zorba tells his English friend, "I like you too much not to tell you something. You lack madness! Without a little madness, you'll never cut the rope that keeps you from being free!"

Robert smiled. "Yes, that's an excellent scene. But I'll tell you what the greatest line is," he said, wagging his finger with fervor. "It is the scene just before that. Zorba and the Englishman sit and eat in stunned silence in the moments just after the collapse of their grand experiment, the end of their collaborative dream. Zorba suddenly bursts into laughter, and says, "What a splendiferous crash, Boss!" Robert leaned back in his seat with satisfaction. "Now that is a great line!"

March 1993

"Mrs. Eleni says that you are lazy. She tells Mom that you never help with the housework," Ellie said as she threw the pink plastic ball at me. There was a double thud in my chest as both the ball and Ellie's words hit me. It was unlike Ellie to gossip. At the sophisticated age of twelve-going-on-thirty, Ellie could not usually be bothered with the petty chatter of the adults around her.

"Ella! Ella! Come, on!" yelled Yiorgos, Ellie's eight-year-old brother. "Throw the ball!" I continued our game in lieu of our informal English practice, as hurt and indignation welled up in me. I pried Ellie for more information about the discussion she'd overheard.

"My mom told Mrs. Eleni that you aren't so lazy and that you are always helpful when you are here with us." Seeing that I was upset, Ellie, who lived on the first-floor flat of our three-floor building, gave the typical Greek shrug of the shoulders and lift of the eyebrows and chin meaning, "Forget it. It doesn't matter." She added, "My mom told Mrs. Eleni that you are a good girl. Forget it! Po, Po! Kyria Eleni says a lot of things." She emphasized the latter with a dramatic upward lift of her hand. I was frequently amused by the kids' adult mannerisms, and how much one could express in Greek without uttering a word.

As I absentmindedly continued my game of ball with Yiorgos and Ellie, who often dragged me downstairs to play with them (with great encouragement from their mother, who insisted they practice their English with me) I realized that over the months, I had taken increasing comfort in their company, for there was no ambiguity with them. No mixed messages, no hypocrisy. They had become my biggest fans since my arrival in Greece, frequently inviting me on outings and bestowing upon me their drawings and other artistic works. Recently their flat had begun to feel like a welcome refuge from the stresses upstairs, and the growing feeling that I was an unwelcome burden to the family I lived with, rather than the "adopted" daughter that I wanted to be. Moreover, because Ellie's parents were more well-traveled and university educated, I felt better understood and accepted by them. While they too questioned my unmarried status, and lack of marriage aspirations, they seemed to appreciate my curiosity about the world.

As I abandoned the game of ball to gaze over the balcony at the Thursday morning open market, I tried to shrug off Eleni's accusation as just another complaint by a dissatisfied housewife who thrived on gossip and drama. But the words still stung. I fought back the lump in my throat as I watched the men play backgammon across the street in the local *kafenio* (coffeehouse), their worry beads effortlessly scurrying through their fingers. A heated conversation about the possibility of war breaking out in

Skopje, Macedonia drifted up from the street below. "How dare the Macedonians use the Greek star of Alexander the Great on their flag!" and "Macedonia is Greek!" I heard the common refrain I'd been hearing for many months. The topic turned to Clinton and his lack of foreign-policy experience and his favoritism toward the Turks. At that moment I saw Eleni cross the street to buy bread, and my thoughts drifted back to my own situation.

As much as I wanted to declare my innocence, Eleni's accusations contained an element of truth: I did not, in fact, help much with the housework. At some point over the months, I had grown tired of being told by Eleni and Roula, my older host sister who lived in the flat below, that I didn't know how to clean, and had given up trying. They insisted that I only made more work for them, that we Americans are not skilled in the finer arts of housekeeping.

I had to admit, it was not an art form I appreciated much. It appeared rather obsessive to me. But in the first weeks after my arrival, I had eagerly participated in the various tasks: sponging the marble floors of the joint living room and dining room; airing the white lace curtains and the synthetic Persian carpets by hanging them over the front balcony; dusting the glassware, glass table, glass cabinets, and diverse memorabilia, including cheap wooden plates from Roula's years of study in Yugoslavia, some Venetian blown glass from Murano, a San Francisco cable car that had been filled with caramels when I first came bearing gifts to this summer host family eight years ago, and a few other items that, in my mind, did not merit open display. I guessed that they were miscellaneous items that my host father, Thymios, had collected from the Olympic Airways crew members he drove home on a nightly basis.

Next to a German beer stein and an old Danish-butter-cookie tin now containing needles and thread, was a picture taken of me, Thymios, and my host sister Litsa (three years my junior) during my first stay with them at age sixteen. We were eating cotton candy next to Thymios's stand at one of the local parks where he sold it at various name-day celebrations in the summer and autumn months. (Orthodox Greeks celebrate their "name days," or their days of baptism, on which they are given their names— usually in honor of a well-known saint.) On the evening the photo was taken, Litsa taught me that in Greek, cotton candy is called "crone's hair." I am laughing heartily in the picture as Thymios teases me with the cotton candy, draping tufts of it over my ears as I eat my own, and Litsa is laughing and rolling her eyes at her father's antics. His lack of English never stopped him from joking and teasing me on a regular basis. His joviality, combined with his short and slightly round frame, always gave me the impression of a small Santa Claus.

The picture was taken the same week that Thymios took Litsa and me to work with him on his nightly bus run. Upon his return from the airport and his last employee drop-off, Thymios took great delight in pointing out all the gays and transvestites loitering around Omonia, the hub of downtown Athens. At sixteen, having come from a sheltered life in a small town in California, I was quite amazed by the sights. I remember arguing with Litsa about the sex of the people she was pointing out. Certainly these were women, and not men! Thymios laughed at my disbelief.

But more memorable to me than seeing my first transvestites that night, was witnessing a fight between a man and a woman on the side of a street. From the bus window, the three of us watched a screaming match between a man and a woman turn into a physical struggle. Intrigued by the drama, Thymios pulled the bus over, just as the man picked up the woman and threw her roughly against the hood of his car. She managed to break loose and, taking off her high-heeled shoes, began to hit him with one. At this, Thymios began to cheer and clap. I didn't understand what he was saying to Litsa in Greek. Both acted as if they were watching a soccer match. While the couple's screaming and fighting escalated, Thymios's amusement grew in proportion to my horror and agitation. Feeling powerless and outraged, I urged Litsa to tell her father to do something. How could Thymios find this amusing? How could he not *do* anything? Although I didn't know what to do, I couldn't just stand and watch. When I made for the door of the bus Thymios closed it and told Litsa to tell me that we couldn't interfere in a domestic fight. Besides, the woman was probably just a whore.

After what felt like hours, Thymios left the scene, and I was left perplexed and angry. How could this affectionate Santa Claus be amused by a woman getting beaten? His reaction seemed to contradict his kind and compassionate nature. I had almost forgotten this upsetting episode until I'd seen the picture in one of my zealous dusting forays. Just as I had forgotten the scene in *Zorba* in which the widow gets stoned and ultimately killed by the villagers. Why had I remembered the dancing and not the stoning? This was my first confrontation with the complexities and subtleties of culture. In my inability to understand, I had judged, and then discarded what I could not integrate. I was beginning to realize that my attachment to the world as it should be prevented me from a deeper understanding and acceptance of the world as it is.

How far this family had come since they first opened their home to me eight years prior! That first summer, they had only recently finished the third-floor flat where we now lived, and the two flats below had been barren concrete floors. I remember my shock when Litsa told me that Thymios did not keep money in the bank; he had paid in cash for the land and building, which lay only a few kilometers from Omonia Square. Because of this, furnishings trickled in one at a time. In fact, my first day with my host family had been spent sitting in a huge, hot, and fanless light-fixture shop, sweat dripping down the backs of my knees, while the family inspected light fixtures for several hours. Meanwhile, I wondered where all the lovely whitewashed houses with blue doors were, as I scrutinized the foreign signs and names on buildings through the shop's windows. I remember being relieved to see that all the women did not dress in black and gray, like the pictures in the library books my Dad had checked out for me when he had learned my country placement.

But how long ago those days now seemed. Not only were all three flats furnished and occupied, but there was even a partial room on the roof, now rented to a Polish woman my age, waiting to get a visa to Canada. Eva was only too happy to find a sympathetic ear, and often invited me up for some coffee and conversation. We both wondered how the single salary of a bus driver who moonlighted as a cotton-candy seller managed to build this humble castle. But Thymios's workaholism was well-known. Working seven days a week, he only came home for the main meal at lunch and midnight dinners. Despite the deep under-eye bags and premature gray that betrayed his lifestyle, Thymios always mustered energy for clowning and laughter, perhaps as an antidote to his wife, who rarely smiled or laughed, except when he was around. Ten years his junior, she had married at the age of fourteen while working in a textile factory. Despite Eleni's premature old-lady mannerisms, she often gave the impression of being a child trapped in the life of a woman. Perhaps it was a missed childhood that permitted her to be a trusted confidante for her youngest daughter Litsa, who held nothing back—not even her sex life—from her mother, and often bonded with her through secret smoking sessions on the balcony. (Since Thymios could not tolerate smoking due to respiratory problems, Eleni and Litsa alternated playing lookout on the balcony and learned to detect the subtle sounds of his car's arrival and the turning of the lock on the street below.)

While I was welcomed as a member of the Secret Smoking

Society, I apparently did not have the credentials to make me a potential member of the Good Greek Housewife Society. Not only could I not clean house but I couldn't cook! Well, more specifically, I couldn't peel potatoes, a house staple. I tried to explain that with a potato peeler I might stand a chance. But as it was, I was competing with women who had been peeling potatoes with knives since the age of three, and I lacked their ease and efficiency. My slow pace in the kitchen amused them, as did my other un-Greek habits such as consuming coffee in the largest available mug, sporting socks instead of slippers and—the worst—spontaneously smiling at strangers.

Eventually, disheartened by the consensus that I was useless at both cooking and cleaning, I stopped trying. I let the law of comparable advantage prevail, and let them do what they did best. (As for what *I* did best, well, that seemed yet to be determined.) My host mother had given up trying to teach me needlepoint after only one session when, with great surprise and solemnity, she and my host sisters digested the news that I did not possess a dowry. What planet did we Americans come from, they asked themselves. Did we not learn anything practical about marriage and womanhood? How was I going to get a husband when I had nothing to offer? What security did I have?

One of the first Greek phrases I learned upon my return to Dodonis 64, Lofos Skouze, Athens, was *"Dhen exho prika"* (I don't have a dowry). People laughed heartily when I gave this response to the question of why I was not yet married at the ripened age of twenty-four. How could I explain to this family that I wanted so much to belong to, to whom I felt deep gratitude for opening a new world to me at the impressionable age of sixteen, that I had so many other things I wanted to do in life before getting married? With a degree in International Relations under my belt, and goodwill-ambassador ambitions, I was ready to burst out onto the scene. Exactly which scene, I wasn't sure. But it was certain to be important and world-saving in nature. But in this family's eyes, I might as well have been an alien, for what else would explain my decision to leave my family and country, especially without a husband in tow? Or at least the intent of soon finding one?

How could I explain to them why I had come?

More importantly, though, could I explain it to myself? Why did I now find myself in this relative state of misery, with my self-esteem dependent on the accolades of two children who enjoyed playing with me while I amused them with my newfound Greek words and phrases? The impetus for my return to Greece—a weeklong conference in Crete, intended as a prelude to the Beijing UN Conference on Women—seemed worlds away now. Learning of this conference the spring before graduation, I had plotted fund-raising strategies to attend. It then dawned on me that if I managed to earn enough money to get myself halfway across the world, I might as well stay a while. When the Kourtis visited me in the U.S., I had been reinspired to connect more deeply with this family of mine. Because of this desire to connect, and the desire to live and work abroad, it made sense to exploit this opportunity.

But these were just the rational reasons I tried to use for my irrational desire to return to Greece. Somewhere in me lurked the suspicion that I was lost and searching for something. That feeling had overcome me as I stood in the San Francisco airport, waiting to board the flight to Athens. Glancing up at the Alitalia departure board, I had suddenly felt a wave of anxiety and a heaviness in my stomach. *Why don't I go back to Italy?* I thought. (I'd spent my junior year of college there.) *At least there I can speak the language!* Something inside me asked, *What are you doing? Why are you going?* But I pretended I had not heard.

Of course I knew what I was doing! I was looking for Zorba, the teacher who could help me find madness—the madness that would make me free. Surely this land and people who could give birth to Zorba had something to teach me. I hoped he still lurked in this land of ancient gods and rocks, amidst the yellow Athenian smog, sprawling apartment buildings, and Albanian squatters. From this place, and these people, I wanted to learn to dance until I dropped, to embrace life as Zorba did. I wanted the freedom that came with expressing the emotions, passions, and spontaneity that we Americans have been trained to tame or sublimate. I also wanted to get back to the simplicity I had enjoyed during my first stay. There had been something uniquely liberating about having only one choice of coffee and two bread options, rather than two aisles of cereal choices to negotiate. There was something refreshing about having to go to two different stores to satisfy my culinary and feminine hygiene needs. On some level, I sought to escape the celebrated American "convenience" of life, which too often felt like a barrier from life. I wanted to inhale both the sweet fumes of the freshly baked bread from the neighborhood bakery and the acrid smells of the hanging meat at the butcher next door. I didn't want the "easy listening" of Muzak to inform my "shopping experience." I wanted to not take a warm shower for granted. And, on a less conscious level, I wanted my Greek family to know that not all Americans value pursuit of the American Dream above all else; that dancing on the beach to bouzouki music was equally, if not more, valuable than a house in the suburbs.

And now, here I was, only six months after my arrival in Zorba country, feeling more like throwing myself off the balcony than dancing on it. I had wanted to be known by my family, but instead, found myself feeling not only unknown, but misunderstood. I found myself pouring out my misery in letters home, to which I would receive the vexing reply: "Why don't you come home?" Letters from the boyfriend I had left behind with only a vague mission statement of my plans in Greece, asked me what was keeping me here. His parents wondered what I was trying to prove.

The truth was, I didn't know. But I knew I couldn't return home a failure. I had never failed in my life, and I was loath to begin now. How could I return home, without having accomplished anything? How could I leave this family, to whom I felt indebted, before redeeming myself? Before proving my gratitude to them by mastering their language? Besides, Opportunity was certainly about to knock, and I didn't want to miss it. I was convinced that if I just stuck it out longer, life would improve.

I was off to a rather inauspicious start, however. After a month of agitated joblessness in Athens, I found a position as a nanny. On day one, I returned home in a state of despair, realizing what a mistake I had made. Why had I made this commitment when I never really liked baby-sitting or staying at home in the first place? Where had my wits gone? On day four of my vocational misery, when Dimitri—a spoiled boy who demanded constant entertainment—spit his Corn Flakes all over me, a wave of great anger swept through me, followed by a wave of absolute clarity: I had NOT worked my way through college and earned high grades to end up as a nanny with chewed-up Corn Flakes down the front of my blouse. This was NOT what my life in Athens was going to be about. This was NOT the type of madness I had in mind.

I made it to day five only because of deeply entrenched Catholic guilt. I had agreed to the job; how could I quit so soon, leaving the Very Nice Mother without a nanny? But on day five, when Very Nice Mother explained to me that she could not trust Maria, the young Filipina live-in maid, to teach her children proper English, as she came from a culture that lacks etiquette and intelligence, my guilt loosened its grip. When I called Very Nice Mother that evening to explain that I had made a very regretful mistake in accepting the position, she cursed me and refused to pay me for my five excruciating days.

After this episode, my Greek family decided that I was not only anti-children, but also spoiled and allergic to hard work. I redeemed myself momentarily when I began teaching part-time, but quickly lost ground when they found out that I had taken on an unpaid internship at the Hellenic Foundation for Defense and Foreign Policy. Weeks after I began my internship, and during a moment of sisterly love, Litsa let me know that the family (read: EVERYONE in the neighborhood and greater Athens area) thought I was a fool! "In Greece," Litsa explained, "only a fool would work for free."

I had stopped counting the cultural mishaps and misunder-standings at this point. Fortunately, my students were often more benevolent bearers of cultural enlightenment. In the classroom, my cultural "transgressions" were often met with laughter rather than judgment, and many delighted in playing the Oracle of Greek Tra-dition. Most recently, my Oracles had enlightened me on the sub-ject of the "Evil Eye." I had been continuously amazed by my family's sincere belief in its powers. Litsa attributed her intense headaches to exposure to somebody's Evil Eye, usually inflicted out of jealousy, and to cure her, Eleni would place her hands on Litsa's head and utter certain words to break the spell. My students con-curred, telling me that their mothers knew the words, but they could not divulge them. If transmitted, the words had to be written rather than spoken. Even my bribes and blue eyes, considered much more potent in casting an Evil Eye, failed to make them reveal the magic words. My students teasingly displayed their pro-tective gear: decorative blue-eye beads worn on bracelets and necklaces to ward off the powers of the covetous eye. I must have seen dozens of these when Roula's baby girl was born—pinned on her pajamas, in her crib, and on a gold chain around her neck. In fact, Roula would not take her newborn outside for forty days, as she was too susceptible to the power of its gaze.

I, however, was proving susceptible not to the Evil Eye, but to the opinions of my Greek family, transmitted to me by the neighbors' twelve-year-old daughter. Where was my blue-eyed trinket, my protection? Where was Zorba? Why was he proving so elusive?

April 1993

Entering the kitchen, I plopped my books and folders full of essays down on the table and greeted Litsa and my host mother, who were seated in the living room watching TV. I announced that I was going to make some Nescafe and grade essays in the kitchen. Eleni looked at her watch, and exchanged a look with Litsa, regarding the notion of drinking coffee at 10:30 in the evening, I imagined. Consuming numerous cups of coffee and tea had become my method of coping with the freezing temperatures and poorly insulated flat. As I lit the Bunsen burner, the howling wind threw more hail at the sliding-glass door of the balcony, and the draft extinguished the flame. It seemed the perfect metaphor for the day's events. Much of my retreat into the kitchen was a result of the tension I sensed in the living room. Roula had clearly told Eleni and Litsa about my clash with her that afternoon. The knot in my stomach had not dissipated with the passing hours.

Litsa entered the kitchen, shut the sliding wooden partition behind her, and sat down. She looked very serious.

"Marci, please tell me that what Roula said is not true." My stomach fell to the floor. Why did she look so grave? How could one short phone call elicit this dire response? "Did you really use the phone to call Jon in the States? I told Mom and Dad that you would never do such a thing." Because the family was on a tight budget, international calls expensive and phone bills not itemized, I usually used pay phones at call centers. I looked at Litsa's pleading eyes, and sadly shook my head. Yes, I had used the phone to call Jon, but it had been a very brief call, and I had left money for the phone call next to Dad's bed.

"Roula said you shut all the doors to sneak the call and then talked for almost an hour." I felt the same groundswell of anger that I had felt that afternoon after my fight with Roula, who had obviously formed her opinion of the incident long before my explanation. The scene in the afternoon had been ugly, as Roula used the opportunity to vent all her pent-up rage. I was a typical selfish American, taking advantage of her family . . . and so ran the tenor of her argument. I explained to Litsa that while I *had* used the phone to call Jon, we had only spoken for ten minutes. I *had* shut the kitchen door, so as not wake up Roula and the baby napping in the next room. While I *should* have called from outside, I had promised to call Jon at this specific time and was running behind schedule.

My explanation proved futile. The look on her face told me

that the verdict was already in. "How could you do this, Marci? I really didn't want to believe Roula." Tears welled up in my eyes as I realized that I had not only disappointed Litsa, but also that I had lost my one ally. Of course the family would believe Roula. After all, she is the REAL daughter. The REAL sister. And it was her word against mine. As Litsa left the room, only anger prevented me from uncontrollable sobs. Litsa returned within minutes to announce that–Roula and her husband were coming upstairs to talk. She might as well have announced the Inquisition. At that moment, Thymios walked in. Looking at his big, tender, disappointed eyes, I felt deep shame and regret. *"Koritzi mou! Ti na kanoume?* (My girl, what are we going to do?)" He made an uncharacteristically serious speech, which I struggled to understand. As he handed me back the money I had left by his bed, I understood that I had offended him with my compensation.

Minutes later the tribunal began. Roula repeated her exaggerated version of my crime, and exhibited the same venom as earlier. After she finished linking me to most of the evils of American political, economic, and cultural imperialism, one of the Inquisitors compassionately suggested that perhaps the defendant wasn't *totally* responsible for all of these. As the trial came to an end, I was in a state of mild shock. All I could think was: "What a splendiferous crash!"

May 1993

"Marci, ella tho. Telefono! Telefono!" Eleni's voice woke me up and I jumped out of bed to grab the phone. It was my best friend's

voice on the other end, "Marci, I need to know if you are coming home in time to be in my wedding or not. It's fine if you're not, just tell me so my mom doesn't make you a bridesmaid's dress."

"Yes, I'm coming home," I told Kim. The words came out before I had even thought about them. I tried them on again for size. "Yes, Kim, I'm still planning on coming home the week before your wedding." Her squeal of delight sounded like it came from the next room.

I wasn't sure why, but it was the right decision. I didn't want to be a good Greek daughter anymore. I wanted to be an independent twenty-four-year-old, in an environment I understood and a culture where I did not have to explain myself.

While I had recovered from the Phone Trial the month before, I was grieving over the realization that my family *did not know me,* and was profoundly shaken that they could harbor such mistrust of me. Litsa had told me that her father was afraid to leave me alone in the house for fear I would use the phone again, as he assumed that I had used the phone many times before to call the States.

I felt betrayed by this family, just as they felt betrayed by me. I finally understood the proverb "the road to Hell is paved with good intentions." Having failed in my ambassadorial mission, I was purposeless. I had nothing, practically speaking, to keep me in Athens. Instead of freedom, I had found failure.

After I hung up the phone with Kim I went to sit in the sun on the front balcony and drink the Nescafe Litsa had made for me. Again the echo haunted me: "What a splendiferous crash!" What a crash, indeed! If only I could call it splendiferous. I had come to Greece in search of joy, simplicity, freedom. Instead, I had found only a sense of frustration and failure. It was a crash I did not yet feel like laughing about.

Peering across the street at the plant-rimmed balcony said to belong to the neighborhood whore, it dawned on me that the real problem was not that my Greek family didn't know me, but that *I* didn't know me. If I knew myself, would I have been so dependent on their approval? Then an equally disturbing thought occurred to me: How could I truly know *them*, without knowing myself? Could any ambassador carry out her mission without clarity about whom and what she is representing? About what she has to offer? Although painful, my "crashes" with my host family had forced me to examine the clash between my own self-image and my reflection in their eyes. The suspicion that I had something to learn from them gnawed at me.

At that moment, I realized why Zorba was so heroic. Zorba had cut the rope of self-deception, of illusion. Zorba's true magic—his madness—came from his self-knowledge. He could live his universal ode to life because he possessed rare self-knowledge, which translated into an acceptance of life—both its music and its crashes. Therein lay his freedom.

It was time to go home. Greece could not give me what I sought. It could only provide a signpost along the road of a much longer journey.

Living the Dream in Paris

Christina Henry de Tessan

"*What* am I going to wear?" I scanned the contents of my closet: mostly jeans and slacks, a black cocktail dress, T-shirts, and nubby sludge-colored sweaters, a yellow silk pantsuit, a couple of short skirts, my favorite worn brown loafers, scuffed black boots, a pair of running shoes. Not exactly the makings for a dress-for-success interview in Paris. But then, that was the question: What is one supposed to wear to a job interview in Paris? I glanced over my options once again, mixing and matching in my head and eliminating one possibility after another. My time might have been better spent preparing to answer questions in French about my professional experience, but no, I just leaned on the closet door—at a fashion crossroads.

In 1964, at the age of twenty-seven, my father moved from Paris to San Francisco. In 1999, at the same age, I undertook the same journey in reverse. When I was a child, my father's decision to come to America had always seemed inevitable. Of course he had moved six thousand miles across an ocean and a continent, left his family and friends behind, found work in the United States and learned to speak English with enviable fluency and a charming accent. He was so firmly established that it never crossed my mind what an epic thing he had done in uprooting himself and starting anew. Although I remember hearing about a few funny linguistic errors in his early days (pronouncing "puddles" as "poodles" is one of my favorites), by the time I was old enough to notice, he spoke English so well that he corrected others' spelling and played Scrabble bilingually and knew everyone in town (had for ages)— he was a San Francisco native in my book. He dropped little hints of a former life occasionally: of zipping around Paris on his scooter as a teenager; of living in Normandy during the War (he recalled the Dentyne the American soldiers passed out to the kids); of cavorting in the Luxembourg gardens after hours with packs of friends.

My trips to France as a child had been great fun, a glimpse into another country and a different era. My grandmother always insisted on telling anyone who would listen that she was a fourth-generation Parisian, and she lived up to standards of which only she knew the existence. Too young to appreciate the age and grandeur of the city, I went to the park (my American mother was horrified at the sign forbidding children from playing on the grass) and for pony rides in the Luxembourg gardens, ogled pastries, got my hair cut at the fancy grown-up coiffeur and generally traipsed around being the "*petite fille Américaine.*" As I became more independent, I explored beyond the confines of the seventeenth arrondissement, venturing over to the hip Left Bank to sip at bitterly charred thimbles of coffee and write grandiloquent thoughts in my journal. In my early twenties, I returned to visit my aging grandmother, revisiting the coiffeur and sighing patiently as my grandmother tried to seduce me—with endless shopping trips— into becoming the *petite Parisienne* she'd always dreamed of. This was all well and good, but I was tired of being a guest, forever hemmed in by family obligations, always checking relatives off a list. I wanted to get to know this place on my own terms, claim it for myself once and for all.

So, full of naive ambition and romantic ideas, my boyfriend and I decided to go. "Paris! Oh I *love* Paris!" people would trill when they heard about our plans, and I would nod dreamily as I pictured our first apartment on a narrow cobblestone street, abundant meals washed down with red wine, picturesque cafés, a casual and intimate familiarity with the Left Bank—all exquisitely stylish and fabulous and *mine*. "But what are you going to do there?" they would ask, and I would glibly explain, "Well, I have a French passport, you see, so I can work over there legally." Uttered with confidence, I convinced myself that this had actually answered their question. While I knew that I would have to make a living over there, my fantasy glossed over the realities of *getting a job*.

So now here we were. We had the darling little apartment—with a huge picture window overlooking the rooftops of the city and a postage stamp of a kitchen with all the appliances in miniature and a partial view of the Eiffel Tower. We had found a place to store the bike on a bathroom hook right above the cat box and figured out how to maneuver the clothes-drying rack that hung from the kitchen ceiling so that it wouldn't smack us on the head. We'd bought a washing machine and an oven, figured out where to buy paint and fungicide, navigated the labyrinth of voice mail, set up a bank account, stocked our shelves with strangely packaged foods. And although these tasks lacked romance, we reveled in each small achievement.

Playing *maison* was great fun, but eventually it came time to find work. And in this matter, all glibness aside, I was profoundly, gut-wrenchingly unprepared. The years of *imparfait* versus *plus-que-parfait,* the endless masculine versus feminine, the essays on nineteenth-century French literature were no use now. American cover-letter etiquette was irrelevant. I vaguely recalled that French cover letters were supposed to be handwritten and that photos were to be sent along with résumés, but I didn't know what to believe. I'd stare blankly at a crisp sheet of ivory-tinted paper and, after waiting futilely for inspiration to strike, I'd decide that laundry needed to be done or that it was time to go buy dinner. This went on for several fruitless days. Finally, after crumpling up several costly sheets of fine paper, I tromped down to a bookstore and discovered an abundant selection of job-hunting titles. After a good laugh while skimming over the sections on handwriting analysis—it's all true and taken very seriously!—I was back at our rickety table, patching together a draft plagiarized from bits and pieces of the various sample letters in the book. I assiduously copied the pompous sign-off, "In awaiting your response, I ask that you receive, Madam, the expression of my most respectful salutations." I recopied my beautiful French letter, with all its archaic terminology, onto my elegant paper with a fountain pen—over and over again—and, exhausted by the entire ordeal, walked my missives over to the post office to go out to publishing houses all over the city.

And then I waited. I knew I should call to follow up, but my confidence in the entire process was waning and I really didn't know what to say. The whole notion that I had thought I could pull off this working-overseas thing was beginning to seem preposterous. As I waited, I received e-mails from friends: "Are you *loving* it? It sounds so romantic." And there *were* romantic, intensely French moments—strolling home from a movie along the Seine at midnight, discovering divey and delicious couscous restaurants in cobblestone alleys, savoring a midnight snack of left-over lemon tart while peering out over the rooftops and sparkling city lights, even the sounds of the market bustling on Saturday mornings—the heavy whine of the hurdy-gurdy; the brassy, off-key marching band; the bustle of commerce unchanged over the years. I went to Audrey Hepburn matinees and Matisse exhibits. I shopped for cheese and olives in the crowded aisles of the open-air markets that appeared twice a week between traffic lanes on the main thoroughfares.

When Dad came to visit, I took him to lunch in a little wine bar he didn't know about. Over massive ham hocks in lentils and a dusty bottle of red wine, we celebrated the fact that I was now fit to show him a few places on his old turf. Paris was coming full circle for him. And as I struggled to adapt, I gained a better understanding of what it had meant for him to move to San Francisco. Judging from my own struggles to build a life in a foreign country, it didn't seem like such a foregone conclusion for him to have stayed in America. In addition, as I got more enmeshed in daily life and saw how confining a certain class of Parisian society can be, how fraught with obligations and rules, I better understood the gloriously liberating appeal of America. Trite, yes, but for the first time, comprehensible. Paris, for all its loveliness, is not a city prone to quirkiness or ebullience. When he set foot in Paris, my father was subjected to unchanging codes of behavior, dress and tradition, and his particular quirks—the down vests he loves so, his habit of wearing his loafers sockless, his culinary whimsy, his jovial enthusiasm—all came under close scrutiny.

Then, lo and behold, one bright summer day a couple of weeks after the letters had gone off, I received a call from a Madame Assouline, the head of a small publishing house, who announced that she would like to see me the following morning. The company's British foreign-rights director would soon be away on maternity leave and they needed someone to replace her temporarily. I tried to stay calm and collected as we set a time, but as soon as I was off the phone, I danced across the floor of our living room.

That is how I found myself despairing over the contents of my closet. Editions Assouline publishes glossy illustrated books on subjects as glamorous and stylish as Chanel and Tiffany, Gucci and Cartier. It was all about being svelte, sleek, and hip. Nubby sweaters and chunky brown loafers simply wouldn't do. I tried on little skirts with fitted T-shirts and teetered on top of the toilet to try to get a full-length glimpse of myself in the mirror. Not quite right. The yellow suit. Too garden party. The pile of clothes mounted on the bed. The chasm between myself and the French yawned wide. Should I dress the way I would in America? Or appear as I thought they thought I should, even if I felt like an imposter? As I mixed and matched, I realized that language fluency and love of a culture, even a passport with République Française emblazoned in gold, do not make for an intuitive understanding of a place. Real cultural integration lurks quietly in the subtleties, waiting to trip you up when you think you know what you're doing. Although I knew that appearance matters deeply to the French, I lacked any natural instinct for the specifics. Finally, I decided: when in doubt, wear black. I hoped to appear neutral and benign enough in a black skirt, white shirt, and black blazer with loafers that I tried valiantly to polish up.

The next morning, I walked up the steps from the metro onto the Place de la Concorde and made my way across the Place Vendome, past the Ritz and Cartier, past Chanel, trying to get one final glimpse of myself in the various windows along the way. I brimmed with purpose and pride—look at me! I'm practically a native! I have an interview! I ignored my churning stomach and overwrought nerves, and tried not to wilt in the stifling heat of the summer day. I turned onto a narrow street and wondered fleetingly whether this might become my daily commute.

I entered the oversized front door and walked through a small courtyard. Formerly a residence, in one of the city's oldest neighborhoods, the building had retained its elegant arched doorways and old-fashioned wooden shutters. Inside, a wide wooden staircase with aging oriental carpet spiraled up around a modern elevator. As I stepped into it, two young women stepped out chatting casually in blazingly fast French. In their skimpy tank tops, strappy sandals, and slinky black pants, they looked as casual and stylish as I did starchy. I should have taken my chances and gone for hip, but alas, too late.

On the top floor, I made my way down a dim, creaky hallway and knocked. After thunderous clomping down the stairs, a harried young woman opened the door and dashed back up. "*Entrez, entrez,*" she yelled to me on her way up. I followed her up into the attic and found myself in a small entryway opening into an office with three desks. The young women glanced over briefly from their computers, surveyed me and went back to their furious typing—no small feat with a cigarette in hand. "*Vous patientez un moment? Martine arrive,*" said the one who'd let me in, emerging from behind a closed door. Yes, of course I will wait. Perched on the edge of an old leather couch, I watched the women tapping away, blowing the ash out of their keyboards occasionally, answering the phone in clipped and professional tones *"Editions Assouline, Bonjour. . . ."* I wondered whether that would ever be me. Could I do that? The graceful old building lacked air conditioning, and the attic trapped the muggy, stifling heat. My shirt stuck to my back. I shifted damply in my confining outfit.

What had I been thinking? I woke up each morning hoping to feel a bit more French, more intimately connected to my family heritage in some incredibly dramatic and clear way, but I was always still just me, a California girl having great fun playing at being French. It was pure folly to have thought that my shiny new French passport would suddenly endow me with insight into the mysterious nuances of the French and their way of interpreting the world. I have never felt so glaringly American as I did that morning, sitting in that attic in the heart of Paris, looking around at the employees of Editions Assouline. Were these really my compatriots?

I was so deeply engrossed in my little identity crisis that I was startled when Martine Assouline finally strode out of her office. Broad-shouldered and tall, in black jeans and a white T-shirt, her thick brown hair pulled back in a youthful ponytail, Martine had once been a model for *Vogue* and other fashion glossies. She greeted me coolly, not unkindly but without any need to put me at ease. I followed her into her office—a large airy space lined with books. Her spacious black desk revealed only a phone, a few pencils, and a few sheets of paper. No computer, no stacks, no clutter.

I sat down across from her at the vast polished desk and

awaited some quippy icebreaker, the what-brought-you-to-France sort of thing. I would have offered some witty remark myself to lighten things up, but it's beyond me to be funny in French. With stony poise, in a deep, flat voice, she launched into her interrogation. I immediately regretted how little time I'd spent skimming over French publishing jargon. With my cursory knowledge of the trade's vocabulary, I described my experience in vague, roundabout terms, along the lines of "Well, yes, in San Francisco, I made books. Yes, well, I *created* books . . . I . . . helped with the . . . writing of them. Yes. . . . That's it." I was just learning in the most agonizingly hard way that business talk is a far different beast from the social chitchat I know so well. In a high-pitched, quavering voice, lightheaded from the stifling, smoky heat and flushed and blushing from my horror at being so tongue-tied, I carried on with my contorted explanations, doubling back and rephrasing, heaping grammatical errors one on top of the other. Martine remained dazzlingly calm throughout, stone-faced, utterly glamorous and French, taking slow, even drags on her cigarette. Sweat trickled down the backs of my knees.

An hour or so later, I emerged into the daylight, dizzy with relief. As I strolled along, I replayed the interview in my mind, trying to gauge its success objectively, but I didn't know how to read through her cold French reserve. I cringed as I replayed some of my bigger gaffes. At one point, I had mentioned working with design layouts and referred to them as "*moquettes.*" She looked mystified. Later, it came to me: the proper word was "*maquette.*"

A moquette is wall-to-carpeting. I also realized how little information I'd gleaned about the position. Bent as I was on projecting a confident image and faking my way through her minefield of questions, I had simply nodded knowingly and casually throughout, with the result that the job itself remained a mystery to me. But at that moment, I only cared that I had survived the interview.

Two weeks later, Martine Assouline left me a message informing me that I had gotten the job. At first, I didn't even understand it was a job offer. I'd never heard formal job-offer language and had no idea what it meant to have *"retenue ma candidature."* It was only when she told me when to begin that I breathed a sigh of relief.

With my first French paycheck, I bought my own pair of strappy sandals.

Conversations in Denmark

Lesley-Ann Brown

In the cold dampness of a Danish winter, I found a community in the most unlikely of places. It was not made up of other writers, Blacks or Americans but of women, just like myself, who found themselves in the new, unfamiliar role of mother. We gathered once a week in each other's homes, drank hot chocolate, nibbled on marzipan bars and breastfed by candlelight—often the only light to be had—as we marveled at how similar yet distinct our respective experiences seemed to be.

There was Tchina, a South African I met when we were both pregnant. I envied her for the ease with which she moved about in this foreign land. "But I've been here longer than you," she'd remind me, her fingers toying with her newly sprouted locks. We had a lot in common: In addition to being new mothers, we were both married to Danish men, living far from home and Black. Her daughter, Malaika, was two months younger than my son, Kai. Sofie, a Dane whose daughter, Nicola, was three months older than Kai, and Anne, another Dane, whose daughter, Nataya, was the oldest by a few months, completed the foursome.

One day on my way to a meeting, I packed Kai up in his pram

and began to walk, each step heavy with a familiar fear. Even after a year here, my eyes still darted about, my heartbeat quickened and I felt exposed and vulnerable. I couldn't shake the nervous and raw feeling of being Black in such a white country. Each passerby was a potential source of some racist comment.

I hadn't always felt like this. There was a time when I walked about Copenhagen with as much confidence as I had in New York. But one day a car sped past me, and the driver yelled "nigger." Although a minor enough offense—I've been called nigger more than once in New York—it was much scarier to hear it here. At least in America, I knew I belonged. But here? My confidence had been shaken tremendously and my once assured steps became more wobbly. I felt that surely, to these people, my Blackness was like the buzz of a fly—not dangerous, but annoying and hard to ignore. I often prayed for the invisibility that Ellison wrote so cursedly about, and I missed being surrounded by other faces as brown as mine more than I had ever thought I would.

Kai slept peacefully as I pushed his pram. I spied an older woman approaching us. I snuffed out the urge to run back inside, into my warm and safe apartment. When the woman and I finally crossed paths, I cringed, remembering stories of bitter older Danes who resented the presence of foreigners. I readied myself for an onslaught of words or, at the very least, a cold blast of negative energy. To my horror, she grabbed my hand, and before I knew what she was doing, peeked in at my son and said, "He's very sweet." My heartbeat slowed and I stepped off more lightly, thanking her for more than she would ever know.

As I approached Tchina's apartment building, I saw all three mothers rocking their prams in an attempt to put their little ones to sleep. We greeted each other and peeked in at each other's babies, marveling at how much they had grown since the week before. I then admitted, "I can't even walk down the street without feeling as if I'm about to have a nervous breakdown."

"Me too." Surprisingly, it was Anne who answered. Why did she feel that way? She was in her own country. She flipped her long red hair over her shoulder and explained, "I feel so clumsy with this big pram. Like I'm in everyone's way and everyone wants me to go home with my baby. As if I shouldn't be in a supermarket or bus."

"I know. Once I was out and someone made a snide remark about how *barnevognes* (prams) are taking over the streets." Sofie laughed nervously and continued, "but we have just as much of a right to be there as they do." Could it be? They were describing exactly how I felt!

"Let's take a walk to the park. Maybe we can get these babies to sleep." As our convoy of prams made its way up the street, we spied a line of prams outside a café, seemingly unattended.

"Isn't that funny?" Tchina mused. "You could never do something like that in South Africa."

"Neither in New York. In fact, this Danish woman left her baby outside a restaurant in the Village, and the child welfare people took her baby away. They gave the baby back of course, but it was front-page news and everything"

Sofie and Anne both expressed surprise at the notion that someone would steal a baby. "It doesn't happen here in Denmark," they assured us.

When we arrived at the park, all babies were asleep except for Sofie's little girl, Nicola. Sofie's face showed signs of stress and, like ours, very little sleep. Her mouse-brown hair was swept back in a ponytail and her smile broke through the weariness of her face. We all looked down at Nicola, who laughed and gurgled back at us, oblivious to the distress she was causing her mother. Sofie continued to rock the pram in that jerky, frantic way that comes out of sheer desperation but that could never lull a baby to sleep. I saw that she needed a break and, since Kai was asleep, offered to take her pram around for a spin. Nicola smiled at me as if she knew what I had suggested. With her little doll nose, blond hair, and blue eyes, she truly is a beauty.

"Would you really?" Sofie automatically took hold of my pram as I did hers and I started for a stroll. The other mothers took a seat on a bench and started to compare notes on how many times their babies had woken up the night before. As I walked through the park I looked at Nicola, who was wide awake and smiling back at me. I couldn't help but think that despite all my fears about Denmark in theory, all my personal interactions had been extremely positive. Sofie, whom I had known from before our pregnancies, opened her home to me regularly for visits, dinners, or even much-needed showers (My husband, Benjamin, and I still lived in a cold-water flat with no shower). Benjamin's mother, Anni, taught me how to knit (a lifelong dream of mine) with a patience that could only be borne out of love. When I first arrived, she was always there to take me around the city, and when I was pregnant, she used to accompany me to the doctor when Benjamin was unable to. She even baby-sat Kai so that I could write.

There was the midwife who offered me prenatal care during those months when I was without healthcare. She even sneaked me into a hospital so that she could accurately gauge how pregnant I was via ultrasound. Throughout all of my visits, she was kind, informative, and never failed to give me any assistance I needed.

And my husband's friends had all taken me in, without question, as a natural extension of their circle. As I walked, more absorbed in my own thoughts than my surroundings, I couldn't help but wonder, what is it then that I am unhappy about? I checked on Nicola, whose eyes had finally closed for sleep. I did miss Brooklyn: taking the train to Nostrand Avenue, past the record stores that blared calypso and reggae into the streets; buying steaming *roti* (a type of wrap with curry inside) from Gloria's and; visiting my family in Forte Green, where their Caribbean-tinged accents warmed everything around. I again looked at Nicola and thought of how different my son, with his brown skin and dark hair, looks from her. I had always thought that my child would be surrounded by others just like him. But then I thought about the mother group and how I feel when I show up and the warm welcome we always greet each other with. I thought about how they smile and accept, regardless of color, and I was reminded of what is here now. I can't help but think—what does it all matter when you have a community of people who love you and whom you love, no matter where you are? I turned the pram around and made my way back to the group.

"Do you like your nurse, Lesley?" Anne was referring to the nurse that visits for free, once a month, for up to a year to check on your baby's progress.

"Yeah, she's really good. What about you, Sofie?"

"Mine is okay. She told me I should breastfeed Nicola every four hours and I don't think that's right."

"What?" We were all surprised, as we had all been told to breastfeed on demand.

"Yeah. But I just think you have to go with what you feel. She's from the old days, you know? Each generation does it differently." We all agreed and recalled the many different pieces of advice we had heard since giving birth, "Definitely don't sleep with your baby" and "You must sleep with your baby." Or, "Wean your baby at six months" versus "Let your baby breastfeed as long as he or she wants."

"What about you, Tchina? Do you like your nurse?"

"Yeah, I do. You know, there're so many cool things about this country. Do you know how spoiled you Danes are?" She teased Anne and Sofie and began to check each point against her fingers, "Free healthcare, insured maternity leave for both mothers and fathers, the dole, free school—even university. Do you know that even if you want to send your child to a private school, the state subsidizes it?"

"Yeah, Benjamin and I could never live this way in the States. I mean—free healthcare? Yeah right." I remembered the four years I was without healthcare in New York and the few times I waited for up to ten hours in a hospital's emergency room for an ailment that never would have progressed as it did had I had access to healthcare.

"But you guys have said before you don't really like it here. If we've got so many perks, what's the problem?" Both Tchina and I looked at each other and, by the intake of her breath, I knew that she would attempt to answer the question first. We'd spoken to each other about the discomfort we felt at all the curious looks and the way Blacks are sometimes portrayed in the media.

"Well, it's not that we don't like it here. It's just weird being such a minority, you know? In South Africa, I mean—"

"Yeah," I continued, "In New York, there are just so many different people, restaurants—"

Anne interrupted, "Yeah, but Denmark has never had a lot of immigrants. I mean, twenty, even ten years ago, you didn't see many people who looked different from us." Sofie shook her head in agreement. (I am constantly amazed at how well most Danes in Copenhagen speak English.) Anne was right, Denmark had been and, to an extent, still is a racially and culturally homogenous society. Even now, immigrants constitute less than 10 percent of the population.

"Yeah, but don't you think it's time Denmark opens its eyes to the issue of race? I mean, what is that whole anti-immigration thing?" (Denmark had recently voted in a party whose platform was based on anti-immigration.)

"I mean, you guys still sell *Little Black Sambo* books and have all these adverts with people in blackface. What's that about?" A recent shampoo ad had featured a white woman with black smeared all over her body, wearing a straw skirt and a bone stuck through her nose. It angered me because it reminded me all too much of blackface: of whites putting on what they could so easily take off.

Sofie shook her head. "But isn't there ignorance wherever you go? Yeah, it embarrasses me when I hear politicians saying ignorant things and people pretending to be black. But that's even more reason for people like us to stay and become part of the dialogue. We shouldn't let people like that take over or say things that go unchallenged. And anyway, nowhere is perfect, right?" We all agreed, although I knew that, for both Tchina and myself, the issue of Black representation would always continue to be unsettling.

Then a small cry came from one of the prams. We were all gripped with fear that it might be our baby—peace was so hard to come by in those early days. It was Tchina's little girl and, as she lifted Malaika out, the others breathed a sigh of relief. "Hey baby."

Her voice was featherlight and full of love. "Did you sleep well?" Careful to ensure that Malaika was guarded against the cold, Tchina returned with her to the bench. We all greeted Malaika and remarked how beautiful she is, with her dark eyes and the curls of dark hair that fall onto her forehead. Tchina held Malaika across her lap, unzipped her coat, unbuttoned her shirt, and allowed Malaika to nurse.

"It's so cool that you can do that here."

"What do you mean? You can't do that in the States?" I rolled my eyes in disbelief at Sofie's question. "Girl, puuleeze. I mean, you can *try*. But you don't see people whipping out their breasts in public just because their child is hungry."

"Really? That's so crazy. Tell me something Lesley—why is it that American films have so much violence and you can't even breastfeed in public? That's weird." Sofie had been to the States and had mentioned this phenomenon to me before. After being here as long as I had been, I could better understand the question from her perspective. Here in Denmark, people are very relaxed about the human body. In the summer entire families bathe in the nude, and women sunbathe topless in parks.

"There are lot of reasons, I guess." I shrugged, not really wanting to get into the far-right, hyper-Christian tendencies that are sometimes absorbed into American culture.

"It's like that in South Africa too. I mean, you would never see a woman breastfeeding in public. It's more something you'd see in a village," Tchina said.

"Really?" We were all very surprised. Surely Africans had held onto *that*.

"We've been just as colonized by consumerism as the rest of the world. That's just it, you know, people attach so much status to formula—"

"It's that way in the States as well," I agreed and Tchina added, "Even though it's a fact that breastfeeding is way more safe than bottle-feeding and cheaper." She then took a look at her daughter contentedly nursing away and continued, "and convenient." We all nodded our heads in agreement. A wind rushed in, stirred the prams a bit, and left a shiver in its wake. Malaika had fallen back asleep and Tchina returned her to the pram. The clouds blanketed the sun.

"Let's go have some coffee." Sofie suggested. We walked in silence through the thick gray mist that had descended on the city until Tchina suggested we buy a bar of chocolate to sneak into the café. I offered to get it and went into a little market. I felt the young storekeeper's curious eyes on me as I grabbed the chocolate and put it on the counter.

"Where are you from?" he asked, first in Danish and, when I gave him the empty look that indicated I didn't understand, then in English.

"New York?" That sounded like a lie. "Brooklyn?" That sounded like a half-truth as well. "Well, my family came from Trinidad and I was born and raised in Brooklyn. Where are you from?"

"Palestine," he answered, as he rang up my chocolate on the register.

"You like it here?" he asked.

"Today? Yeah." I smiled and he laughed. "What about you?" I asked.

"Me? I was born here."

"So, you're Danish?"

He shrugged, "Yes, this is my country. And I am also from Palestine. But for now, I'm staying here. There's too much fighting over there. And here in Denmark? Disneyland." I handed him his money, he handed me my change.

"I know what you mean."

We continued our walk, parked our prams outside the café as our babies slept and, in true Danish style, left them there as we went inside to enjoy a few more minutes of peace before they woke up.

Best Friends and Balaclavas

Erica Jacobs

The first time I heard the term "expat" I was a twenty-year-old, well-tanned college student spending my junior year abroad in West Africa. I was on a program—a planned, educational exchange in which I would, for three hundred and sixty-five days, live and study in Accra, Ghana. The experience was sure to be intense, exotic, eye-opening—all the things a junior year abroad promises to be. The fixed time and the dated return ticket were just fine by me, for I knew—even as I lived in, traveled throughout and absorbed West Africa—that eventually I would go home.

That year other students and I would occasionally spot Them. They'd wander into the campus library or mosey down the next row of stalls in the marketplace. They were the other foreigners. The other white people. The impossible-to-miss expats.

While we donned our dusty backpacks and hitchhiked, sweating, across town, they sped by in Land Rovers, the windows rolled up and the air conditioning cranked so high we could see the small goose bumps that peppered their arms. On the special days when we fished out our cleanest Gap T-shirts and headed to the British High Commission for lunch, they were there dining in short white skirts, tennis rackets in tow. At the one almost–European grocery store, they bought the ten-dollar boxes of imported American cereals the very day the shipment arrived.

They were always, all of them, overly bronzed and inclined to speak slowly. Very slowly. Sometimes they offered us small, forced smiles as they passed. Maybe, I thought, that sedated state was the result of too much Larium, the antimalaria pills. Maybe they had contracted malaria one too many times. But the malaria, the oppressive heat, and the overpriced Special K aside, they stayed. Surely there had to be a good reason for living in West Africa? To visit was one thing, but to live!? I knew they had to be running from something. A prison sentence. A bad marriage. A wicked family. To live permanently in West Africa as a white foreigner, to be an expat, meant that something was wrong with you. Or, at least, that you were strange.

Ten years later, college long over and a handful of jobs under my belt, I resolved to settle down. I was staring at thirty and had decided to move to Los Angeles, my hometown, for good. It was time for me to get back to my L.A.–girl roots, be close to my family, and stay put. So, naturally, one month after my return, I met Him. A sweet, intelligent, insightful, sensitive, strong, and good-smelling guy. I was swooning. The only problem was that he lived in Belfast, Northern Ireland. After a handful of trips back and forth, countless e-mails, and an outrageous phone bill, I too became strange.

After hauling most of my worldly possessions to a small, dark rented storage space in Arcadia and shipping two brown boxes of trinkets, I up and moved to Belfast, effectively becoming one of Them.

Of course, as with any move, there were endless new things to encounter, decipher, decode, and then face up to. I had to do some nesting and make the house look faintly like my own. The boyfriend had never thought to buy things like a toothbrush holder, matching sheets, or knickknacks for the mantel. I needed friends, or at least a friend, one other human being, preferably a female, with whom I could talk about fabulous new restaurants, my fluctuating moods, and which black pants I should wear that night, someone I could consult for advice on the boyfriend. I had to figure out the things that put Belfast on the map and into international newspapers, differentiate between Catholics and Protestants, and try to make sense of the divided communities, the issues and histories at hand. I also needed a job.

A job was the real priority: a place to go each day. A purpose. A routine. The possibility of friends (or, at the very least, colleagues—people forced to interact, and, hey, even talk, with me). Something I could call my own. Responsibility. Stimulation.

Headlines in the *Belfast Telegraph* read "Technology Boom Hits Northern Ireland," "IT Professionals Needed!" Fresh from high-tech California, I had plenty of experience. Fluent in all the B2B, B2C jargon and every new bit of lingo in between, I figured I was exactly what they were looking for. Poised and ready, updated CV in hand, I waved my various credentials at my recruiter and stood by waiting for that perfect offer.

After a month, my recruiter produced a single interview. A start-up Internet company needed a studio manager to run the web development and design teams. Perfect! Or, at least, good enough.

The day of the interview I put on my high-power, out-to-impress red sweater and favorite Armani skirt and called a cab. On the ride over my mind began to race. Start-up Internet company. That could only mean one thing: ultrahip. Think Ping-Pong table, beanbags, Birkenstocks, and longhaired hipsters making websites, experimenting with online animation, finding innovative solutions using cutting-edge technology, conceptualizing creative content. I remembered some of my previous desks. The one in front of a floor-to-ceiling window that looked out at the Bay Bridge in the trendy SOMA district in San Francisco. The southern California office adjacent to a park, a few blocks from the beach. My desk at the children's e-commerce site, filled with toy dinosaurs, colorful picture books, and glitter paint. All of a sudden, the cab turned and I realized I didn't recognize where we were. Perhaps we were heading to the town's warehouse district—the up-and-coming next big thing—where chic restaurants poke out behind deserted buildings and renovated lofts. The taxi continued to turn and eventually headed right past the small (and well, okay, not that hip) warehouse district and right out of town.

I found myself on the border of north Belfast. A housing project sprawled across the few blocks on my left. The Union Jack flag flew from a dozen poles along the avenue. The curbs were all painted red, white, and blue. On my left, an enormous mill emitted the pungent smell of animal feed. It started to rain just as I spotted the large gray building, sandwiched between the mill and Iceland, a grocery store selling only frozen food. An old train rumbled past, blowing out a dark cloud of steam and shaking the windows at the front of the building. At the front door was a small plaque: "Laurel & Hardy slept here!" I held my breath as I walked up the flight of stairs, past the aqua-painted walls reminiscent of public bathrooms in California. Looking down the hallway of former-hotel-rooms-cum-office-space, I spotted the door with a taped-up paper sign.

Inside I was met with floor-to-ceiling bright orange walls. Facing the door was a board covered with ads, icons, and color swatches. Techno music beat out from a small radio and four designers with spiky hair and Diesel jeans stared into new iMacs. Ultrahip, as I'd predicted. Two conservative-looking women approached to shake my hand before shuffling me into a small white room to begin the interview. The two women—managers I soon learned—wore suits. I mean *real* suits, the whole thing— nylons and heels and matching skirts. I was fairly certain it had been at least three years since I had put on nylons and even then it had certainly not been for work.

Despite their serious appearance, the managers were friendly. One of them had an unpronounceable Irish name, a degree from Trinity College, and made mention of summers spent in South

Armagh, so I could assume she was Catholic. The other one, a blond, spoke in a most clipped, almost British, manner and made loving references to Prince Charles (was she really talking about the royals!)—clearly a Protestant. They were smart, quick, eloquent, and each ran a division of the company. They covered the basics—company history, expected growth rate, objectives of the position—and eventually moved on to questions and answers. I tried to embellish as I spoke of my experience and abilities before I settled into my chair, relaxed a bit, and told office anecdotes, imbuing the conversation with bits of innocuous humor. We talked for almost two hours and laughed a great deal. Then, after the interview, they offered me the job.

After choking at the salary, which, when converted to dollars, was exactly half of what I had made in California, I accepted. Within days (and after some quick visa work) I found myself back in the orange office.

Counting the thumping pulse of the techno music as a given, there were, of course, other perks. According to my contract, the workweek was limited to thirty-five hours. The office was only open from nine to five, and the day included a mandatory one-hour lunch break. Unlike at my previous workplaces, they weren't kidding. No one arrived before nine and, at five, the lights went out and the door was locked. With twenty-five vacation days, I knew this was sure to be a good life.

Despite the luxurious schedule, those first weeks were rough.

I was still adjusting to the accent, and understood only half of what was said. All of our clients were referred to only by acronyms, and I couldn't make out what LEDU, DETI, or IFI stood for, let alone what they did or how they related to me. Somehow, I still managed to set up some office procedures, begin art-directing the designers, and slowly shift my job into gear.

At noon, given our low salaries and limited restaurant options, the staff crowded into the small conference room and ate packed lunches at the table while mobile phones rang and individuals typed away text messages to send out between rings and bites. Each week proved a culinary adventure as lunchtime trends swept the office. The first week, while I chewed on my toasted bagels with cream cheese, everyone else seemed to be eating baked beans on toast. The next week, the team moved on to mayonnaise laced with shards of carrot and cabbage. I think they called it coleslaw, but according to my calculations, the ratio of mayonnaise to vegetable was far too high to legally call it a salad of any sort. The group later moved on to a pinkish mayonnaise with a few prawns in it—again lathered on toast. Other weeks brought further adventures—frozen pizzas from Iceland, bananas on toast and sausage rolls.

As my stomach hardened and my palate adjusted to the symphony of smells, I also settled into the job and my relationship with the nylon-wearing managers. I was thrilled to be interacting with young, intelligent, motivated people, and for the first few months I was satisfied simply to have a place to go each day. A place where I was in charge of organizing Web and graphic work, reviewing designs and content, creating schedules and holding meetings. People talked to me all day long. I belonged. I would work all day, come home at night, have some "quiet" time, greet the boyfriend, make dinner with him and hang out. I was happy. Color me full.

But after a few months of this routine, I realized that something was still missing. While I did have a place to go to every day and the relationship with the boyfriend was only getting stronger, I still didn't have that other thing. I believe they call it "friends." I thought of my San Francisco crowd—the lovely ladies who taught me how to shotgun a beer and table dance, who brought me birthday breakfast in bed every year and who came over before a date to tell me I looked fabulous in whatever outfit I had chosen. I also thought of the L.A. girlfriends who saw right through my neurosis, who accurately predicted my decisions and who would come over simply to sit on the couch for five hours and chat. Sure, I laughed with the girls in my Belfast office, gossiped about our weekend escapades, and even occasionally shared an anecdote about my love life over the boiling kettle at midafternoon tea. But the talk was always brief, between meetings or assignments, and confined to the space behind the orange walls in the gray building stuck between Iceland and the feed mill.

Finally, I decided to ask them out. Nervously, I planned the e-mail I would send. It felt like a first date: I worried about rejections, the simple or sweet ways they might say no. Maybe they would ask for my number and never call. Maybe they would say yes and then never commit to a time or place. Maybe they would just say, "I'm busy," and leave it at that, never to mention it again. I waited until after a particularly stressful meeting and then sprung it on them. In a quick e-mail I told them I thought it best that we try talking in a less heated circumstance some time, perhaps over alcohol. We should go for drinks after work the next week. To be safe, I asked them to tell me what days were free, if they were up for it, and then, to best entice, I mentioned some of the new hip spots in town.

Like a teenager asking the cute girl in algebra to the prom, I was sweating. Rejection would leave the possibility of making new friends impossible. If it wasn't going to be the nylon-wearing girls from work, then who? Although desperate for friends, I didn't dare show it. I acted mellow, pretended it was a casual thing, and sat by, checking my e-mail inbox every fourteen minutes or so. By the end of the afternoon I had received two e-mails.

"Sounds great. Let's go to Giraffe Café on Tuesday." And, "Yes, Yes, Yes. Only we can't talk about work all night and I'll go if I'm promised copious amounts of red wine."

Two resounding yeses. I was thrilled.

By the time five o'clock on Tuesday rolled around, the three of us were haggard. Catherine had sweat-stained armpits and Siofra had a new blemish growing on her chin. My hair was frizzy and I was really craving a glass of red wine. As we drove to the restaurant we naturally bitched about work. We had never seen one another outside of the office and we stuck to what we knew. The managing director was spineless, the company's growth was too erratic, what did we think about employee A, or hiring someone to help employee B? We went on in this vein until we were seated and the first bottle of wine was uncorked. By the time the appetizers arrived, we had downed the bottle of Chianti and vowed to drop all mention of anything related to our current employment. Instead, we talked about Siofra's new marriage, Catherine's long-term boyfriend, and my romantic but still new situation with the nomadic boyfriend currently residing in Belfast. Over sweet cod, savory mussels, and salty prosciutto, we fantasized about the glamorous lives we hoped to be leading in five years' time and then talked about more realistic long-term goals. After more wine and louder conversation we switched to our families and our preteen years and finally crossed the street to find a table at the pub.

By our third bottle of wine, the inevitable happened. My Catholic and Protestant tablemates turned to politics, or, as they politely call it here, "The Troubles." Catherine told stories of her friend in the RUC who had detained a now-senior Sinn Fein politician at the site of more than one murder. Siofra talked about the time her car broke down in a housing estate in East Belfast— she'd had to say her name was Sharon and pray she'd get out of there without anyone figuring out she was a Catholic. Catherine told us about the night a team of men in balaclavas showed up next door and killed all the pets of her disabled neighbor because he had stolen a candy bar from the corner store. The following day Ulster Volunteer Force graffiti had appeared on the sidewalk in front of her house. They talked about the time of the hunger strikes in the H-block of the Maze Prison. Margaret Thatcher. The British official, that damned Peter Mandelson. They both agreed on his idiocy. Even I knew enough to agree to that.

Somewhere deep into bottle four (was it Pinot Noir by now?) Catherine and Siofra had both told their toughest stories and let their eyes well up with tears. And that's when Catherine started giggling, acknowledging our sorry state. "Anything beyond heinous is humorous," she declared as she burst into laughter. I was quick to come back, "Laugh to keep from crying." And Siofra, commenting first on my cliché, and then on the situation, just said, "Imagine getting all puffed up in paramilitary gear over a twelve-year-old child's damn candy bar." We cracked up and kept laughing as they taunted me with stories of impossible attempts to avoid the roadblocks and somehow get into our office on so-called Orangemen's Day. Having survived it for almost thirty years, they each howled as they tried to scare me into thinking that I could be shot in July. Safe in the corner of our delicately lit table on a trendy Lisburn road, they guffawed as they told me how the "bonfires reached almost two stories high!" and "all the roads were blocked but the managing director assumed we

should be able to get in and spend the entire day in our office."
"But once inside the building we were fine. I think a few cars were
burned in the lot out front but it couldn't have been more than
one or two." As they taunted me, I shot back with an offer to provide them each with new balaclavas if they'd drive me to work that
week. We laughed, chuckled, giggled, and guffawed. We teared up
at the tougher moments, which brought us right back to the brink
of laughter and kept us, all of us, grinning.

Sometime around midnight I knew I had arrived. I was one of
them. Only, unlike the Land Rover–driving whites in West Africa,
secluded in Euro-stores and air-conditioned cars, I was in the thick
of it—sitting in the middle of a Belfast pub posturing about politics. Rather than talking slowly or donning an impressive tan, I was
pale and becoming versed in paramilitary procedures. I knew then
that as an expat I could do more than move between the isolated
expat settings and circles I had seen in Africa. Here I was feeling
at home with my girls, comfortable in our swapped stories and safe
in the knowledge that we had talked about boys, fears, frantic
times, and families. We had done that thing—confided in each
other—and in doing so, we had connected. The big girls had let
me into their club.

The only thing I hadn't accounted for was that these girls
from the island of Ireland—Catholic and Protestant—could hold
their alcohol better than I could. The next day my head swam, I
had the shakes and dry mouth and made prolonged trips to the

toilet. Still, my cheeks hurt from so much smiling and I had obtained that other, much-needed life ingredient—friends. I knew I would never be a true Belfastian, a member of the community with a history deeply seeded in religion and politics. Being one of the Belfast girls wasn't a game I would win, but it was a game I could enjoy, and one I certainly could play.

Growing Season

Sadie Ackerman

It took me a long time to stop looking for jungle even though I was back in the desert. Back in the place where I had lived my first twenty-plus years, now somehow eclipsed by those few in between. By angle and proximity, my few years in the jungle swept over the larger bulk like the tiny moon blots out the sun and causes twilight in the middle of the day.

I walked closer than I had before to the desert trees, palo verde with pine-needle–like stems and parallel rows of tiny leaves, small enough to turn upright and hide from the heat in the middle of the day. I tried to admire their resilience and suitability for the desert I'd grown up in, but I was now used to big lush elephant ear leaves the size of my torso with stems so thick I'd need a steak knife to cut through them. Sucking in my breath, I stood in the shadow of a single saguaro cactus, trying to remember feeling sheltered by the immense canopy of the rainforest above me. I was exposed here, tiptoeing from one patch of shade to the next, squinting.

I waited to feel like I was back home, fully expecting the feeling to be immediate, remembering how long it had taken me to feel at home in Belize, that country way out on the tip of the Yucatán Peninsula, halfway between Latin America and the Caribbean. I had learned to live there slowly, measuring my progress by the seasons.

During my first monsoon season in the jungle, I was out on a field playing soccer when everyone around me stopped, their eyes on the ground or in the air or scanning all around as if they could squint just so and actually *see* the sound they were straining to hear. Then they took off running and I was left on an empty field listening to the apparent silence, the soccer ball still rolling itself to stillness in the grass. In a moment, I heard the sound, too, very faint, but growing louder. It was like a breeze, then a wind, then like a huge beast roving in the jungle, and then I was soaking wet and running, too. The rain on the huge leaves above my head was nearly deafening. By the time I got to the clotheslines, they were empty except for a section of sopping wet, familiar clothing.

I learned to listen to the jungle that day. The trees, the clouds, the birds, they all became audible to me and then, finally, comprehensible. It seemed like such an innate knowledge, but I had to receive it as the children in that village did, slowly and with wide eyes. I had to defy my own upbringing, which had reared me to leave nature behind at the city limits, to see conquest as my primary mode of relation.

By the next monsoon season, I could hear the rain coming. I knew that an orange morning meant it had rained the night before and probably wouldn't rain again that day (good day for laundry!). I knew how to store up enough rainwater to drink during the dry season. I knew when I woke up to parrots squawking noisily and flying their crazy, love-blinded flight patterns that the citrus harvest was fast approaching. These were the kinds of things I had learned about living in Belize on the scale of the cycle of seasons and the tilting axis of the Earth.

On a smaller scale, I had learned thousands of things about getting through a single day: how to speak Creole, how to hold tightly onto laundry and get a good rinse from a waterfall, how to cook in an outdoor kitchen. I landed in a dirt-floored house with thatched roofing where I shared my new way of life with scorpions and geckos, in a place where the nearest market was a half-day's walk away and occurred only on Wednesdays and Saturdays. In my time there, I succeeded: I felt at home; I made myself indispensable in my community. And then, after caving, rock climbing, avoiding six-foot boas, and learning to walk through the jungle at night without fear, I did the most courageous thing of all: I tried to come back.

"Back home," people kept saying. As if by saying it they could remind me it was true and as if by hearing it I would feel as if it were. I hit the ground stumbling, tried to pick up where I had left off and live as if I had returned merely from an innocuous vacation. I had to speak aloud to myself like a second-party instructor. Each time I spoke, I consciously hammered out the rounded Creole vowels, "Get up if you can't sleep," I said in front of the dark windowpane that blocked my senses from the world outside.

"Don't lie here in hermetically sealed silence. Stock the cupboards instead."

So I found myself in Safeway at 2:00 A.M., staring at an entire aisle of pasta: twenty different shapes, each available in half a dozen different brands. I stood there gape-mouthed like Dorothy's first vision of Technicolor. I'd forgotten how to choose. The calm, instructive voice in my head was silent.

Finally, it kicked in. "Look away," it said, in the same even, coaxing tone as when I'd almost driven my car off the road thinking I had to actually read all of the signs and billboards. So I stared at the gleaming, garishly white tile floor. There was no way I could choose. I walked to produce.

The rows and piles of fruit were familiar, their skins and colors more organic and natural to my eyes and nose. I felt closer to the local women in Belize and their wool blankets, spread with food from their own gardens. Martha always had the plumpest limes—perfect for juicing—but Magdalena's were cheaper and better for garnishes. I touched the small, hard limes in their tidy pile at Safeway. "See?" I thought to myself, "it is more *convenient* to have them at waist level. No bending, no squatting, no bartering. This is *easier.*" I picked out my fruit. I pushed my cart along the smooth tile. I smiled at the produce stocker as he arranged a pyramid of pineapples. And then I got mad. Not the internally monologued find-a-way-to-make-it-productive mad, but the irrational ridiculous furious-at-the-whole-world mad.

What did this pimple-faced produce boy see when he looked

at me? It would hardly help to explain that I was not some lunatic pissed off at pasta at 2:00 A.M., but that I was *changed*. That I wasn't *home* anymore. And what good would it do if I told him? I doubted he could point to Belize on a globe if his life depended on it—even though most kids there can identify all fifty U.S. states.

I surveyed the well-stocked produce department; I could only tell what season it was by looking very closely, not at the fruit, but at the price tags. Were limes ten for a dollar or twenty-five cents apiece? I had never realized the impact that this kind of isolation from natural cycles and rhythms has on its recipients, let alone the people who grow the limes and the pineapples piled up in front of me. Was it possible that I had been there, on the other end, when these very pineapples were harvested and boxed up and exported to this country where I now stood, rolling one over in my hand and deliberating in the middle of the night?

"Are you finding everything you need?" he asked. And I can't say why, but I turned around and left without a word, abandoning my grocery cart right there in produce and leaving my car in the lot, forgetting it was even possible that I had driven. As I stomped home, I raged. All around me I saw concrete, asphalt, bricks, and huge sheets of glass separating me from earth. The urban American lifestyle had taught me to live isolated from nature, creating an emptiness and a longing in me that I couldn't pinpoint until I had lived elsewhere. I had only briefly felt stirrings of it before, staring up from the bottom of the Grand Canyon at a spectacular desert sunset or standing on a ridge projecting out from Mount Rainier beneath a sky overflowing with stars. But never had I felt it every day as I ate, washed my clothes, and worked. I was willing to fight to get that connection back.

I walked by several homes perched fearlessly on the edge of the Tanque Verde wash, oblivious to the flooding and erosion at work beneath them at a happy pace on the geological scale. *Tear it down,* I willed the water. *Come busting on through. Shock these people senseless with your ability to cross their borders of fear and control. Take out every dam, every retaining wall, every concrete-sprayed hillside. Grab a slab of clay and yank it out from under those buildings. You can.*

When I finished my tirade of a walk, I went inside my house, remembering my car as I unlocked the front door. Suddenly shamefaced and exhausted, I crept inside and fell into bed. As I lay there, it occurred to me that I wasn't angry at the produce guy or at the homeowners along the wash or at any other American. I was angry at the parts within myself that reflected certain American tendencies whether I consented to them or not. I was angry that I liked being able to shop in the middle of the night and that I liked coming home to a bed that didn't reek of mildew and sweat.

But from my always-wet-and-smelly Central American bed, I could hear the rain. I never had to squint through the glass or crane my neck to listen for rain—I had to shout to someone on the other side of the room and make sure everything near the walls could stand to get a little wet. I experienced a connectedness to the natural world I suddenly found difficult to forge in my hometown.

Fortunately, this anger was temporary. The desert was a good metaphor for this stony-faced period of mine. In the desert, the growing season is practically invisible. It's all about rain in the middle of winter and roots sinking way, way down, unseen. Like a desert wildflower, I sucked up the small rains when they came and plunged roots down deep within myself, so that when spring finally did come, I was ready with a bright bursting bloom that seemed to come out of nowhere. When I opened my eyes, this is what I saw:

I saw that I had lived and adapted. I had made not only the obvious adaptations in going to Belize, but also those taken for granted in the seemingly simple act of coming home. I saw weeds growing up through cracks of concrete, cracks of asphalt. I saw bird nests in the lighted letters above storefronts. I saw a palm tree that managed to spring up out of a storm drain down the street from my house. As it was too expensive to pull out the sidewalk, the drain and part of the road to dig it out, the city resigned itself to coming by twice a year to cut back the unruly branches. I winked at its stubborn beauty every time I walked by and I think it winked back at mine. I saw reminder after reminder that nature's strong fingers continue to probe out the faults of our urban empire and remind us that she still rules the foundations on which we sit.

I saw the differences in two opposing ways of life, and saw myself in the middle equally suited and unsuited for each. And I saw these not as a battle raging, but as a balance vacillating, slowly bending to accommodate the shifting weight of each moment of existence. Today I must sweep the earth back outside. Tomorrow I will want to taste the rain.

Kashmar

Julie van Arcken

When I realized that I was probably going to spend the rest of my life in a Ukrainian prison, I stopped caring that my hair looked like crap.

The scene was going wrong. My character was supposed to get through security with a nod and a smile. I wanted to explain to the guard that the movie of my life was not supposed to be a dismal prison drama.

Throughout my twenties, I pretended that I was living in a movie. Since at age twenty-seven I had failed to achieve any of the normal measures of success—buying a house, getting married, having a family, making a lot of money—I tried to compensate by taking dramatic action. And, as my high school reunion approached, I wanted to make sure that the latest scenes from my living movie contained lots of intrigue and on-location work that I could brag about to my dull, provincial classmates. I would show them that I wasn't just an awkward, bookish girl, but a mysterious expatriate journalist! And since that day's script called for me to fly from Kiev to Paris with a hidden cache of hard currency, I had decided to play the part of a jet-setting lady smuggler.

But the haircut I had gotten the night before was all wrong for the role. I wanted to look like a James Bond or Alfred Hitchcock character—the mysterious, well-dressed woman traveling alone. Instead, my short and ragged haircut seemed more appropriate for the *Midnight Express* nightmare the day was turning into.

A Kievan would have described my situation as a *kashmar*, a catchall phrase Russian speakers use when things go wrong. It was taken from the French *cauchemar*, meaning nightmare. Locals use it for everything from minor hassles to the economic depression. Standing in line to pay an electricity bill is a kashmar, as was the mayoral election, the situation in the Balkans, the price of tomatoes. Until the armed airport security guard singled me out and took me to a special room for further questioning and searching, my kashmar of the moment had been my ugly haircut.

I hadn't gotten my hair cut since I had arrived several months earlier. My limited language skills had deterred me from visiting the salon near the office. The only person I knew who spoke less Russian than I did was a British coworker at the English-language weekly where I was a copyeditor and arts writer. One time I asked him to meet me in Maidan Nezalezhnosti, Kiev's main square, and he told me he had never heard of it. When I explained, he said, "Oh, you mean Independence Square," a term I'd only seen once, on a map the government designed in the early '90s for all the English-speaking tourists who never came.

His girlfriend, a generous and gracious woman, was his constant companion and translator. I had been meaning to take them up on their standing invitation to come to their apartment and meet their friends, as I didn't know many people outside work. So when he said that a neighbor cut his hair and she would be glad to cut mine, I knew it was time for a visit. A good hairdresser would rank up there with two other recent finds, frozen broccoli and Drano.

My British coworker—and his hairdresser neighbor—lived in a communist-era high-rise apartment building. Almost all the Americans I knew lived in turn-of-the-century buildings near the center of town. My own flat, a run-down studio with twelve-foot ceilings and crystal chandeliers, was one block south of a reconstructed thousand-year-old fortress and one block north of the downtown McDonald's.

I would sometimes try to brighten my dim and drafty room, whose wallpaper was not only ugly but stained, with tulips, which would stay fresh for a week because the room was nearly as cold as the ancient refrigerator in which I kept my Spanish vegetables, German milk, and bottled water. I was never comfortable eating locally grown food, which was not only heavy and bland but possibly radioactive as well, having grown in soil within a hundred miles of Chernobyl.

Most expatriates in Ukraine eventually overcame their apprehension about the local produce and meat. My college friend, who had invited me to come to Kiev after he became editor of the English-language weekly, ate local vegetables and dairy products, only shunning berries, mushrooms, and freshwater fish. When I went to his spacious, renovated apartment a couple of blocks away from mine and stayed up late watching BBC, I would occasionally have a bowl of cereal with his Ukrainian milk. Not only did it cost three times less than the imported milk I used, it was also widely available. Sometimes I had to search through five or six shops before finding one that had German milk in stock. But the good shops were all clustered in the center of town, and I could walk to all the places where I bought groceries.

My British coworker's building was on the outskirts of town, and he gave me complicated directions I knew I would have trouble explaining to a taxi driver. He lived there because his girlfriend owned the flat, which she'd been living in since Soviet times. They both wanted to move to a nicer apartment closer to the town's center, but it was impossible for them to sell their place because the building was falling over. When I met them outside their building in the evening, I couldn't tell that it leaned to one side, and inside the floors seemed level. But the sixteen-story building's tilt, which got measurably worse each year, had recently stopped the elevators, as their shafts were no longer perpendicular to the ground.

"Do they know when it's going to fall over?" I asked. In a way I hoped to be scared about my evening there, to add a little cinematic tension to the situation. I liked being close to danger. I had witnessed midnight strip searches by militia in the fields of Chiapas; I had been stranded in and hitchhiked out of Nicaragua; I had traveled in the Balkans during the war. When my college friend became editor of the English-language weekly and told me he'd pay me well to come out and copyedit it, the only thing I knew about Ukraine was that it was one of the former Soviet states struggling with its independence. But that sounded good to me: to live in adverse circumstances but make a lot of money while telling the world about injustice, corruption, and poverty in the land of the former enemy. Glamour, intrigue, adventure.

I never wanted to stand directly in harm's way; I only wanted to watch it slink past. I had always been quiet and shy, but as I got older I tried to reinvent myself by taking bold and dramatic steps. In high school and college classes, I never raised my hand to ask a question. Sometimes I even had trouble addressing a room full of friends. And when girlfriends of mine married, I was always happy to be chosen as a bridesmaid, who needed only to stand around in a fancy dress, rather than the maid of honor, who had to make a toast at the reception.

But I didn't always want to be an awkward wallflower with Walter Mitty fantasies of leading an exciting and important life. So I would force myself to commit to plans I was not just apprehensive about but *terrified* to follow through with. When asked to live abroad, it was easy to say yes. And of course after I said yes, I had to go. Sometimes pretending that my life wasn't my own but that of an interesting movie character made getting on planes and interviewing strangers easier. In my recurring role as intrepid girl reporter, visiting an apartment in a tilting high-rise in the former Soviet Union was no problem.

"No one knows, or no one is saying, but we're definitely going to move before it topples over. Soon." All the residents had vague plans to move, a classic kashmar.

We climbed the twelve stories to his apartment, where his girl-friend tried to talk me into eating dinner, but I had just eaten a large meal. After refusing her offer of food, which I knew was rude but hoped to get away with as a foreigner, I felt more obligated to drink with her—first Georgian red wine, then vodka. She told me about her life in Soviet times, and to me it didn't sound much different from her current situation.

She stayed home most of the time, living off small disability payments and occasionally doing some translation work. She told me her life had been ruined in her teens. She was one of Ukraine's most promising young ice skaters until she injured her knee at a tournament at age fourteen. And at nineteen, she explained, she went to the hospital with great abdominal pain, and the surgeons removed not only her appendix but her uterus as well. The conversation was like others I had had with English-speaking Ukrainians, whose reasons for telling me their griev-ances I never fully understood. I wondered if they expected me to answer for my own good fortune, to have been born in a country with competent doctors and well-paying jobs, or if they wanted me to explain to them what I was doing there when I could be in America.

Her kitchen, like the rest of the apartment, was dark and cramped, and we moved into the living room when neighbors started arriving, crowding the tiny space. "It's like this all the time," my coworker said. "People over at all hours. This is an open house."

Their next-door neighbor, a star of the 1988 Soviet Olympic track team, came over first. Another coworker of mine had written a story about him, and the accompanying photo showed him standing in front of a Soviet flag that hung in his apartment. He explained: "I knew at the time that this would be the last Soviet Olympic team, and that's why I took the flag, the last one that would ever be used in the games." I understood. As the photographer knew, the flag was an important prop in the movie of his life.

Another former ice skater came over, and then a painter. My coworker invited us all to smoke hash with him, and we did. Then in came a woman with a skittish, saucer-eyed Persian cat. Before he escaped from her arms to run all over the house, hiding under furniture, I told her that I admired the big, white cat.

Whenever I knew the appropriate words, I liked to compliment people, usually on their clothes or cooking. I had found that just two or three words ("beautiful cat," "pretty coat," "very delicious soup") would be enough to make someone want to talk to me. Although I couldn't say much back, I understood most of what people said and knew enough to get by. At the paper, all the text I edited was in English, and when I wrote stories, I only interviewed other Americans and Europeans for short arts pieces. Even though I took language lessons several times a week, I hadn't made nearly as much progress as I had hoped to.

Although I have always been an even-keeled person, during my first week in Kiev I sometimes had to fight off panic. I didn't have any local currency and I didn't know how to get any, I didn't know my own address, I didn't know where I worked, I didn't know how to get anywhere on the metro and not only did I not understand Russian or Ukrainian, I couldn't even decipher the alphabet. In fact, I wasn't even sure how to work the locks on the door. Those first days were exciting, but after the initial bold leaps from bewilderment to acclimation, I now had to work very hard for small rewards in cultural competence. Since I didn't need to know the Russian past tense to see the sights or order a meal or write a story about Belgian entrepreneurs, it was hard to make myself study my friend's hand-me-down lesson book instead of going out drinking, or even staying late at the office.

That evening I was pretty sure there was no more glamorous place to be, not even for intrepid girl reporters, in all Kiev. After all, there I was, a single female expatriate journalist hanging out drinking and smoking hash with an artist, a filmmaker, and an Olympic athlete, in a collapsing apartment building in the former Soviet Union, the night before I was to jet off to Paris with a load of smuggled cash. If that didn't sound like a great movie scene, then nothing in my whole life would. In any case, it was certainly more interesting than spending a Wednesday night in Portland. At home I had been working at a series of worthless temp jobs and going out with cute waiters and sales clerks to the same bars I had been going to since I had been able to pass for legal. My big goal was to get enough sleep to wake up and drive to some office park by eight the next morning.

The hairdresser arrived and had a glass of vodka with the other guests. I thanked her for agreeing to cut my hair, and we went back into the dark kitchen. My coworker's girlfriend was busy filling glasses for all the other guests, so I tried to speak for myself, pointing to the ends of my hair. "A little," I said, hoping she would understand that I only wanted a trim. When I saw that she was cutting off large chunks of hair, I swallowed hard to keep from vomiting.

I didn't mind having straggly hair in dismal, wintry Kiev, but I wanted to look chic and cosmopolitan in Paris. After seven cold months in Kiev, the character of plucky American girl journalist in the former Soviet Union, which had appealed so much to the clerical temp I had portrayed back in the States, was no longer very glamorous to me. I wanted to have a really good time in Paris, staying in the center of town, buying beautiful clothes, and practicing my passable French (so much better than my Russian!) on suave, attractive men. I also looked forward to eating out in Paris, not only because the street vendors served better food than some of Kiev's best restaurants but because I could hope that another Latin Quarter waiter would compliment me on my pronunciation of "*steak au poivre.*" And it was nice to consider everything on a menu without factoring in the likelihood of radiation poisoning. And I could see all the movies I wanted. The entertainment guide *Pariscope* bragged that every week it listed 1,000 films, most of which were in English with

French subtitles. In Kiev, I had once gotten excited that three American films were coming to town, only to find out *Hard Target* and *Lethal Weapon 4* were dubbed in Russian.

With my haircut—such as it was—completed, I uttered one loud good-bye to everyone and left. Barely able to walk straight, I started my slow and treacherous twelve-floor descent. Every lightbulb in the stairway had been stolen, so it was almost completely dark. On many landings the windows were broken, and snow, ice, and broken glass covered the steps. I got home fine, but I was stoned, drunk, and maudlin, so when I looked at my hair in the mirror I cried for the first time since I had arrived. Kashmar.

I woke up too late to worry about my swollen, red face, and short, asymmetrical hairdo. I had to figure out how much cash I was going to try to take out of the country and where I was going to put it. All I had was a stack of the hundred-dollar bills with which I was paid each month. The thousand dollars in cash that the Ukrainian government allowed noncitizens to take out of the country certainly wasn't going to be enough for this two-week trip, especially as I was going to need new makeup as well as new clothes in order to get over the haircut. I decided to bring an extra four hundred dollars. I talked myself into believing that it didn't really matter where I put it—the dozen people I had asked had never been searched on their way out of Kiev. I had always liked to use books as props. So when my friend asked me to bring him my copy of *Crime and Punishment*, there was no question of where I would stash the extra cash.

I wasn't worried until I got to the airport and started writing out my lies on the customs form. Everywhere armed guards in Soviet-style khaki uniforms were watching me. Ideas careened through my head—I could try to hide the four hundred dollars and come back and get it later, I could try to spend four hundred dollars on vodka and trinkets, I could flush it down the toilet, I could even declare the extra money and see what they said. The only possibility I rejected entirely was to do anything that would justify a body-cavity search, my worst horror.

I went to the bathroom, which was mercifully empty, but I worried about electronic surveillance. Even if they didn't have cameras in the stalls, surely they could see from under the door that I was tucking a couple bills in my shoe. Besides, this was a Soviet-built airport—the staff could probably see you in the dark if they wanted to. I headed for the checkpoint, trying not to walk strangely even though the shoe I had just put the money in was tied much tighter than the one whose laces had loosened over the course of the day.

I didn't want to betray my anxiety, so I tried hard to pretend this was all just a movie. I chose the line with the most handsome customs officer, who looked a little like Rutger Hauer. His English wasn't very good and he asked me in a thick accent if I had, as my form stated, only one thousand dollars on me. I said yes. Then he asked me if I had any drugs, and I said no, and then he asked again about the money. "That's correct, just a thousand dollars." Then he asked me again if I only had one thousand dollars on me. Kashmar.

I wondered if I should stick to the script or if I should break down and confess about the extra four hundred dollars. How much milder would my punishment be if I gave up? Was this questioning going as badly as I thought it was? How could I have ever cared about a haircut?

"Yes, just a thousand dollars," I repeated. He asked me five times about the money before asking me to follow him to the search room.

Several guards in khaki uniforms that could have been left over from Soviet days were standing around in the small, beige room lined with stainless steel tables. I looked around for other women, other tourists, privacy curtains, torture devices, rubber gloves. But there were only guards, X-ray machines, and steel tables.

Rutger Hauer asked me to empty my backpack. I handed him my wallet, which contained the maximum allowable amount of cash, and he counted through the bills twice. He asked me to continue removing items from my pack, and I hoped to bribe him when we got to the book. Or would that make things even worse? That had to be a separate crime.

He couldn't have failed to notice my shaking hands as I removed my camera. He asked again about the money. Did I really only have one thousand dollars on me? I hated him for prolonging my anguish, making me reconsider what stance I should take. I just wanted to give myself up to whatever horrible fate was in store for me. In a movie, this would be the part where the main character gets hauled off in handcuffs. I couldn't believe I had ever been foolish enough to have gotten myself into this. Intrigue and adventure were vastly overrated. Why couldn't I have cast myself in a nice romantic comedy instead? I mumbled, "Y-y-yes."

I remembered how I had thought that stowing the extra money in *Crime and Punishment*, which I would soon have to remove from my backpack, would make for a funny mass e-mail message about my successful little smuggling venture and my fabulous trip to Paris. I also remembered an article I had read about how the Council of Europe had criticized Ukraine for executing hundreds of people without much cause. Getting lightheaded at the thought that my day would end not in Paris but in prison, I thought about how upset my mother would be.

Then the guard asked me if I was a student. "No," I said. "I work here. I'm a journalist."

"Which paper?"

I told him, and he laughed. He told another security guard that I worked for the English-language paper, and he snickered too. Then he told me I could pack up my stuff and go. As with so many other things in this foreign place, I never understood what happened.

After my Paris trip, which started in terror but ended at my favorite department store, I knew I couldn't make a permanent home in Kiev. Bleakness, poverty, and injustice may be compelling challenges, but they aren't good foundations for a home. Paradoxically, deciding to leave gave me an equanimity that allowed me to settle into the city during my remaining time there. I started to enjoy meeting people with whom I didn't have much in common—I didn't need to, as they wouldn't be lifelong friends.

My Paris clothes and makeup didn't help my hair, but a thirty-dollar minidress I bought on sale in Montparnasse did help me charm a Ukrainian stock analyst, a South African businessman, and a British macroeconomist. When I got back to Ukraine, I stayed out late drinking at the same expat bars everyone else went to, and my life became less like a movie and more like a TV show, with the same characters week after week. The random airport incident was my only encounter with the law; after that I was never even asked for identification on the street. But even after I started to feel at home in the city, I didn't want to stay. Not just because Kiev lacked the luxury of Paris and the comfort of Portland, but because it was no longer exciting. It wasn't that Ukraine was too scary; it wasn't scary enough.

About the Contributors

Sadie Ackerman writes—in spare moments of respite from her husband and two-year-old son—on a laptop computer that has been to nine states and five countries. She is currently trying to publish a novel based on her work and travels in Belize, Central America.

Kate Baldus lived for a year in Dhaka, Bangladesh, where she taught English in a private university. She later returned to live in the north of the country, where she worked as a teacher-trainer for Peace Corps volunteers. She now lives in New York City.

Eliza Bonner recently returned to the United States from Rio de Janeiro, Brazil, where she lived for five years. She worked in the international energy industry for several years after receiving her master's in international management from the American Graduate School of International Management (Thunderbird), and worked as the managing director of the Brazil office of a financial communications firm. Eliza is also a freelance writer and translator, and is fluent in Portuguese and Spanish. She has published several business articles, some poetry, and a short story, and is now working on a collection of children's stories and a collection of short stories. She currently lives in Colorado with her Argentine husband and her Brazilian cat.

Lesley-Ann Brown lives in Copenhagen, Denmark, with her husband and their two-year-old son, Kai. She worked for four years with Marie Brown Associates and is now working on her novel, "Dreaming in

Brooklyn." She also intends to write more about her experiences as an African American in Denmark.

Emmeline Chang is a freelance writer and editor in New York. She teaches fiction and nonfiction at Gotham Writers' Workshop as well as at bookstores throughout the city. Emmeline has an MFA from Columbia University and has been a resident at Ragdale and Millay colonies. Her recent writing appears in www.mrbellersneighborhood.com, ACM: *Another Chicago Magazine, Ten* magazine and *BigCityLit.* She is currently working on a series of essays about New York and a collection of short stories about tea. Her website is www.emmelinechang.com.

Mandy Dowd is a poet and artist who lives in the south of France. Her poems and essays have appeared in anthologies and numerous magazines, including *American Letters & Commentary, Artweek,* and *Five Fingers Review.* Her sculptures and installations have been shown in San Francisco and in France. *The Altarpiece,* her chapbook, was published by Goats + Compasses Press.

Laura Fokkena has lived in Europe, North America, and the Middle East. She earned a master's degree at the University of Iowa before moving to Boston, where she currently writes, teaches, and watches her daughter grow up.

Juleigh Howard-Hobson has lived in northern California since she returned to the U.S. She is quite happily married to a Golden State golden boy she met while they were both West Coast punk rockers. They have three children that they homebirthed and now homeschool. She has written one novel, one novella, and numerous essays that are scattered in various zines and e-zines across the globe. In her spare time she works on novel number two. Her dad still resides in Sydney; occasionally he sends her Arnott's Iced Vo Vo biscuits.

Gina Hyams lived in Mexico with her husband and young daughter from January 17, 1997 to January 19, 2001. There she worked as a correspondent for Fodors Travel Publications and contributed articles to Salon.com and *Newsweek*. She is the author of *Day of the Dead Box* and *Mexicasa: The Enchanting Inns and Haciendas of Mexico* (both published by Chronicle Books). Now in Oakland, California, she is writing a book about the history, lore, and rituals of incense around the world.

Erica Jacobs is an L.A. girl on the run. A former book editor, she left the San Francisco publishing scene to try out the high-tech prospects in southern California. After a stint in L.A., she jumped across the pond and became the creative director at a U.K. company that produces websites and offers graphic-design solutions. She currently lives and works in Belfast, Northern Ireland.

Marci Laughlin has her master's degree in Middle East studies from the Jackson School and her BA in international relations and Italian from the University of California, Davis. She grew up in Modesto, California and after a stint in Seattle, Washington, moved to Turkey to teach.

Stephanie Loleng is a freelance writer living in Oakland. She has written for websites, including AOL and LookSmart as well as for the offline Filipino cultural and environmental magazine, *Call of Nature*. Often suffering from a travel bug, Stephanie finds it hard not to strap on a backpack and hit the open road in search of more story ideas.

Leza Lowitz lived in Japan from 1990-1994, where she taught writing and American literature at Rikkyo University and at Tokyo University (Todai). She has published two books of poems, *Yoga Poems: Lines to Unfold By*, which received the 2001 PEN Oakland Josephine Miles Award for Best Book of Poetry, and *Old Ways to Fold New Paper*. Other honors include individual fellowships from the NEA and NEH, a California Arts

Council grant in poetry, the Money for Women/Barbara Deming Memorial Award in fiction, the *Japanophile* fiction award, the PEN Syndicated Fiction Award, and the *Tokyo Journal* Fiction Translation Award. Lowitz has also published six books of translations, including the award-winning anthologies of contemporary Japanese women's poetry, *A Long Rainy Season* and *Other Side River*. For the past decade, Lowitz has been corresponding editor to Japan for Mänoa (University of Hawaii) and a regular book reviewer for the *Japan Times*. She is author of a travel book, *Beautiful Japan*. Her expatriate fiction has appeared in *Prairie Schooner* and the anthologies *The Broken Bridge: Expatriate Writing from Literary Japan; An Inn Near Kyoto: Writing by American Women Abroad* and *They Only Laughed Later: Tales of Women on the Move*. Lowitz has just finished a novel with her husband, the Japanese writer Shogo Oketani.

Emily Wise Miller began her career as editor of Fodor's Berkeley Guides to Italy. Since then she has worked as an editor of illustrated books, a restaurant critic, and an overpaid dot-com drone. She has written about food, travel, and other subjects for various newspapers and magazines, including *San Francisco* magazine, *Surface,* and *Salon*. A chronic Italophile, she has spent time in Venice and Perugia, and currently lives in Florence, Italy, with her husband, an art historian.

Born in California, **Rhiannon Paine** has lived in England (five years) and Toyko (eighteen months). In 1999, Academy Chicago published her book about her experiences in Japan, *Too Late for the Festival: An American Salary-Woman in Japan*. Paine's travel essays have appeared in two travel anthologies from New Rivers Press, *The House on Via Gambito* and *An Inn Near Kyoto*. She is currently at work on a book about her first trip to England in 1973.

Angeli Primlani is a journalist, writer, poet, playwright, and Web designer from an obscure place in rural North Carolina best known for a terrible flood that killed a lot of pigs. The worst job she ever had was market research interviewer. The second-worst job she ever had was managing the clown band at Carowinds amusement park. She currently lives in Chicago and is working on one master's degree and two novels. Her nonfiction has appeared in the *Prague Post, The Economist's Business Central Europe, Vancouver,* Canada's *Terminal City,* Chicago's *Daily Southtown* and *Daily Herald* and the *Illinois Times.* Her fiction and poetry have appeared in small press publications. She designed and launched the *Prague Post Online* and the National Training and Information Center/Disclosure website.

Karen Rosenberg grew up in New York City and currently lives in Seattle. She writes both fiction and nonfiction and her work has appeared in various literary journals and magazines. Her work also appeared in another Seal Press anthology, *Sex and Single Girls.* She is a doctoral student in women's studies at the University of Washington.

Tonya Ward Singer taught English at Qingdao University in China during the 1995–1996 academic year. She now is a bilingual Spanish-English teacher in Santa Rosa, California, where she also writes professional books and articles for teachers. She married a vegetarian, and has long since retired from cooking chicken.

Julie van Arcken took her first trip abroad, to visit the families of her British mother and Dutch-Indonesian father, when she was six months old. She grew up in Oregon and spent a few years at the University of Washington before dropping out to move to Prague, where she worked for an English-language newspaper. A few years later she returned to Eastern Europe to copyedit and write for a weekly in Kiev, Ukraine. She currently resides in Seattle, where she works as a copyeditor for

Amazon.com. She has traveled to about thirty countries, mostly in Europe and Central America, and can read menus in a dozen languages. Her favorite cities are Barcelona, Istanbul, and Portland, Oregon.

Deryn P. Verity has enjoyed the expatriate life in Serbia and Slovenia (in the former Yugoslavia); Osaka, Japan; Bangkok, Thailand; and Warsaw and Krakow, Poland, while working as a teacher and teacher-trainer. A specialist in English as a second language, applied linguistics, and second-language pedagogy, she has a PhD in linguistics and has published academic articles on psycholinguistics and language acquisition. Her travels and professional activity have taken her to Australia, Russia, Ukraine, Hong Kong, Canada, Italy, Hungary, France, Germany, Czech Republic, Slovakia, and Great Britain. She currently is based in New Jersey and awaiting her next move.

Meg Wirth works in the field of public health and has a master's degree in international development. Most recently she worked for three years for the Rockefeller Foundation, and previously contributed to health projects in the Appalachian region of the United States and in Indonesia. She coedited a volume called *Challenging Inequities in Health,* published in 2001 by Oxford University Press, and currently is living in Hong Kong and working on migrant-worker issues.

About the Editor

Christina Henry de Tessan has worked in publishing in San Francisco and Seattle, and as a freelance book translator, editor, and book reviewer in Paris. She recently coedited *A Woman Alone: Travel Tales from Around the Globe*. She lives on an island outside Seattle with her husband.

Selected titles from Adventura Books

The Unsavvy Traveler: Women's Comic Tales of Catastrophe edited by Rosemary Caperton, Anne Mathews, and Lucie Ocenas. $15.95, 1-58005-058-1. Twenty-five gut-wrenchingly funny responses to the question: What happens when trips go wrong?

A Woman Alone edited by Faith Conlon, Ingrid Emerick and Christina Henry de Tessan. $15.95, 1-58005-059-X. A collection of rousing stories by women who travel solo.

Journey Across Tibet: A Young Woman's Trek Across the Rooftop of the World by Sorrel Wilby. Foreword by the Dalai Lama. $16.95, 1-58005-053-0. An inspiring story that captures the sensibility of a remote land and its people.

Dream of a Thousand Lives: A Sojourn in Thailand by Karen Connelly. $14.95, 1-58005-062-X. The award-winning account of a young woman immersed in the heart of Thailand.

East Toward Dawn: A Woman's Solo Journey Around the World by Nan Watkins. $14.95, 1-58005-064-6. After the loss of her son and the end of a marriage, the author sets out in search of joy and renewal in travel.

The Curve of Time: The Classic Memoir of a Woman and her Children Who Explored the Coastal Waters of the Pacific Northwest, second edition by M. Wylie Blanchet, foreword by Timothy Egan. $15.95, 1-58005-072-7. The timeless memoir of a pioneering, courageous woman who acted as both mother and captain of the twenty-five foot boat that became her family's home during the long Northwest summers.

Hot Flashes from Abroad: Women's Travel Tales and Adventures edited by Jean Gould. $16.95, 1-878067-55-7. The women in this inspirational collection—each over the age of fifty—prove once and for all that verve will always trump age.

Seal Press publishes many outdoor and travel books by women writers. Please visit our Web site at **www.sealpress.com**.